W9-AUI-447

TCP/IP JumpStart™: Internet Protocol Basics

Andrew G. Blank

SYBEX®

San Francisco ◆ London

Associate Publisher: Neil Edde

Acquisitions and Developmental Editor: Heather O'Connor

Editor: Donna Crossman

Production Editor: Kelly Winquist

Technical Editor: Michelle A. Roudebush

Book Designer: Maureen Forys and Kate Kaminski, Happenstance Type-O-Rama

Graphic Illustrator: Jerry Williams!

Electronic Publishing Specialist: Maureen Forys, Happenstance Type-O-Rama

Proofreaders: Emily Hsuan, Yariv Rabinovitch, Nancy Riddiough

Indexer: Nancy Guenther

Cover Designer: Archer Design

Cover Illustrator/Photographer: Archer Design

*To my inspiration, my encourager, my perfect match,
my best friend, and the love of my life, my wife Suzie,
you have had a profound and awesome impact on
my life. I love you very much.*

*To my son A.J. and my daughter Amber, I treasure
your love and have tremendous pride in both of you;
Daddy loves you so much.*

Acknowledgments

Several people have assisted me in many ways while writing this book. I'd like to acknowledge their contributions and offer my sincere appreciation.

I appreciate several devoted people at Sybex. I have had the privilege of working closely with some very talented people, especially Kelly Winquist and Heather O'Connor. Donna Crossman did an exceptional job of editing my garbled-up thoughts into complete sentences. Many thanks to the Sybex production department, including proofreaders Emily Hsuan, Nancy Riddiough, and Yariv Rabinovitch, indexer Nancy Guenther, and Maureen Forys, who diligently turned text into print. I appreciate the technical insight of Michelle Roudebush and the selfless assistance of Sara Richardson. I applaud the imagination and creativity of Jerry Williams in turning my sketches into artwork. What an awesome honor to work with all of you!

I'd like to acknowledge the encouragement and prayers of my family and friends. All things are possible!

Contents

Introduction   *xiv*

Chapter 1 ◆ The Origin of TCP/IP and the Internet   **1**
  What Is TCP/IP?   2
    Features of TCP/IP   3
  The Origins of the Internet: ARPAnet   4
    ARPAnet's Requirements   5
  Requests for Comments   6
  The Birth of TCP/IP   7
  Design Goals of TCP/IP   8
  Moving Data across the Network   9
    Moving Data on a Circuit-Switched Network   9
    Moving Data on a Packet-Switched Network   10
  Why Use TCP/IP?   12

Chapter 2 ◆ Protocols   **16**
  What Are Protocols?   18
    Protocols Move Packets of Data   20
  Why We Need Protocols and Standards   22
  The OSI Reference Model   23
    The Seven Layers of the OSI Model   24
    Responsibilities of Each Layer   25
    How the OSI Model Is Used   28
  TCP/IP and the DoD Model   29

Chapter 3 ◆ The Network Interface and Internet Layers   **32**
  The Network Interface Layer   34
    Hardware Address   36
  The Internet Layer   38
    Internet Protocol (IP)   39
    Address Resolution Protocol (ARP)   43
    Internet Control Message Protocol (ICMP)   47
    Internet Group Management Protocol (IGMP)   49

Chapter 4 ◆ The Transport Layer   **54**
  Understanding the Transport Layer   56
  Understanding Transmission Control Protocol   58
    Using a Three-Way Handshake   58
    Organizing Data and Guaranteeing Delivery   60

Understanding User Datagram Protocol   61
   UDP Communication   62

Chapter 5 ◆ The Application Layer   66
   Understanding the Application Layer   68
   Understanding Ports and Sockets   68
      Well-Known Ports   70
   File Transfer Protocol (FTP)   71
      How FTP Works   72
   Hypertext Transfer Protocol (HTTP)   74

Chapter 6 ◆ IP Addressing   78
   What Is IP Addressing?   80
   Numbering Systems   80
      Reviewing Binary and Decimal Numbering Systems   82
      Converting Binary Numbers to Decimal   83
      Converting Decimal Numbers to Binary   84
   IP Addresses   90
   IP Address Classes   92
      Class A Addresses   92
      Class B Addresses   94
      Class C Addresses   95
      Class D Addresses   96
      Class E Addresses   96
   IP Address Class Summary   97

Chapter 7 ◆ Addressing IP Hosts   100
   Installing and Assigning IP Addresses   102
      Manual IP Address Configuration   102
      Installing TCP/IP on Windows XP   103
      Installing TCP/IP on Windows 2000   106
      Installing TCP/IP on Windows NT   110
      Installing TCP/IP on Windows 95/98   114
      Dynamic Host Configuration Protocol (DHCP)   116
   Obtaining an IP Address from a DHCP Server   118
      DHCP Discover   118
      DHCP Offer   119
      DHCP Request   121
      DHCP Acknowledgment   124

Contents

DHCP Leases   126
   DHCP IP Address Renewal   127
Reserving DHCP IP Addresses   129
Setting the Lease Duration   130
Setting DHCP Scopes and Options   131

Chapter 8 ◆ Introduction to Subnet Masks   134

What Is a Subnet Mask?   136
   Network and Host   138
   Identifying a Local or Remote Network   139
Standard Subnet Masks   142
   Class A Addresses   142
   Class B Addresses   142
   Class C Addresses   142

Chapter 9 ◆ Using Custom Subnet Masks   146

Custom Subnet Masks   148
   Creating Additional Networks   150
   Subnetting Rules   150
   Creating a Custom Subnet Mask   151
Class A Subnet Masks   171
Class B Subnet Masks   172
Class C Subnet Masks   173

Chapter 10 ◆ Supernetting and CIDR   178

IP Address Allocation   180
   Limitations of the Classful System   180
   The Trouble with Class B   181
Supernetting   183
Classless Inter-Domain Routing (CIDR)   186

Chapter 11 ◆ Name Resolution   190

Understanding Name Resolution   192
   What Is Host Name Resolution?   193
   What Is NetBIOS Name Resolution?   194
   NetBIOS Name Resolution vs. Host Name Resolution 195
Understanding Host Name Resolution   196
   Local Host (HOSTNAME)   198
   The HOSTS file   200

Domain Name System (DNS)   202
NetBIOS Name Cache   203
Windows Internet Naming Service (WINS)   205
Broadcast   206
The LMHOSTS file   208
The Host Name Resolution Cycle   212
Understanding NetBIOS Name Resolution   213
The NetBIOS Name Resolution Cycle   214

Chapter 12 ◆ Domain Name System (DNS)   **218**
What Is DNS?   220
DNS on the Internet   221
Name Resolution Using DNS   222
Querying a DNS Server   223
Querying Name Servers   224
Completing Resolution   226
Understanding Recursive and Iterative Queries   226
Maintaining a Database   228
Maintaining a DNS Server   229
Primary Name Server   229
Secondary Name Server   229
DNS Zone Transfer   230
Caching-Only Server   231
Record Types in DNS   231

Chapter 13 ◆ Dynamic DNS   **236**
What Is Dynamic DNS?   238
Configure Windows 2000 Server for Dynamic Update   241
Dynamic DNS on the Internet   247
Benefits of Dynamic DNS   247

Chapter 14 ◆ Windows Internet Naming Service (WINS)   **250**
NetBIOS Applications   252
NetBIOS Name Resolution Process without WINS   252
NetBIOS Name Resolution Process with WINS   257
WINS Manager   262

Contents

Chapter 15 ◆ IP Version 6   **266**

  The Need for a New Version of TCP/IP   268
  IPv6 Addressing   269
    IPv4 Addresses and IPv6 Addresses   269
    Harry—The Next Generation   270
    The New Hexadecimal IPv6 Addresses   271
    Double-Colon Notation   272
    IPv6 Special Addresses   274
    IPv6 Documentation   274
  Improvements of IPv6   275
  The Transition Plan to IPv6   276

Appendix A ◆ Answers to Review Questions   **281**

Appendix B ◆ Glossary   **293**

Appendix C ◆ Acronym Expansion Guide   **303**

Appendix D ◆ What's on the Web Site   **307**

Index   *310*

Introduction

This book introduces TCP/IP to a person with any level of computer skills or computer background knowledge. My hope in writing this book is to explain in a simple way some concepts that may be considered difficult. My ambition is to write a book that makes no assumptions and that leads a TCP/IP beginner to an intermediate understanding of TCP/IP. This book isn't boringly technical; each topic is covered to sufficient depth but not to an extreme.

As a network administrator and instructor, I have several years' experience working in the computer industry and specifically with TCP/IP. Pulling from this experience, I've tried to present the relevant material in an interesting way, and I've included what I have found to be the most important concepts. The book is filled with several simple examples, diagrams, and screen captures in an effort to make the TCP/IP protocol more tangible. Many of the graphics include this book's mascot, whose name is Harry. Harry the Host represents a device attached to a network and using TCP/IP.

This book is neither operating system-specific nor software-specific. Concepts are presented so that the reader can gain an understanding of the topic without being tied to a particular platform. Many books about TCP/IP are test-prep books or programmer guides to TCP/IP. This book is different because it is not focused on passing a test and teaching answers to questions. It is not a certification preparation book, although it can be an excellent supplement. Anyone studying for a TCP/IP exam will find this book useful for fine-tuning any concepts that they do not thoroughly understand.

Someone who may be interested in a particular topic within TCP/IP can pick up the book and get a quick, thorough understanding. Many executives and IS decision-makers need to be conversant with TCP/IP so that they can talk with their staff and other professionals. This is the perfect book to provide that understanding.

Who Should Read This Book?

TCP/IP JumpStart is designed to teach the fundamentals of the TCP/IP protocol stack to people who are fairly new to the topic.

This book will be useful to:

- ◆ People interested in learning more about TCP/IP
- ◆ Decision-makers who need to know the fundamentals in order to make valid, informed choices

- Individuals interested in pursuing networking certifications
- Administrators who feel they are missing some of the foundational information about TCP/IP
- Small business owners interested in understanding the protocol they will likely use on their networks
- Those interested in learning more about how data moves across the Internet
- Instructors teaching a TCP/IP fundamentals course
- Students enrolled in a TCP/IP fundamentals course

What This Book Covers

Working with TCP/IP has been an interesting, exciting, and rewarding experience. As I continue to learn about computers and TCP/IP, the more I see the need to continue learning. No matter what sector of the computer industry you're employed in, TCP/IP is an important foundational topic that you must understand; TCP/IP is the current and future standard protocol.

TCP/IP JumpStart contains many drawings and charts that help create a comfortable learning environment. It provides many real-world analogies that you will be able to relate to and through which the TCP/IP protocol will become tangible. These analogies provide a simple way to understand the technical process that is occurring through TCP/IP.

This book continues to build your understanding about TCP/IP progressively, like climbing a ladder. Here is how the information is presented:

Chapter 1   This chapter provides an overview of where TCP/IP and the Internet came from and how they are related. A lot of good Internet trivia appears in this chapter.

Chapters 2–5   These chapters describe what a protocol is and what the OSI and DoD models are. These chapters include a discussion of what happens at each layer in the DoD model and why the model is important.

Chapters 6–10   These chapters describe TCP/IP addressing—what IP addresses look like and how they are implemented. You'll learn how to assign IP addresses both manually and through Dynamic Host Configuration Protocol (DHCP). You'll learn all about DHCP. You'll also learn about subnet masks: what they are, what they do, and how to create them.

Chapter 11–14   These chapters focus on name resolution methods and implementations. You'll learn why name resolution is needed and the steps taken to resolve names. You'll learn about Domain Name System (DNS), Dynamic DNS, and Windows Internet Naming Service (WINS).

Chapter 15   You'll learn about the future of TCP/IP: the transition to a new version of IP in the next few years. This chapter gives you a heads-up on what to expect, and tells you how to find out more.

Making the Most of This Book

At the beginning of each chapter of *TCP/IP JumpStart*, you'll find a list of topics that you can expect to learn about within that chapter. As you read through the chapter, you'll notice that when a topic continues to the next page you'll see this icon at the bottom outside corner of the page:

When a topic ends, you'll see this icon:

To help you soak up new material easily, I've highlighted **new terms** in bold and defined them in the page margins. And to give you some hands-on experience, there are Test It Out sections that let you practice what you've just learned. In addition, several special elements highlight important information:

NOTE

Notes provide extra information and references to related information.

TIP

Tips are insights that help you perform tasks more easily and effectively.

WARNING

Warnings let you know about things you should do—or shouldn't do—as you learn more about TCP/IP.

At the end of each chapter, you can test your knowledge of the chapter's relevant topics by answering the review questions. (You'll find the answers to the review questions in Appendix A.)

There's also some special material for your reference. If you'd like to quickly look up the meaning of a term, Appendix B is a glossary of terms that have been introduced throughout the book. If you are wondering what certain acronyms stand for, Appendix C is an acronym guide spelling out the acronyms used in this book. Because TCP/IP is a current technology and is likely to constantly change, a Web site has been set up to accompany this book. Appendix D describes the materials that you will find on the *TCP/IP JumpStart* companion Web site.

Chapter

1

The Origin of TCP/IP and the Internet

Two people can communicate effectively when they agree to use a common language. They could speak English, Spanish, French, or even sign language, but they must use the same language.

Computers work the same way. Transmission Control Protocol/Internet Protocol (TCP/IP) is like a language that computers speak. More specifically, TCP/IP is a set of rules that defines how two computers address each other and send data to each other. This set of rules is called a protocol. Multiple protocols that are grouped together form a protocol suite and work together as a protocol stack.

TCP/IP is a strong, fast, scalable, and efficient suite of protocols. This protocol stack is the de facto protocol of the Internet. As information exchange via the Internet becomes more widespread, more individuals and companies will need to understand TCP/IP.

In this first chapter you'll look at the origins of TCP/IP. You will learn about:

 The features of TCP/IP

 ARPAnet

 TCP's method of moving data

 Requests for Comments (RFCs)

 The benefits of using TCP/IP

What Is TCP/IP?

TCP/IP is a set of **protocols** that enable communication between computers. There was a time when it was not important for computers to communicate with each other. There was no need for a common protocol. But as computers became networked, the need arose for computers to agree on certain protocols.

Today, a **network administrator** can choose from many protocols, but the TCP/IP protocol is the most widely used. Part of the reason is that TCP/IP is the protocol of choice on the Internet—the world's largest network. If you want a computer to communicate on the Internet, it'll have to use TCP/IP.

protocols
Rules or standards that govern communications.

network administrator
A person who installs, monitors, and troubleshoots a network.

> **NOTE**
>
> When multiple protocols work together, the group is collectively known as a protocol suite or protocol stack. TCP/IP is an example of a protocol suite (it describes multiple protocols that work together). The implementation of TCP/IP is described as a protocol stack. Both terms are used interchangeably, yet their definitions vary slightly.

Another reason for TCP/IP's popularity is that it is compatible with almost every computer in the world. The TCP/IP stack is supported by current versions of all the major operating systems and network operating systems—including Windows 95/98, Windows NT, Windows 2000, Windows XP, Linux, Unix, and NetWare.

Unlike proprietary protocols developed by hardware and software vendors to make their equipment work, TCP/IP enjoys support from a variety of hardware and software vendors. Examples of companies that have products that work with TCP/IP include Microsoft, Novell, IBM, Apple, and Red Hat. Many other companies also support the TCP/IP protocol suite.

TCP/IP is sometimes referred to as "the language of the Internet." In addition to being the official language of the Internet, TCP/IP is also the official language of many smaller networks. For all the computers that are attached to the Internet to communicate effectively, they must agree on a language. Just like every human language has certain rules so that the people involved in the conversation understand what the other is saying, a computer language needs a set of rules so that computers can effectively communicate. Some of the rules of a language that computers use to communicate include determining when to send data and when to receive data.

Features of TCP/IP

TCP/IP has been in a use for more than 20 years, and time has proven it to be a tested and stable protocol suite. TCP/IP has many features and benefits. In this section, you will learn about some of the most important ones.

Support from Vendors

As stated earlier, TCP/IP receives support from many hardware and software vendors. This means that the TCP/IP suite is not tied to the development efforts of a single company. Instead, the choice to use TCP/IP on a network can be based on the purpose of the network and not on the hardware or software that has been purchased.

Interoperability

One of the major reasons why the TCP/IP suite has gained popularity and acceptance so universally is that it can be installed and used on virtually every platform. For example, using TCP/IP, a Unix host can communicate and transfer data to a DOS host or a Windows host. A **host** is another name for a computer or device on a network. TCP/IP eliminates the cross-platform boundaries.

Flexibility

TCP/IP is an extremely flexible protocol suite, and in later chapters you will learn about some features that contribute to this flexibility. Examples of TCP/IP's flexibility include the latitude an administrator has in assigning and reassigning addresses. An administrator can automatically or manually assign an IP address to a host, and a TCP/IP host can convert easy-to-remember names, such as www.sybex.com, to a TCP/IP address.

Routability

A limitation of many protocols is their difficulty moving data from one segment of the network to another. TCP/IP is exceptionally well adapted to the process of routing data from one segment of the network to another, or from a host on a network in one part of the world to a host on a network in another part of the world.

In the following sections, you will learn about how these features of TCP/IP grew out of the military's need for a reliable, flexible networking standard.

---

host
Any device (such as a workstation, server, mainframe, or printer) on a network or internetwork that has a TCP/IP address.

The Origins of the Internet: ARPAnet

ARPAnet
The Advanced Research Projects Agency's super-network–the predecessor of the Internet.

Network Control Protocol (NCP)
The protocol used before TCP/IP.

Understanding the roots of the Internet will give you insight into the development of TCP/IP and many of its rules and standards. If you know why TCP/IP was created and how it evolved, the TCP/IP protocol suite is easier to understand.

The predecessor of today's Internet was **ARPAnet**, a supernetwork that was created by the Advanced Research Projects Agency (ARPA) and launched in 1969. This network was created in response to the potential threat of nuclear attack from the Soviet Union. One of ARPA's primary goals was to design a fault-tolerant network that would enable U.S. military leaders to stay in contact in case of nuclear war. By the standards of the time, this fault-tolerant network seemed to be almost science fiction. ARPA set out on a mission to create a network with what seemed to be impossible requirements.

NOTE

In the late 1950s, the United States Department of Defense (DoD), under the guidance of one of America's leading think tanks, the RAND corporation, formed the Advanced Research Projects Agency (ARPA).

The protocol, or language of choice, used on the ARPAnet was called **Network Control Protocol (NCP)**–TCP/IP had not yet been developed. As the ARPAnet grew, however, a new protocol was needed because NCP simply didn't fulfill all the needs of a larger network. The NCP protocol was similar to a human language that has only a few words. The language might enable a few people to communicate, but as you include more people who want to talk about many more subjects, you have to improve the language.

The ARPAnet project had some specific goals and requirements. To reach these goals and meet these requirements, some of the top computer minds worked in a collaborative effort with little financial or public glory. Many of the top computer minds that worked on the ARPAnet were affiliated with major universities. It was not the intention of the project leaders to create the worldwide network that exists today, but fantastic growth soon followed the ARPAnet's humble beginnings.

ARPAnet's Requirements

To fulfill the needs of the military, the new ARPAnet had to meet the following requirements:

No one point more critical than any other   Because the network needed to be able to withstand a nuclear war, there could be no one critical part of the network and no single point of failure. If there were any critical parts of the network, enemies could target that area and eliminate communications.

Redundant routes to any destination   Because any location on the network could be taken down by enemies in the event of a war, there had to be multiple routes from any source to any destination on the network. Without redundant routes, any one location could become a critical communications link and a potential point of failure.

On-the-fly rerouting of data   If any part of the network failed, the network had to be able to reroute data to its destination on-the-fly.

Ability to connect different types of computers over different types of networks   This network could not be tied to just one operating system or hardware type. Because universities, government agencies, and corporations often rely on different types of Local Area Networks (LANs) and network operating systems, interoperability among these many networks was critical. Connecting to the network should not dictate that a lot of new hardware had to be purchased; rather, the existing hardware should suffice.

Not controlled by a single corporation   If one corporation had a monopoly on this network, the network would grow to boost the corporation instead of the usefulness and effectiveness of the network. This network needed to be a cooperative effort among many engineers who were working to improve the network for the sake of the supernetwork, not that of a corporation.

By December of 1969 the ARPAnet had four hosts. The ARPAnet consisted of computers at the University of California at Los Angeles, the University of California at Santa Barbara, the University of Utah, and Stanford Research Institute. The ARPAnet set the foundation for what would grow up to be the Internet.

Requests for Comments

To improve the technology that was being used on the ARPAnet, a system was designed to encourage and facilitate correspondence among the engineers who were developing this new network. This system, which is still in use today, relies on **Requests for Comments (RFCs)** to provide feedback and collaboration among engineers. An RFC is a paper that has been written by an engineer, a team of engineers, or just someone with a better idea, to define a new technology or enhance an existing technology.

Request for Comments (RFC)
A paper thoroughly describing a new protocol or technology.

The process of submitting RFCs was designed to be a "bulletin board" for posting technical theories. The old-school way of writing a thesis or book was too slow. RFCs provided an informal and fast way to share new technologies and ideas for enhancements. After an RFC is written and posted, it can be evaluated, critiqued, and used by other engineers and developers. If another engineer or developer can improve on the theory or standard, the RFC provides an open forum in which to do so. Many of these papers are long, painstakingly technical, and in most cases good reading material for someone with difficulty sleeping.

Internet Engineering Task Force (IETF)
A governing body of the Internet.

An RFC can be submitted for review to the **Internet Engineering Task Force (IETF)**. Engineers from the IETF review the papers that are submitted and assign a number to each. From that point on, the RFC number becomes the effective "name" of the paper. For example, the first RFC, which is about host software, is called RFC 1. RFC 1 was submitted in 1969 by a developer named Steve Crocker. There are currently more than 3,000 RFCs.

As the ARPAnet was growing and researchers and engineers were making improvements, they used RFCs as a tool to strengthen and ensure the network's foundation. TCP/IP is a child of the RFC method of development—no corporation makes money when you install TCP/IP. Using RFCs has been the method of growing the ARPAnet with the best network minds contributing.

TIP

It is possible for anyone to write and publish an RFC. Instructions on how to write and submit an RFC are detailed in RFC 2223. Today, RFCs are posted on many Web sites. Appendix D describes this book's companion Web site, which has links to RFC 2223 and other RFC Web sites.

The Birth of TCP/IP

As stated earlier, the "language" spoken by hosts on the ARPAnet in 1969 was called NCP. However, NCP had too many limitations and was not robust enough for the supernetwork, which was beginning to grow out of control. The limitations of NCP and the growth of the ARPAnet lead to research and development of a new network language.

In 1974 Vint Cerf and Bob Kahn, two Internet pioneers, published "A Protocol for Packet Network Interconnection." This paper describes the **Transmission Control Protocol (TCP)**, which is a protocol in the protocol suite that would eventually replace NCP.

The TCP protocol describes the host-to-host portion of a communication. TCP explains how two hosts can set up this communication and how they can stay in touch with each other as data is being transferred. NCP did not resolve these issues to the extent that TCP was able to.

As you will learn in later chapters, TCP is responsible for making sure that the data gets through to the other host. It keeps track of what is sent and retransmits anything that did not get through. If any message is too large for one package, TCP splits the message into several packages and makes sure that they all arrive correctly. After they have arrived, TCP at the other end puts all the packages back together in the proper order.

By 1978, testing and further development of this language led to a new suite of protocols called **Transmission Control Protocol/Internet Protocol (TCP/IP)**. In 1982, it was decided that TCP/IP would replace NCP as the standard language of the ARPAnet. RFC 801 describes how and why the transition from NCP to TCP was to take place. On January 1, 1983, ARPAnet switched over to TCP/IP and the network continued to grow exponentially.

In 1990, the ARPAnet ceased to exist. The Internet has since grown from ARPAnet's roots, and TCP/IP has evolved to meet the changing requirements of the Internet.

Transmission Control Protocol (TCP)
The protocol describing communication between hosts.

Transmission Control Protocol/ Internet Protocol (TCP/IP)
The suite of protocols that when combined create the "language of the Internet."

Design Goals of TCP/IP

TCP/IP has evolved to its current state. The protocols within the TCP/IP suite have been tested, modified, and improved over time. The original TCP/IP protocol suite had several design goals that intended to make it a viable protocol for the large, evolving internetwork. Some of these goals included:

Hardware independence   A protocol suite that could be used on a Mac, PC, mainframe, or any other computer.

Software independence   A protocol suite that could be used by different software vendors and applications. This would enable a host on one site to communicate with a host on another site, without having the same software configuration.

Failure recovery and the ability to handle high error rates   A protocol suite that featured automatic recovery from any dropped or lost data. This protocol must be able to recover from an outage of any host on any part of the network and at any point in a data transfer.

Efficient protocol with low overhead   A protocol suite that had a minimal amount of "extra" data moving with the data being transferred. This extra data, called overhead, functions as packaging for the data being transferred and enables the data transmission. Overhead is similar to an envelope used to send a letter, or a box used to send a bigger item—having too much overhead is as efficient as using a large crate to send someone a necklace.

Ability to add new networks to the internetwork without service disruption   A protocol suite that enabled new, independent networks to join this network of networks without bringing down the larger internetwork.

Routable Data   A protocol suite on which data could make its way through an internetwork of computers to any possible destination. For this to be possible, a single and meaningful addressing scheme must be used so that every computer that is moving the data can compute the best path of every piece of data as it moves through the network.

The TCP/IP protocol suite has evolved to meet these goals. Throughout this book, you will learn how TCP/IP has met and surpassed these original design goals.

Moving Data across the Network

Creating this new "super network" introduced many new concepts and challenges for the pioneering engineers. One of the most critical issues was how to move data across the network. Older communications protocols relied on a circuit-switched technology. TCP/IP, however, introduced a new way of moving data across a network. The protocol suite set a new standard for communications and data transport by using a packet-switched network.

TCP/IP's method of moving data and information helped the protocol suite fulfill several of the requirements for the growing ARPAnet supernetwork. In the following sections, you'll learn about how circuit-switched and packet-switched communications methods work.

Moving Data on a Circuit-Switched Network

Historically, data has moved through a **circuit-switched network**. In a circuit-switched network, data moves across the same path throughout the entire communication. An example of a circuit-switched network is the telephone system. When you make a telephone call, a single path (also called a circuit) is established between the caller and the recipient. For the rest of the conversation, the voice data keeps moving through the same circuit. If you were to make a call and get a very staticky connection, you would hang up and try again. This way you could get a different circuit, hopefully one with less static. Early network data transmissions followed this type of pathway.

In the illustration below, notice that although the data could take multiple routes, all the data moves from the source to the destination along the same path. In a circuit-switched network, data communication moves along a single, established route.

circuit-switched network
A network on which all data in a communication takes the same path.

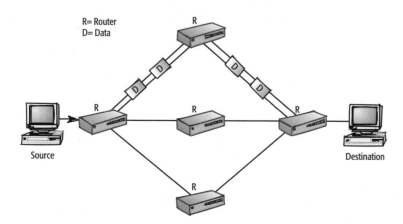

9

Moving Data on a Packet-Switched Network

packet-switched network
A network on which the data in a communication takes several paths.

packet
A unit of data that is prepared for transmission onto a network.

A circuit-switched network was unacceptable for both the ARPAnet and the Internet. Data had to be able to move through different routes so that if one circuit went down or got staticky, it didn't affect communication on the rest of the network. Instead, data simply would take a different route.

The Internet uses a **packet-switched network**. On a packet-switched network, the computer that is sending the data fragments the data into smaller, more manageable chunks. These chunks are called **packets**. Each packet is then individually addressed and sent to its intended recipient. As the several packets make their way through the network, each packet finds its own way to the receiver. The receiving computer reassembles the packets into the original message.

The illustration below shows how TCP/IP moves data. Notice that there are several routes that the data packets can follow from the source to the destination. Unlike the illustration on the preceding page, the data packets here use a variety of routes—some follow the same path, while others follow different paths. Each packet follows its own route, and data is reassembled at the destination. This is how information moves on a packet-switched network.

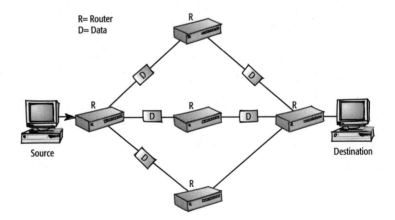

R= Router
D= Data

Source

Destination

Understanding How a Packet-Switched Network Functions

To help you understand how a packet-switched network moves data, let's look at a similar real-world situation.

Let's say that I take my son's soccer team to an arcade and restaurant for a team party. I have the whole team outside of the arcade. My task is to get the team to the other side of the arcade, to my wife who is waiting for them in the restaurant. In this analogy, the team represents the complete file on one host, and each child represents a data packet. One of my goals is to lose as few of the kids as possible.

While we are standing outside, it is easy to put the team in order; all the children are wearing numbered jerseys. I tell the kids that we will meet on the other side of the arcade in a restaurant for pizza and that they should all move as fast as possible through the arcade and to the restaurant.

After I open the door and say, "go," the kids enter one at a time. Entering the arcade one at a time represents the fragmenting and sending of the file. Just as each of the kids has a numbered jersey, each packet has a number so that the receiving host can put the data back together.

Now picture a dozen six-year-olds moving through the arcade. Some of the children will take a short route; others will take a long route. Possibly, they'll all take the same route, though it is much more likely that they will all take different routes. Some will get hung up at certain spots, but others will move through faster. My wife is in the restaurant waiting to receive the team. As they start arriving at the restaurant, she can reassemble the children (packets) in the correct order because they all have a number on their backs. If any are missing, she will wait just a bit for the stragglers and then send back a message that she is missing part of the team (file).

After I receive a message that she is missing a child (a packet), I can resend the missing part. I do not need to resend the entire team (all the packets), just the missing child (packet or packets).

Please note, however, I would not go look for the lost child, I would just put the same numbered jersey on a clone of the lost child and send him into the arcade to find the restaurant.

Why Use TCP/IP?

TCP/IP offers many advantages over other network protocols and protocol suites. Here is a summary of some of the benefits of using the TCP/IP protocol suite:

Widely published, open standard   TCP/IP is not a secret. It is not proprietary or owned by any corporation. Because it is a published protocol with no secrets, any computer engineer is able to improve or enhance the protocol by publishing an RFC.

Compatible with different computer systems   TCP/IP enables any system to communicate with any other system. It is like a universal language that would enable people from any country to communicate effectively with people from any other country.

Works on different hardware and network configurations   TCP/IP is accepted and can be configured for virtually every network created.

Routable protocol   TCP/IP can figure out the path of every piece of data as it moves through the network. Because TCP/IP is a routable protocol, the size of any TCP/IP network is virtually unlimited.

Reliable, efficient data delivery   TCP/IP can guarantee that the data is transferred to another host.

Single addressing scheme   TCP/IP uses a single and relatively simple addressing scheme. You will learn about TCP/IP's addressing in Chapter 6. An administrator can transfer knowledge of TCP/IP to any TCP/IP network without relearning the addressing scheme.

The Internet has become a necessity for business, and it soon will be a necessity at home. Many businesses, large and small, are connected to the Internet and are using TCP/IP as the protocol of choice for their internal networks. As more and more homes connect to the Internet, those computers will also use the TCP/IP protocol suite. The commercial implications of the Internet have changed the dynamic of every business model that has ever been taught.

The Origin of TCP/IP and the Internet

TCP/IP is the standard for a communications protocol on the Internet. You cannot connect to the Internet without using TCP/IP. Whether you build a network at home with two hosts or you manage an **internetwork** at your business with 100,000 hosts, TCP/IP is a communications protocol that will work effectively. TCP/IP can scale to any size environment and is robust enough to connect different types of LANs.

These are a few of the many reasons why network administrators choose to use TCP/IP as the protocol on their networks.

internetwork
Several smaller networks connected together.

Review Questions

1. The Internet was originally called:

    _____

2. List three requirements that the military mandated of this new network.

    _____

    _____

    _____

3. Another name for a computer on a TCP/IP network is:

    _____

4. Describe packet-switched and circuit-switched networks.

    _____

5. What is an RFC?

    _____

6. What protocol did TCP/IP replace?

    _____

7. True or False: TCP/IP is one protocol.

    _____

8. What is IETF?

    _____

9. List four benefits of using TCP/IP.

_____

_____

_____

_____

10. What year was the change made from NCP to TCP/IP?

_____

chapter

2

Protocols

In the first chapter, you learned how the Internet grew from the ARPAnet and how TCP/IP was developed. As the computer network industry has grown, rules and standards have evolved. These rules and standards have formed the TCP/IP protocol into a popular and robust standard used by computers to communicate. This chapter examines why protocols are important and how they enable communication between hosts.

In this chapter you will learn about:

 Protocols

 Packets

 The seven layers of the OSI model

 The four layers of the DoD model

What Are Protocols?

A protocol is a rule or a set of rules and standards for communicating that computers use when they send data back and forth. Both the sender and receiver involved in data transfer must recognize and observe the same protocols.

To exchange data, the sending and the receiving computers, also called hosts, must agree on what the data will look like. When one host is sending another host a whole bunch of 1s and 0s, both hosts have to agree on the meaning and placement of each 1 and each 0. Part of the information that is sent represents addresses and part is data—each host has a unique address, just as you have a unique address on your street. And just like a letter being delivered to your address, data is delivered to the appropriate host based on its address. The hosts that send the information must understand how to find the correct address among the data so that the data can be routed to its destination.

When hosts begin communicating with each other, they first must agree on what protocols to use. This is similar to two people who are going to have a conversation: They have to agree on which language to use and what the rules for the conversation will be. They must agree on who will talk first, how to address the other, how to acknowledge that the information is understood, and how to finish or close the conversation. In the following illustration, Harry the Host is trying to set up communication with another host. The first thing that they need to agree on is the language, or protocols, to use.

Harry   Gary

Protocols

A group of protocols is called a **protocol suite** or a **protocol stack**. A single protocol addresses one particular issue that helps to enable communication—for example, defining what an address looks like. When combined with other protocols, the protocol group that results is called a protocol suite. TCP/IP, for example, is a protocol suite. At a computer that is communicating on a network, the software that packages the data and prepares it for transmission is called a protocol stack. When a computer is receiving data, the data moves up through the protocol stack.

Protocol suites are typically referred to by just a couple of the protocols in the suite. Rather than refer to a suite by a name that might include as many as 20 protocols, you can simply reference it by an easier-to-use and more friendly name. Many protocol suites are in use today. Some are proprietary protocols that have limited use. These are developed for specific purposes to meet some particular need of the hardware or software involved.

Some of the popular protocol suites in today's network communications include:

IPX/SPX   This is the protocol suite that Novell has implemented with its operating system. The acronym stands for Internetwork Packet Exchange/Sequenced Packet Exchange.

AppleTalk   This is the protocol suite that Apple has implemented with its operating system.

TCP/IP   This is the protocol suite that has been made a standard of the Internet. Anyone who would like to use the Internet must use the TCP/IP suite.

Some of the questions that a protocol might answer include:

- What type of cable or transmission media is used to connect hosts on the network?
- How is data transmitted on the transmission media?
- How do the hosts on the network know when to transmit data?
- How does each host know how much data can be transmitted at a time?
- How can hosts using different operating systems communicate?
- How can a host check the data received for transmissions?

protocol suite
A combination of protocols.

protocol stack
Protocols that send and receive data.

19

Protocols Move Packets of Data

When data is sent from one host to another, the Transmission Control Protocol of TCP/IP divides the data into more manageable "chunks." As explained in Chapter 1, these chunks are called packets. The protocol determines how the packets are formed and addressed—the packets are like crates that are used to ship the data.

Each of the packets has a set of **headers** applied to it. The headers usually include addressing and routing information, which makes it possible to reassemble the packets and have the original data at the destination. The headers are applied to the packets for the same reason that you'd apply labels to a package that you are sending. Several headers may be applied to each packet.

A host sending data to another host is like me sending a package to somebody else —for instance, sending a bicycle to my sister in another state. The bicycle represents data that is going to be transferred to another host. To send the bicycle, I have to follow certain rules, or protocols. I put the bicycle into a package, or maybe more than one package if it doesn't fit into a single package. In this example, the packages represent packets.

Even after the bicycle is inside the packages, it is not going anywhere until I put some addressing information on it. There are protocols for putting addresses on the packages: I must use my sister's correct name as well as her correct address. The address label must include the pieces of information necessary to get the packages to the correct destination—for example, her street address, city, state, and zip code. This is similar to TCP/IP putting addressing information headers on the packets that are being transmitted. I also put my return address on the labels, which is similar to a data packet including its source information. There is a proper place for all this addressing information, and I must correctly fill it in on every package or it will not get there. Finally, I indicate the order in which to open the packages by writing "1 of 6," "2 of 6," etc. on them. This will let my sister know which package to open first, second, and so on so that she can easily reassemble the bike.

After the packages are ready to go, I need to decide which delivery service to use. The packages' format depends on the delivery service I choose: If I use Federal Express, I will put the packages into FedEx boxes; if I use United Parcel Service, I will put the packages into a UPS format. Similarly, packets are encapsulated into a format that is appropriate for the physical network that the sending host is located on. If the host is on an Ethernet network, the packet must be in the appropriate format to travel on an Ethernet network. If it's on a Token Ring network, it must be in the Token Ring format. **Encapsulation** is a fancy word for wrapping up the packet into the appropriate package or format.

headers

Bits of information attached to each packet that usually include addressing and routing details; the information acts like a little sticky note on the packet.

encapsulation

The wrapping of a packet into the appropriate package or format.

Because I'm on a UPS route, I call Mike, the UPS man, and ask him to pick up the packages. Neither Mike nor I actually deliver the packages. Instead, the data, packaged in the appropriate format, moves through the transport system, being transferred from one location to the next. The packages might take different routes, but they will get to the same destination. They are delivered to the destination based on the address that I put on the labels. If there is a problem with the delivery, the system will let me know because I put my return address on the packages.

After the packages arrive, my sister opens them. She can reassemble the bicycle based on the information that was on the labels. Similarly, the recipient of the data packet can assemble the data based on the information in the packets' headers.

My sister discards the packing material after she uses the pertinent information from the labels. All she really wants is the bicycle; the packaging was used only to send the bicycle to the correct destination and in the correct order. When using TCP/IP to transport data, a packet is built with several headers, which are discarded after the important information has been used and the data has been delivered to the requesting application.

The illustration below shows Harry the Host sending data to Sally the Host. Notice that the data has been fragmented into several packets and that each packet includes sequence numbers. As the receiving host, Sally reassembles the data back to its unfragmented format.

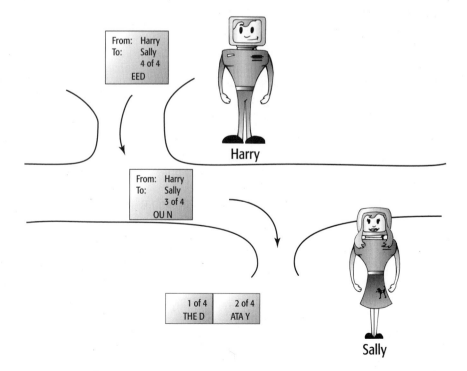

Why We Need Protocols and Standards

Rules—or protocols and standards—are important to ensure compatibility between different kinds of things. As more and more hardware and software vendors began joining the technology explosion, there was no guarantee that any of their products would be able to work with one another. A system had to be put in place so that hardware and software consumers would not get burned by buying incompatible systems.

For example, let's say that I own a small business and I want to buy some new computer equipment. I go out and find some hardware and software that will make my business run smoother and more effectively. All the vendors tell me how great their hardware and software is, so I buy it. I've been sold the dream of how my new automated office will function and how I'll have nothing but spare time. I've been told that everything works together and that my small business will be successful as a result.

However, I bought some hardware from one vendor, some software from another, some other hardware from another vendor, and more software from yet another. And guess what? None of the stuff works together. I just spent a ton of money, and now I'm spending all my time calling for support. All the nice support people are telling me it's the other vendor's software or hardware that is causing the problem.

To keep this scenario from happening, standards and protocols were developed. If the hardware and software vendors were all working with the same guidelines—the same standards and protocols—then their hardware and software should all work together. The hardware vendor would continue to make money selling his hardware, the software vendor would continue to make money selling his software, and I would make money in my small- to medium-sized automated business. I would be happy to buy more hardware and software because it works and it serves my purposes.

Developing protocols is an ongoing, ever changing science. New protocols are constantly under development and testing, and they are improved as the need arises. As the industry is increasing so dynamically and rapidly, more protocols are unleashed to handle the boom. However, before a protocol is accepted and widely implemented, it has to pass rigorous testing. A standard framework is used to help design, compare, test, and evaluate protocols.

The OSI Reference Model

For network communications to take place, hundreds of questions must be answered by a set of protocols. Evaluating and working with these hundreds of questions would be unmanageable. So, in 1977 the **International Organization for Standardization (ISO)** adopted the **Open Standards Interconnection (OSI)** model. The OSI model breaks down the many tasks involved in moving data from one host to another. Now instead of having hundreds of questions to answer, the OSI model gives us a reference to work with. The hundreds of questions are divided into seven smaller, more manageable groups of questions. The seven groups are called **layers**.

The OSI reference model is exactly that; it is only a model. If we continue to think of the model as a set of questions that have to be answered, then the protocols are the answers. Any one protocol may answer only a few of the questions or, in other words, address specific layers in the model. By combining multiple protocols into a protocol suite, we can answer all the questions posed by the model.

The OSI model was created by first making a list of most computer networking topics, such as routing, reliability, and sequencing. From this list, all of the topics were categorized by how they are used in network communications. Within each layer, several topics are discussed. Breaking down this huge task of data communication into seven layers makes the task more manageable.

NOTE

The seven layers of the OSI model are explained in the following sections.

The OSI reference model functions as a baseline for comparison to any protocol suite. As such you can use the OSI model—or the DoD model, which you'll learn about later in this chapter—to help you understand how the parts of TCP/IP work.

This baseline function of the OSI model is similar to a model home. When designing your new home, a model can be used as a baseline. Everyone in the neighborhood also uses the model home as reference to help make the choices in the new homes that they are building. All the homes will vary slightly from the model, but the model provides a means for comparison. In the same way, you can compare any protocol suite to the OSI reference model because protocols are designed from this model. The OSI model acts as a baseline for creating and comparing networking protocols.

International Organization for Standardization (ISO)
The organization that ratified the OSI model.

Open Standards Interconnection model (OSI)
A seven-layer model used to break down the many tasks involved in moving data from one host to another.

layer
A portion of the OSI model that is used to categorize specific concerns.

The Seven Layers of the OSI Model

The goal of the OSI model is to break down the task of data communication into simple steps. These steps are called layers, and the OSI model is made up of seven distinct layers. Each layer has certain responsibilities.

The seven layers of the OSI model are:

◇ Application
◇ Presentation
◇ Session
◇ Transport
◇ Network
◇ Data-Link
◇ Physical

You will learn about the responsibilities of each of these layers in the following sections. The OSI model is a method of compartmentalizing data-communication topics in a way that can help a network administrator when troubleshooting.

What's Your Favorite Layer of the OSI Model?

Here's an interesting party topic and excellent conversation starter. Recently I had a heated discussion with a colleague that lasted almost an hour. We were arguing about which is our favorite layer of the OSI model, and I was amazed at how fast we dug in our heels to defend which layer and why. I found myself deeply loyal to the Physical layer, while my colleague had the opinion that the Presentation layer is best. My point was that all of the important "blue-collar" stuff happens at the Physical layer. The Physical layer works down in the trenches getting bits onto the wire and taking them off. He pointed out that the Presentation layer is so important because it uses compression and encryption. As the discussion got more heated, I found myself thinking of the Presentation layer as a wimpy layer while building up the many important tasks that the Physical layer handles!

Since this discussion, I teach that this is actually a tremendous way to learn the OSI model. Find another network administrator and defend your favorite layer. Come up with valid reasons why you like and don't like each layer. Then take turns defending different layers.

Responsibilities of Each Layer

The purpose of each layer in the OSI model is to provide services to the layer above it while shielding the upper level from what happens below. The higher layers do not need to know how the data got there or what happened at the lower layers.

The following illustration shows how data moves through the seven layers of the OSI model. Here, Harry the Host is transmitting data onto a network. He could be saving a file from his word processing application to a file server, for example. As the data moves down the seven layers toward the network, each layer puts a little bit of information called a header on the packet. The exact contents of each header depend on the protocols enabled at each layer of the protocol suite.

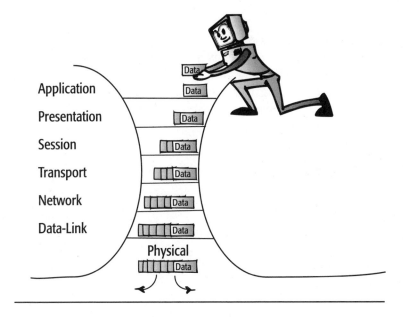

The Application Layer

The top layer of the OSI model is the Application layer. The purpose of the Application layer is to manage communications between applications. A standard Application layer program such as FTP or SMTP interacts with a program that is running at the local workstation. The programmer who has written a word processing application writes the program to interact with a standard application that exists at the Application layer. The word processor uses the standard network application to save, copy, or delete files. This is the layer where the applications receive data and request data. All other layers work for this layer. Think of the Application layer as the CEO of the OSI model.

The Presentation Layer

The Presentation layer is the layer below the Application layer and above the Session layer. The Presentation layer adds structure to packets of data being exchanged. The primary job of the Presentation layer is to ensure that the message gets transmitted in a language or syntax that the receiving computer can understand. The protocols at the Presentation layer may translate the data into an understandable syntax and then compress and maybe encrypt the data before passing it down to the Session layer. Some people may choose this as their favorite layer because it presents the data to the Application layer and the Application layer is so important.

The Session Layer

The Session layer is below the Presentation layer. It controls the dialog during communications. The Session layer protocols set up sessions, or connections. These protocols cover such topics as how to establish a connection, how to use a connection, and how to break down the connection when a session is completed. After a connection is established, the Session layer protocols check for transmission errors. The Session layer also adds control headers to the data packets during the exchange of data.

The Transport Layer

Below the Session layer is the Transport layer. The Transport layer can guarantee that packets are received. The Transport layer also can establish a connection and send acknowledgments as packets are received. The protocols in this layer provide the means to establish, maintain, and release connections for the hosts involved in communication.

The Network Layer

The Network layer, which is below the Transport layer, is responsible for routing the packet based on its logical address. The Network layer fragments and reassembles packets if necessary. It also moves the packets of data from the source to the destination and across networks if necessary. Many people may choose this layer of the OSI model as their favorite because this is where routing happens.

The Data-Link Layer

Below the Network layer is the Data-Link layer, which is where the data is pre-pared for final delivery to the network. The packet is encapsulated into a frame (which is a term used to describe the bundle of binary data). Protocols at this layer aid in the addressing and error detection of data being transferred.

The Data-Link layer is made up of two sublayers: the Logical Link Control (LLC) sublayer and the Media Access Control (MAC) sublayer. Each sublayer provides its own services. The LLC sublayer is the interface between Network layer proto-cols and the media access method, for example, Ethernet or Token Ring. The MAC sublayer handles the connection to the physical media, such as twisted-pair or coaxial cabling.

The Physical Layer

At the bottom of the OSI model is the Physical layer. The topics at this layer determine how the sending and receiving bits of data move along the network's wire. Think of the actual bits moving from the network card on your computer to the wire on the network. I call this the "John Madden layer," because this is truly a blue-collar layer. This layer works down in the trenches putting the bits on the wire and taking them off of the wire. At this layer we talk about the data in bits and packets.

Mnemonics to Help You Remember the Seven Layers

Remembering the order of the OSI model's seven layers will be helpful in any dis-cussion of any protocol or protocol suite. Some mnemonics that might help you remember the seven layers are:

From top to bottom:

All People Seem To Need Data Processing

Aunt Paula Says To Never Drink Poison

From bottom to top:

Please Do Not Throw Sausage Pizza Away

Please Do Not Take Sales Persons' Advice

Paul Dumped Nancy To See Paula Abdul

How the OSI Model Is Used

Packet creation starts at the top of the OSI model. The Application layer gets the data to be transmitted and passes the packet down to the Presentation layer, where another header is put on the packet. The Presentation layer passes the packet down, and each layer puts a header on the packet until the Physical layer gets the packet. The Physical layer merges the packet onto the network wire, and the data continues on its way to the destination.

At the destination, the packet moves in the opposite direction, from the bottom of the model to the top. The Physical layer at the destination protocol stack takes the packet off of the wire and passes it up to the Data-Link layer. The Data-Link layer examines the header that the sending Data-Link layer put on the packet. If this is not the destination for this packet, the packet is discarded. If this is the destination for this packet, the Data-Link layer protocols strip off the Data-Link header that the sender had put onto the packet and pass the rest of the packet up to the Network layer. This continues at every layer until the data reaches the top of the stack.

In this way, each layer of the sending host communicates with the same layer of the receiving host. This is called **peer-layer communication**.

The illustration below depicts peer-layer communication. Each layer in the sending host communicates with its peer layer in the receiving host. Notice that each layer has specific responsibilities that aid in communicating with the other host.

peer-layer communication

A type of communication in which each layer of the sending host communicates with the same layer of the receiving host.

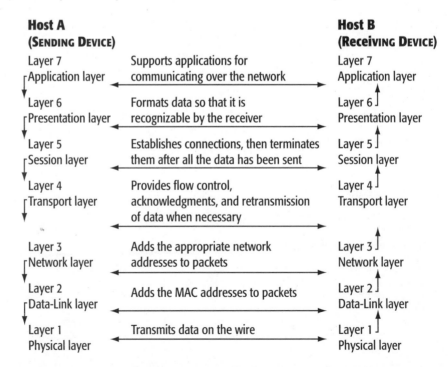

Host A (SENDING DEVICE)		Host B (RECEIVING DEVICE)
Layer 7 Application layer	Supports applications for communicating over the network	Layer 7 Application layer
Layer 6 Presentation layer	Formats data so that it is recognizable by the receiver	Layer 6 Presentation layer
Layer 5 Session layer	Establishes connections, then terminates them after all the data has been sent	Layer 5 Session layer
Layer 4 Transport layer	Provides flow control, acknowledgments, and retransmission of data when necessary	Layer 4 Transport layer
Layer 3 Network layer	Adds the appropriate network addresses to packets	Layer 3 Network layer
Layer 2 Data-Link layer	Adds the MAC addresses to packets	Layer 2 Data-Link layer
Layer 1 Physical layer	Transmits data on the wire	Layer 1 Physical layer

TCP/IP and the DoD Model

The TCP/IP protocol suite was developed before the OSI model was published. As a result, it does not use the OSI model as a reference. TCP/IP was developed using the **Department of Defense (DoD)** reference model. It's important to be familiar with the OSI model, though, because OSI is used to compare the TCP/IP suite with other protocol suites.

Unlike the OSI model, the DoD reference model has four layers. Still, the DoD model answers the same questions about network communications as the OSI model. In the following chapters, you will learn about each of the layers in the DoD model.

The four layers of the DoD model are

Application   Covers the same topics as the Application, Presentation, and Session layers in the OSI model. The Application layer is covered in detail in Chapter 5.

Transport   Covers the topics of Transport from the OSI model. The Transport layer is covered in detail in Chapter 4.

Internet   Covers the topics of Network from the OSI model. The Internet layer is examined in detail in Chapter 3.

Network Interface Layer   Covers the topics of Data-Link and Physical from the OSI model. The Network Interface layer is examined in detail in Chapter 3.

The following table compares the OSI and DoD models. Notice how some of the layers in the DoD model encompass several layers of the OSI model.

OSI Model	DoD or TCP/IP Model
Application layer	Application layer
Presentation layer	
Session layer	
Transport layer	Transport layer
Network layer	Internet layer
Data-Link layer	Network Interface layer
Physical layer	

Department of Defense (DoD)
The branch of the United States military maintaining national defense.

Review Questions

Terms to Know
- ❑ protocol suite
- ❑ protocol stack
- ❑ headers
- ❑ encapsulation
- ❑ ISO
- ❑ OSI
- ❑ layers
- ❑ peer-layer communication
- ❑ DoD

1. What is a protocol?

   _____

2. What is a packet?

   _____

3. Why was the OSI model created?

   _____

4. List the seven layers of the OSI model.

   _____

   _____

   _____

   _____

   _____

   _____

   _____

5. List the four layers of the DoD model.

   _____

   _____

   _____

   _____

6. List three protocol suites.

_____

_____

_____

7. Data is moved across the network in manageable chunks of data called

_____

8. Labels on a package are analogous to _____ on a packet.

9. Which layer of the OSI model has been divided into two sublayers, and what are they?

_____

10. What is your favorite layer of the OSI model and why?

_____

_____

11. What is your least favorite layer of the OSI model and why?

_____

_____

Chapter

3

The Network Interface and Internet Layers

The Network Interface layer and the Internet layer address and route packets. These layers interact with the network by defining how the packets are moved to and from the network. Protocols place headers onto the packet like labels being placed on a package that is being mailed. As each packet is received at a host, it is examined to see if it needs to be processed or discarded.

In this chapter you will learn about:

 The Network Interface layer

 Hardware addresses

 Broadcast addresses

 The Internet layer

 Internet Protocol (IP)

 Address Resolution Protocol (ARP)

 Internet Control Message Protocol (ICMP)

 Internet Group Message Protocol (IGMP)

The Network Interface Layer

The lowest layer in the TCP/IP stack is the **Network Interface layer**. The primary responsibility of the Network Interface layer is to define how a computer connects to a network. This is an important part of the data delivery process because data must be delivered to a particular host through a connection to a network, and data leaving a host has to follow the rules of the network that it is on.

Network Interface layer
Lowest layer of the DoD model, it acts as a host's connection, or interface, to the network.

network topology
Describes how a network is connected and how each host knows when and how to transmit and receive data.

The TCP/IP Network Interface layer does not regulate the type of network that the host is on, but the network that the host is on dictates the driver that the Network Interface layer uses. The host can be on an Ethernet, Token Ring, or Fiber Distributed Data Interface (FDDI), for instance, or on any other **network topology**. The host has to follow the rules for transmitting and receiving data according to the topology of the network.

One way to understand how the host interacts with the Network Interface layer is to compare it to a similar real-life example. For instance, say you are going to send a get-well-soon card and a chocolate cake to your grandmother in the hospital. You are in charge of packaging and addressing the cake and card, but then you turn it over to another system for delivery. You might use one of the private companies offering overnight services or you might use the United States Postal Service; that is not the critical component of this transaction. You must follow the rules established by the service you are using, such as how to address the package, how much to pay for postage, and how to include your return address. When Grandma receives the package, it doesn't really matter how it got there, she is just pleased that it did. How the Network Interface layer at a host interacts with the network that it is connected to is analogous to how you would interact with the postal service.

NOTE

The Network Interface layer is sometimes referred to as the Data-Link layer.

The Network Interface layer is like the receiving department of the hospital. Employees there receive many packages and must decide which to pass up to patients. After they see that your package is addressed correctly, they pass it up to your grandmother. She processes the package by opening it to eat the cake and read the card that you sent.

Similarly, the Network Interface layer is used to receive packets and to send packets. As a packet is received by a network card, the Network Interface layer acts like the receiving department at the hospital and determines whether to pass the packet up the protocol stack for processing based on the hardware address. As a packet is being created, it eventually gets passed down to the Network Interface layer to be put onto the network.

At the Network Interface layer, a header is applied that contains addressing information. Contained within the header is an address called a hardware address, which you will learn about in the next section. The following graphic shows several hosts on a network. Each host has a mailbox through which it sends packets out onto the network and receives packets from the network.

Hardware Address

Within every packet of data is a header that contains addressing information. This header enables the packet to arrive at the correct location. This addressing information comes from a physical address that is burned into every **network interface card** when the card is manufactured. This address will not change for the life of the card. This burned-in address can be called any of the following:

◇ Hardware address

◇ Media Access Control (MAC) address

◇ Ethernet address

◇ Physical address

◇ Network Interface Card (NIC) address

The hardware address is unique to all the network cards ever manufactured. It is a 12-character hexadecimal address. A hardware address looks similar to this:

00:A0:C9:0F:92:A5

NOTE

The three most common numbering systems used in the computer industry are **binary**, **decimal**, and **hexadecimal**. The hexadecimal numbering system uses the same 0 to 9 digits as decimal, then uses A, B, C, D, E, and F to represent 10, 11, 12, 13, 14, and 15. The decimal 16 is represented in hexadecimal as 10.

The first six of these hexadecimal characters represent the manufacturer and are unique to the network card's manufacturer. The last six characters form a unique serial number that the card's manufacturer has assigned to it.

Therefore, if a network card manufacturer doesn't use the same serial number twice, and no two manufacturers use the same manufacturer ID, no two network cards will ever have the same hardware address. In the same way that a Social Security number uniquely identifies a person, a hardware address uniquely identifies a network card.

network interface card

A piece of hardware that is used to connect a host to a network; every host must have one in order to connect to a network.

binary

The base-2 numbering system that computers use to represent data; it consists of only two numbers, 0 and 1.

decimal

A numbering system that uses 0, 1, 2, 3, 4, 5, 6, 7, 8, 9.

hexadecimal

A base-16 numbering system containing 16 sequential numbers (including 0) as base units before adding a new position for the next number; the hexadecimal system uses the numbers 0–9 and then the letters A–F.

TIP

For all TCP/IP communication to occur, the sender/builder of the packet must know the destination hardware address.

broadcast packet
A packet that is addressed to all hosts; the broadcast address is a universal address enabling all hosts to receive the packet.

For a TCP/IP packet to be delivered, it must contain the destination's hardware address. As each packet arrives at the network interface card, the portion of the packet that contains the target hardware address is examined to see whether the packet is intended for that host. If the target hardware address matches that of the receiving network interface card, or if the packet was broadcast, the packet is passed up the stack for processing. If the packet's target hardware address is different, then the packet is discarded.

This process is similar to going to the mailbox to check the mail. You may look through the mail while you are still standing at the mailbox. As you are looking at the pieces, you check to see to whom each letter is addressed. If it is addressed to you, you begin to process it; if it is not to you, you ignore it. If an envelope is addressed to "resident," you also start to process it and see whether it applies to you. The address of "resident" is like a broadcast address in a packet: The broadcast mail is sent out hoping to find someone that it applies to.

Broadcast Packets

Every packet must be addressed to a host. As the packets move through the network, every host will examine every packet to see if each is addressed to that host's unique hardware address.

A packet may be intended for all hosts on a network. This type of packet is called a **broadcast packet**. A broadcast packet contains the target hardware address of FF:FF:FF:FF:FF:FF.

The Internet Layer

The **Internet layer** of the TCP/IP model lies between the Network Interface layer and the Transport layer. (The Transport layer is discussed in Chapter 4.) The Internet layer contains the protocols that are responsible for addressing and **routing** of packets. The Internet layer contains several protocols, including:

- ◇ Internet Protocol (IP)
- ◇ Address Resolution Protocol (ARP)
- ◇ Internet Control Message Protocol (ICMP)
- ◇ Internet Group Message Protocol (IGMP)

In the following sections, you will learn about each of these protocols.

In the preceding section, you learned that for TCP/IP communication to be successful, the packet examined by the Network Interface layer must have a hardware address in its header. As the packet moves up to the Internet layer, it also needs to contain an **IP address**. Using the IP address, the Internet layer provides the necessary protocols to determine the hardware address for routing the packet to the destination.

NOTE

IP addressing is covered in detail in Chapter 6.

The illustration below shows the protocols at the Internet layer. Each of these protocols is discussed in the following sections.

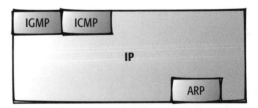

Internet layer

Layer between the Network Interface and Transport layers of the DoD model; protocols at the Internet layer focus on addressing.

routing

The process of determining which is the next path to send a packet so that it gets to its destination.

IP address

An address that IP uses to identify a unique network and host.

38

Internet Protocol (IP)

The Internet Protocol is the primary protocol at the Internet layer of the TCP/IP stack. This protocol is responsible for determining the source and destination IP addresses of every packet.

The network administrator assigns every host on a network a unique IP address. Whereas the hardware address refers to the physical network card, the IP address refers to a **logical address** that the network administrator has assigned to the host. Every host on a TCP/IP network has a unique IP address. An example of an IP address is:

        192.168.2.51

This logical address is assigned by the administrator to the host and must be unique on its network. A portion of the IP address describes the TCP/IP network that the host is on, and a portion describes the unique host address on that network.

The street address where you live is like a logical address. A letter that is addressed to you will be delivered to your house because of this logical address. If you move to another house, your address will change, and letters to you will have to be sent to this new address—but the one who the letter is being delivered to, you, is still the same.

As a packet is being passed down the TCP/IP stack, a source and target IP address are put into an IP header. IP determines whether the destination is local or remote as compared to the source host. The target is local if IP determines that the target is on the same network, and it is remote if the target is on another network. IP can make this determination based on the IP address of the target and the **subnet mask** of the source host.

The subnet mask is a required parameter of every TCP/IP address that is used to separate the network and host portions of that address.

NOTE

Subnet masks are covered in Chapter 7.

logical address
This address can be modified; it refers only to the host.

subnet mask
A parameter included with every IP address that highlights the network portion of the IP address.

Determining Whether the Destination is Local or Remote

IP needs to determine how to get a packet to the destination. If the destination is addressed to a host on the local network, TCP/IP can communicate directly with the destination host. If the host is on a **remote network**, TCP/IP needs to send the packet through the **default gateway**.

remote network

A network other than the one that the host is on; a remote network is on the other side of a router.

A default gateway, also called a **router**, is the address of a host on the network that offers a route off of the network. In other words, the default gateway is the door providing access off of the network.

default gateway

A parameter included with the router's IP address that packets are sent to en route to a remote network.

TCP/IP's communication process is similar to mailing a package. If you want to send a package to someone who lives on the same street that you do, you'd be able to deliver it yourself. If you mail a package to someone who lives on any other street, the package would go to the post office, and then the post office could figure out how to get the package to its destination. The post office is like a default gateway.

router

A host that interfaces with other networks and can move packets from one network to another.

In the illustration below, the router is like a post office that routes the packets to the correct network.

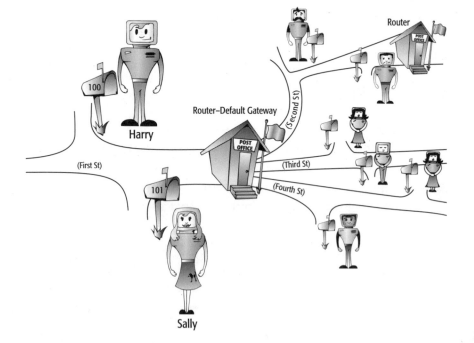

The next illustration shows Harry the Host sending a packet to Sally the Host. The IP protocol in Harry's TCP/IP stack will examine the destination address (Sally's) and determine that Sally is local to Harry. The destination host is local when IP determines that both the sending and destination hosts have the same network portion in their IP addresses.

routing table
A table that contains the addresses indicating the best routes to other networks.

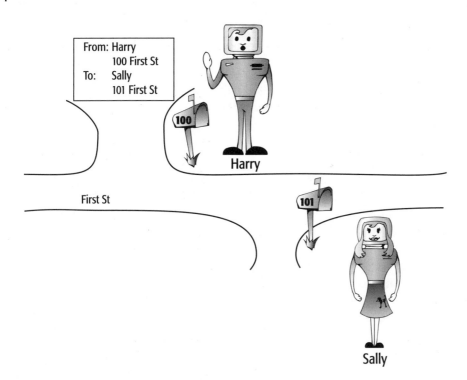

If the target host is local, IP needs to get the hardware address for the target. If the target host is remote, IP looks in its **routing table** for an explicit route to that network. If there is an explicit route, IP needs to get the hardware address of the gateway listed in the routing table. If there is no explicit route, IP needs to get the hardware address for the default gateway.

Determining the Hardware Address

The following flowchart outlines the decision process that TCP/IP uses to decide whose hardware address is required to send a packet.

Address Resolution Protocol (ARP)
A protocol used to translate an IP address to a hardware address.

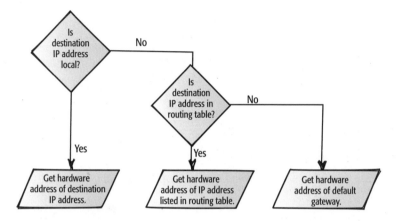

When assigning the IP address of the host, a network administrator will type in the address of the default gateway as one of the TCP/IP parameters. (The packet will be sent to the default gateway's hardware address if the packet is destined for another network.) The default gateway then determines whether the target IP address is on one of its other interfaces or whether the default gateway needs to forward the packet to another router.

Using another analogy, this is similar to going to an airport and trying to get to a destination. If there is a direct route from the airport to your destination, you are sent to your destination. If no direct route exists, you are sent on a route that will get you closer to your destination. If the target is on one of the other interfaces, IP can send the packet through that interface onto the destination network. IP on the gateway strips off the original IP header and puts a new IP header on the packet. The gateway is now the source, and the destination of the packet is either the actual target or the next gateway on its way to the target network.

In the next step, IP uses the **Address Resolution Protocol (ARP)** to get the hardware address of the destination host. ARP is like a detective who will find the hardware address of the destination host based on the IP address that the Internet Protocol is asking for.

Address Resolution Protocol (ARP)

ARP is a protocol that can **resolve** an IP address to a hardware address. After the hardware address is resolved, ARP maintains that information for a short time. Because the host wants to communicate with another host, but only has the IP address, ARP will ask, "Hey, what is your hardware address?" and wait for an answer.

The first place that ARP looks to resolve an IP address to a hardware address is in **ARP cache**. ARP cache is an area in random access memory (RAM) where ARP keeps the IP and hardware addresses that have been resolved. If ARP can find the IP and hardware addresses in ARP cache, the packet is addressed to the hardware address with no further resolution. If the IP address is not in ARP cache, ARP will initiate an **ARP request** broadcast.

After an IP address is resolved to a hardware address, it is stored in ARP cache for two minutes. If IP requests resolution again to the same IP address within those two minutes, the entry will stay in ARP cache another two minutes. An entry can stay in ARP cache for a maximum of ten minutes; then it will be removed from cache regardless of whether it has been referenced within the last two minutes.

The screen capture below shows the ARP cache. The cache contains three types of entries: the IP address in the first column, the hardware address in the second column, and an indication of how the entry got into ARP cache in the third column. An entry in ARP cache is dynamic when an address has been discovered through broadcast, and static when the address has been manually added.

```
C:\>ARP -A

Interface: 209.132.94.125 on Interface 2
  Internet Address        Physical Address        Type
  209.132.94.113          00-a0-24-35-d1-df       dynamic
  209.132.94.114          00-a0-24-87-f0-f0       dynamic
  209.132.94.115          00-a0-24-87-ec-e2       dynamic
  209.132.94.119          00-a0-24-87-f3-c0       dynamic
  209.132.94.120          00-a0-24-87-f3-b3       dynamic
  209.132.94.121          00-a0-24-87-f3-bf       dynamic

C:\>_
```

resolve
To translate a logical to a physical address.

ARP cache
An area in RAM that holds recently resolved IP-to-hardware address resolutions.

ARP request
A broadcast packet that seeks to resolve an IP address to a hardware address.

Using Broadcast to Resolve a Hardware Address

If ARP does not find the IP address in ARP cache, the ARP protocol initiates an ARP request. This request is broadcast on the local network. In the following illustration, Harry's ARP is trying to get resolution for the IP address of 209.132.94.101. ARP broadcasts a packet onto the network that basically says:

"HEY, WHOEVER IS 209.132.94.101, I NEED YOUR HARDWARE ADDRESS!"

The ARP broadcast is addressed to every host by setting the destination hardware address to FF:FF:FF:FF:FF:FF. The ARP broadcast contains the IP address of the requested destination so that the intended recipient is identified. The ARP broadcast also contains the source's hardware address. Including the source's hardware address expedites the reply from the destination host. After the destination receives and recognizes that the ARP broadcast is intended for it, the destination puts the source IP address and hardware address into its own ARP cache. Because the source's hardware address is in ARP cache, the address will already be known when the ARP reply is sent back to the original source.

The Network Interface and Internet Layers

As the ARP packet is received at each host, the network interface card takes the packet off of the wire and passes it up through the Network Interface layer to the Internet layer and ARP. ARP at the destination examines the packet to see whether the packet is asking for that host's hardware address. If the ARP request is not for that host, the packet is discarded. If it does have that host's hardware address, the IP and hardware address of the source is put into ARP cache and an ARP reply to the source is created. The target's hardware address is included in the **ARP reply**. When the ARP reply is received, the IP and hardware addresses are placed into ARP cache for two minutes.

In the illustration below, Sally the host responds to the ARP request with a packet that contains her IP address and hardware address. This ARP reply is sent directly to Harry because the ARP request had his IP and hardware addresses.

ARP reply
A packet that is returned to the sender of the ARP request and that includes the IP address and hardware address that was requested.

Harry

Hey 209.132.94.100 with the hardware address of 00:10:4B:74:91:12, I am 209.132.94.101 and my hardware address is 00:10:4B:6F:B3:F2.

Sally

ARP Packets

The following screen shot shows two ARP packets that were captured from a network. The first packet says that it is an ARP request and the target IP is 209.132.94.101.

The bottom portion of the graphic shows the contents of the first packet. You can see that the ARP request packet was broadcast to all hosts (destination FFFFFFFFFFFF) in the ETHERNET section. This ARP request came from a source host whose hardware address is 00104B749112. In the ARP section of this packet, the sender's hardware and protocol addresses and the target's protocol address are filled in, but not the target's hardware address. The purpose of this packet is to request that the host with the protocol address of 209.132.94.101 reply and fill in the hardware address section.

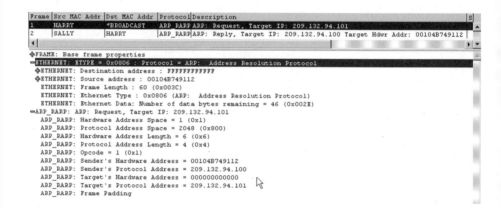

The following screen shot shows the contents of the ARP reply. The reply is a new packet and is sent from the target host. The target host is now the sender because it is sending back the requested information. In this reply packet, the source lets the destination know the source's hardware address.

Internet Control Message Protocol (ICMP)

ICMP is a protocol used primarily for sending error messages, performing diagnostics, and controlling the flow of data. An example of an error message and of flow control is an ICMP **source-quench** packet sent by a router to a source host to tell the host to slow down because the router is overloaded.

Routers let hosts send data as fast as possible—unless traffic at the router is getting too heavy. Then, a router will send the host a source-quench message as an ICMP packet, requesting that the host slow down. After the host receives a source-quench message, the host will slow down and then slowly increase the speed again until another source-quench message is sent.

The router's action is similar to a real-life situation you might be familiar with. When driving in the car with the kids in the back, I will let them play and get louder until finally I will send back a source-quench message. The message says, "You'd better quiet down; you're getting too loud!" The kids will immediately quiet down. Then they will slowly start ramping up again until I have to send back another source-quench message. The kids will make as much noise as they can get away with in the same way that the hosts will constantly be trying to send data as fast as the router can handle it.

Performing Diagnostics with ICMP and Ping

As stated earlier, the ICMP protocol is used for performing diagnostics. An example of using ICMP as a diagnostic tool is with the **Ping** utility. Ping stands for Packet InterNet Groper.

An administrator uses the Ping utility to send four ICMP echo request packets to the destination host and to ask that the destination host reply to these packets. ICMP places a small amount of data and requests that the data get sent back. If the data returns, the administrator can assume successful connectivity to the destination. If the ICMP packet does not return, then a connectivity problem exists.

To ping another host from a command prompt, type:

```
Ping ip address
```

source-quench
An ICMP packet that is sent to slow down the transmission at the source.

Ping
Packet InterNet Groper; a software utility that tests connectivity between two TCP/IP hosts.

Examining Ping Packets

In the screen shot below, the source host (209.132.94.100) pinged the destination host (209.132.94.101).

Frame	Src MAC Addr	Dst MAC Addr	Protocol	Description	S
33	HARRY	*BROADCAST	ARP_RARP	ARP: Request, Target IP: 209.132.94.101	
34	SALLY	HARRY	ARP_RARP	ARP: Reply, Target IP: 209.132.94.100 Target Hdwr Addr: 00104B749112	
35	HARRY	SALLY	ICMP	Echo, From 209.132.94.100 To 209.132.94.101	2
36	SALLY	HARRY	ICMP	Echo Reply, To 209.132.94.100 From 209.132.94.101	S.
37	HARRY	SALLY	ICMP	Echo, From 209.132.94.100 To 209.132.94.101	2
38	SALLY	HARRY	ICMP	Echo Reply, To 209.132.94.100 From 209.132.94.101	S.
39	HARRY	SALLY	ICMP	Echo, From 209.132.94.100 To 209.132.94.101	2
40	SALLY	HARRY	ICMP	Echo Reply, To 209.132.94.100 From 209.132.94.101	S.
41	HARRY	SALLY	ICMP	Echo, From 209.132.94.100 To 209.132.94.101	2
42	SALLY	HARRY	ICMP	Echo Reply, To 209.132.94.100 From 209.132.94.101	S.

The screen shot shows:

1. (Frame 1) An ARP request is broadcast for the target 209.132.94.101.

2. (Frame 2) An ARP reply is sent to the source at 209.132.94.100 with the target's hardware address.

3. (Frame 3) An ICMP packet is sent from the source 209.132.94.100 to the destination 209.132.94.101 requesting an "echo."

4. (Frame 4) An ICMP echo reply is sent from the destination 209.132.94.101 to the source 209.132.94.100.

5. (Frames 5–10) Steps 3 and 4 are repeated three more times.

Looking at captured packets is like eavesdropping on the hosts' conversation. Sending a little ICMP packet to another host is an excellent method of testing connectivity. It takes virtually no overhead for the destination to respond with an ICMP reply.

Although almost no overhead is required, some sites, such as www.microsoft.com, will not respond to ICMP request packets. The enormous amount of ping-request traffic Microsoft was receiving caused the overhead to get excessive, and so their servers no longer reply to such requests. A network administrator has set up a filter as well so that ICMP echo packets are filtered or dropped at the **firewall** for security purposes. A company may not want outsiders pinging or "groping" inside their network.

firewall

An application that prevents certain types of data from passing from a public network to an internal, private network.

48

Internet Group Management Protocol (IGMP)

IGMP is a protocol that enables one host to send one **stream** of data to many hosts at the same time. Most TCP/IP connections consist of one host sending data to one other host, or possibly to all hosts via a broadcast. In contrast, IGMP packets are directed to a **reserved IP address**, and any hosts that would like to receive the data stream have to listen at the address. In other words, the host does not wait to receive data at its own address—it has to actively request the data that is sent to the reserved IP address.

The destination IP address used by IGMP is called a **multicast address.** These reserved IP addresses cannot be assigned to a host. With special software, a TCP/IP host can "listen" for data that is being sent to a multicast address. When several hosts are listening for data at a specific address and data is sent to that address, all the hosts receive the data. All these packets contain an IGMP header.

stream
A series of packets sent without waiting for acknowledgments.

reserved IP address
An IP address that cannot be used as a valid host address.

multicast address
A reserved IP address that IGMP uses for streaming data.

NOTE

Multicast addresses are covered in detail in Chapter 6.

Many devices on a network use IGMP packets to exchange data. Some routing protocols use IGMP to exchange routing tables. Windows Internet Naming Service (WINS) can use IGMP to exchange databases. Across the Internet, many sites are using IGMP packets to move streams of data to many hosts concurrently.

The concept of multicast is similar to a garden hose that has a bunch of small pinholes in it. As a stream of water gushes down the hose, the water is received by many. The water represents the one stream of data and the pinholes represent the hosts that receive it. In this way, the stream is sent only once, but many can receive it.

Sending Streaming Audio and Video with IGMP

IGMP can be used as the protocol for sending streaming audio or streaming video when the data needs to go from one source to many receivers. Rather than address and track each packet to every host, which would be impossible, the data is streamed to a multicast address, and the recipients listen and receive at that address.

Again, multicasting is like a garden hose with several small holes in it: The water is not directed to any one place, but it is dispersed to many. The following illustration shows a server sending some IGMP audio packets. The host "sings" the broadcast. Some of the other hosts listen and some don't. Whether Harry gets the data is not important to the sender.

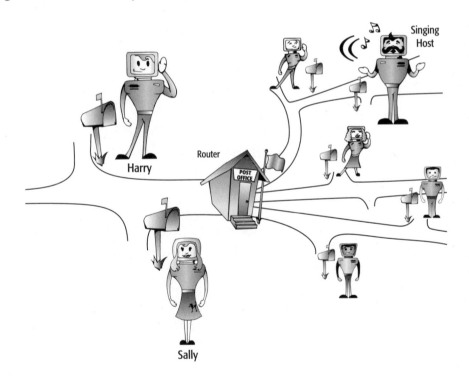

Some of the largest multimedia files that get transferred through the Internet include audio and video files. Streaming is a technique for transferring such data in a way that enables it to be processed as a steady and continuous flow. Without streaming, large multimedia files get broken up into smaller packets and reach end users in a hit-or-miss order. As the application is trying to display the data, the out-of-order pattern results in an unacceptable, choppy presentation.

Because of the growing popularity of the Internet and the demand for these large multimedia files to arrive in a smooth, orderly fashion, streaming technologies are becoming increasingly important. Most users do not have fast enough access to download large multimedia files quickly. With streaming, Web browsers can start displaying the data before the entire file has been transmitted.

In the streaming process, the host receiving the data collects the data and sends it up the protocol stack to the application that is processing the data. The application converts the data to sound or pictures and presents it as one smooth flow of information. If the host receiving the stream receives the data faster than it can be processed, that host needs to temporarily save the excess data in a buffer so that it can be presented by the application in a smooth manner. If the data isn't received quickly enough, though, the presentation of the data will not be smooth; it will be choppy and staticky.

Review Questions

Terms to Know

❏ Network Interface layer
❏ network topology
❏ network interface card
❏ binary
❏ decimal
❏ hexadecimal
❏ broadcast packet
❏ Internet layer
❏ routing
❏ IP address
❏ logical address
❏ subnet mask
❏ remote network

1. List three other names for *hardware address*.

_____

_____

_____

2. What hardware address is a broadcast packet addressed to?

_____

3. List four protocols at the Internet layer.

_____

_____

_____

_____

4. List two responsibilities of IP.

_____

_____

5. What protocol resolves an IP address to a hardware address?

_____

6. How long will IP-to-hardware address resolution stay in ARP cache?

_____

7. What hardware address is an ARP request sent to?

_____

8. What hardware address is an ARP reply sent to?

_____

9. What software utility uses ICMP?

_____

10. What information is contained in an ARP request?

_____

11. What information is contained in an ARP reply?

_____

12. List three examples of a network topology.

_____

_____

_____

13. When is the hardware address assigned to the network interface card?

_____

14. How many characters does the hardware address contain?

_____

Terms to Know
- ❏ default gateway
- ❏ router
- ❏ routing table
- ❏ ARP
- ❏ resolve
- ❏ ARP cache
- ❏ ARP request
- ❏ ARP reply
- ❏ source-quench
- ❏ ping
- ❏ firewall
- ❏ stream
- ❏ reserved IP address
- ❏ multicast address

53

Chapter

4

The Transport Layer

The Transport layer determines whether the sender and the receiver will set up a connection before communicating and how often they will send acknowledgments of that connection to each other.

The Transport layer has only two protocols:

 Transmission Control Protocol (TCP)

 User Datagram Protocol (UDP)

Whereas TCP sets up a connection and sends acknowledgments, UDP does not. UDP can move data faster, but TCP guarantees delivery. Both are explained in this chapter.

Understanding the Transport Layer

The protocols at the Transport layer deliver data to and receive data from the Transport layer protocols of other hosts. The other host can be on the local network or on a network thousands of miles away. In some documentation, the Transport layer is also called the Host-to-Host layer.

The Transport layer of the TCP/IP protocol suite consists of only two protocols, TCP and UDP. TCP provides connection-oriented, reliable communication, and UDP provides connectionless, unreliable communication. TCP is slower and typically used for transferring large amounts of data to ensure that the data won't have to be sent again. UDP is faster and typically used for transferring small amounts of data.

Connection-oriented means that a connection is established as the communication begins. During this connection, certain information is exchanged to set the parameters of the main communication. Questions such as the following are answered:

- ◇ How much data can each host receive at a time?
- ◇ What sequence numbers should the hosts use in this connection?
- ◇ What acknowledgment numbers should be used in this connection?
- ◇ How long should each host wait for acknowledgments before resending data?

Reliable means that an acknowledgment will be sent back to the sending host throughout the communication to verify receipt of the packets. As each segment of data is received at the destination, an acknowledgment is sent to the sender within a specified period. If an acknowledgment is not sent within that time, the sender resends the data. If the receiver of the data gets the data in a damaged condition, the damaged packet is simply discarded. The recipient sends no acknowledgment for the damaged packet, and because the sender receives no acknowledgment, the data is re-sent.

The screen capture below shows the TCP portion of a packet. Notice the sequence and acknowledgment numbers: Frame 1 is sent from Harry to the FTP server to establish the connection; the sequence numbers are 2714368-2714371. Frame 2 is sent from the FTP server (and delivered by Harry's default gateway) and displays an acknowledgment for 2714369.

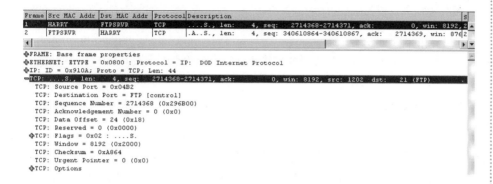

```
Frame Src MAC Addr  Dst MAC Addr  Protocol Description                                                              S
1     HARRY         FTPSRVR       TCP      ....S., len:    4, seq:  2714368-2714371, ack:         0, win: 8192, 2
2     FTPSRVR       HARRY         TCP      .A..S., len:    4, seq: 340610864-340610867, ack:  2714369, win: 876 2

⊕FRAME: Base frame properties
⊕ETHERNET: ETYPE = 0x0800 : Protocol = IP:  DOD Internet Protocol
⊕IP: ID = 0x910A; Proto = TCP; Len: 44
⊟TCP: ....S., len:    4, seq:  2714368-2714371, ack:         0, win: 8192, src: 1202  dst:   21 (FTP)
     TCP: Source Port = 0x04B2
     TCP: Destination Port = FTP [control]
     TCP: Sequence Number = 2714368 (0x296B00)
     TCP: Acknowledgement Number = 0 (0x0)
     TCP: Data Offset = 24 (0x18)
     TCP: Reserved = 0 (0x0000)
  ⊕TCP: Flags = 0x02 : ....S.
     TCP: Window = 8192 (0x2000)
     TCP: Checksum = 0xA864
     TCP: Urgent Pointer = 0 (0x0)
  ⊕TCP: Options
```

Unlike TCP, UDP provides connectionless, unreliable communication. *Connectionless* means that no connection is established before data transfer begins. The sending host does not send any setup packets to the destination; it just starts sending. This process is similar to the service that has an operator announcing the correct time when you call a designated telephone number. The operator continually sends out the current time; if nobody gets it, that's okay. The communication is considered unreliable because there will be no acknowledgments that the data was received at the destination. In addition, this type of packet contains a small header at the Transport layer, and because there is no connection to establish and no acknowledgment to wait for, data can be transferred faster.

The screen capture below shows the UDP portion of a packet. Notice that the UDP header is very small compared to the TCP portion of the packet shown above. The UDP portion has no sequence numbers nor acknowledgments. The packet is simply sent out, and hopefully the recipient gets it.

```
Frame Src MAC Addr  Dst MAC Addr  Protocol Description                                       S
1     HARRY         *BROADCAST    DHCP     Discover       (xid=5F444C10)                     0
2     DHCPSRVR      *BROADCAST    DHCP     Offer          (xid=5F444C10)                     1

⊕FRAME: Base frame properties
⊕ETHERNET: ETYPE = 0x0800 : Protocol = IP:  DOD Internet Protocol
⊕IP: ID = 0xF400; Proto = UDP; Len: 328
⊟UDP: IP Multicast:  Src Port: BOOTP Client, (68); Dst Port: BOOTP Server (67); Length = 308 (0x134)
     UDP: Source Port = BOOTP Client
     UDP: Destination Port = BOOTP Server
     UDP: Total length = 308 (0x134) bytes
     UDP: UDP Checksum = 0x23A5
     UDP: Data: Number of data bytes remaining = 300 (0x012C)
  ⊕DHCP: Discover          (xid=5F444C10)
```

Understanding Transmission Control Protocol

Transmission Control Protocol (TCP)

Protocol at the Transport layer that is connection oriented and guarantees delivery of packets. TCP is responsible for ensuring that a message is divided into the packets that IP manages and for reassembling the packets into the complete message at the other end.

Transmission Control Protocol (TCP) is the protocol that connects the sending host and the receiving host to each other. TCP is a **connection-oriented** protocol, which means that the two hosts that are communicating know about each other. One of the first aspects they determine is how to communicate with each other, where to send data, and how it will be received. The protocol guarantees delivery of packets by sending **acknowledgments** after each packet is received.

Before a sender begins sending data to a receiver, a short conversation takes place. The conversation is initiated by the TCP protocol at the Transport layer of the sending host. The protocol sends a packet to the receiving host to set up the communication for transferring data.

connection-oriented

A type of protocol in which a connection is established and maintained until the message or messages to be exchanged by the application programs at each end have been exchanged.

TCP is similar to the protocol for using a walkie-talkie. The first person tries to set up a connection by asking, "Hello, are you there?" The other person responds with, "Yes, I'm here, go ahead." Then a conversation begins, and every time one person gives some information, the other needs to respond with an acknowledgment that the information was received. Several times in the walkie-talkie conversation, the one receiving the information says, "Okay, got it, keep going."

Using a Three-Way Handshake

acknowledgments

A packet sent by a host to confirm receipt of a packet. The sending host waits for an acknowledgment packet before sending additional data. The destination host sends acknowledgments as packets are received.

A conversation is started with a **three-way handshake**. In the first step of this process, the initiator of the conversation sends a packet to the other host requesting that they start a conversation. In the second step, the destination host sends back an acknowledgment that agrees to set up the communication and sets some parameters. In the final step, the initiator sends back one more packet that is a confirmation of the connection.

A good analogy for the three-way handshake is a secretary placing a call for an executive. The secretary acts like TCP when initiating the call for the executive. The secretary sets up the call with the destination executive and possibly lays down some guidelines. After the destination executive and the secretary have agreed, the "real" conversation begins between the executives.

The three-way handshake is used to set up TCP/IP communication, for example, when requesting a Web page. In the following dialog, Harry the Host is setting up a conversation with Wally the Web Server. The Web server is a host on the Internet that listens for requests and responds by sending Web pages. This is a sample of the process used to set up a conversation between any two hosts so that TCP/IP communication can occur.

> **Harry:** "Hello, I would like to connect to you and make some requests from you. Please send a packet to me to acknowledge that you received this. Please send it to my port 1076; that's where I'll be listening for your response."

> **Wally:** "Hi, I am acknowledging receipt of a packet from you. I would be happy to set up a connection with you. Please acknowledge that you received this packet."

> **Harry:** "All right, I'm acknowledging receipt of a packet from you. Thanks for acknowledging me. Let's get started."

In the illustration below, Harry the Host sets up communication with Wally the Web Server.

three-way handshake
A three-step conversation initiated by TCP to set up a connection between hosts.

Then the conversation continues like this:

> **Harry:** "Hi, it's me. I'd like you to send me your home page."

> **Wally:** "Here's some of it. Let me know when you've got it, and I'll send you more."

> **Harry:** "Got it; let me have more."

> **Wally:** "Here's some more; let me know when you've got it."

Organizing Data and Guaranteeing Delivery

sequence numbers

Numbers in a header that indicate the order of packets. If packets get out of order en route to the destination host, this numbering system enables packets to be rearranged in order at the destination host.

TCP is a connection-oriented protocol because the connection is set up and used for the entire conversation. As packets are moved between the hosts having the conversation, TCP provides the connection. Each packet has a TCP header that includes **sequence numbers**, acknowledgment numbers, addresses, and other pieces of connection information.

TCP is also responsible for dividing the data into smaller packets if the data is too large to fit into a single packet. TCP on the destination host reassembles the packets so that the data is presented to the Application layer all put back together.

After a packet is sent, the sending host waits for an acknowledgment before sending more data. This is the feature of TCP that guarantees delivery of packets. If an acknowledgment is not received at the sending host, the sender resends the packet.

Every TCP packet that is received by the receiver triggers TCP to send back an acknowledgment packet. If the sending host does not receive the acknowledgment, then something must have gone wrong. Rather than send out a search-and-rescue party to try to find the packet, TCP on the host simply retransmits the missing packet.

Many times my wife tells me that she would like me to at least respond to something she is saying. I listen to her talk and instead of immediately responding, I think through what she's saying. Or maybe I just pretend to listen while I think about a baseball game, and I forget to respond. She says, "Are you listening to me?" What she wants is a response before she sends me more information. I could respond with a grunt or a nod of my head, and that would let her know that I received the data and I'm ready for more. Likewise, TCP would just like an acknowledgment before sending more data.

Understanding User Datagram Protocol

User Datagram Protocol (UDP) is the protocol used at the Transport layer for **connectionless**, non-guaranteed communication. Unlike TCP, UDP does not set up a connection and does not use acknowledgments.

Instead, UDP just blasts out the packets. If the receiver gets the packet, great; if not, oh well. If a UDP packet gets lost or never arrives at the destination, the sender doesn't know nor care about it. When an application uses UDP, no connection gets set up before a conversation starts—the sender just sends.

In other words, UDP is similar to me teaching a class on television. I send out the data but I'm not waiting for you to acknowledge any of the data. It is not specifically going to anyone, but I'm hoping that you're watching. This communication method is much faster than teaching you in my classroom. In my classroom, I'd be looking for your acknowledgments before continuing to the next topic. On television, I don't have to wait; I'm hoping that you get it, but I don't know. As a matter of fact, you may have left the room to get a soda and a sandwich. Still, I keep on sending the data because I'm not waiting for your acknowledgments.

UDP is useful when TCP would be too complex, too slow, or just unnecessary.

UDP provides a few details in the UDP header that are used to get the packet to the right port at the destination host. One of the parameters in the small UDP header is the port number. The 16-bit UDP port number indicates the location of the service that the host is looking for.

Another value that is placed into the UDP header is a checksum. The sending host calculates the checksum by using a special algorithm and then places the checksum into the UDP header. The algorithm applies an equation to the data that is being sent (all the 1s and 0s). The checksum is used by the receiving host to verify that the packet was received intact. The recipient applies the same algorithm to the received packet, and if the value matches the UDP checksum value, the packet was received intact. If the values are different, the packet is simply discarded and ignored.

User Datagram Protocol (UDP)
A protocol offering a limited amount of service when messages are exchanged between hosts. No connection is set up and no acknowledgments are expected.

connectionless
Communication that occurs without a connection first being set up.

UDP Communication

In terms of computers, a host may use UDP to make a request of some service, not knowing where that service is located. A UDP conversation is similar to one Harry the Host might have when looking for a Dynamic Host Configuration Protocol (DHCP) server. He doesn't send a request to the DHCP server because he doesn't know where it is. There is no acknowledgment that anyone received the packet. However, Donna the DHCP server does hear his request and responds.

The short conversation would be like this:

> **Harry:** "Hey, I'm looking for a DHCP server."
>
> **Donna:** "I am a DHCP server."

When Harry sends out the UDP packet, no connection is set up nor does Harry wait for an acknowledgment of packet receipt. Harry waits for the answer to the request, but not for an acknowledgment.

When UDP is used, the connection and guarantee of the packets are usually the responsibility of a higher layer. The application that resides at a higher layer is responsible for making sure that the UDP packets are getting to their destinations correctly.

Throughout this chapter you have learned the differences between TCP and UDP. One of the most striking comparisons is the size of the header at the Transport layer.

The screen capture below is the layout of the TCP header from the actual RFC in which TCP is described. RFC 761 details TCP; here is the author's header description:

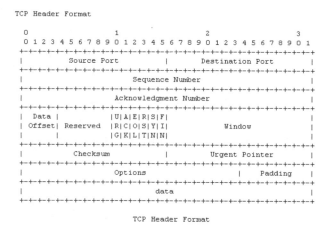

Notice how large and complicated this header looks.

Compare the TCP header to the simple, relatively small header of UDP, which is detailed in RFC 768.

```
0          7 8      15 16    23 24     31
+--------+--------+--------+--------+
|     Source      |   Destination   |
|      Port       |      Port       |
+--------+--------+--------+--------+
|                 |                 |
|     Length      |    Checksum     |
+--------+--------+--------+--------+
|
|         data octets ...
+--------------- ...

      User Datagram Header Format
```

Review Questions

Terms to Know
- ❏ TCP
- ❏ connection-oriented
- ❏ acknowledgments
- ❏ three-way
  handshake
- ❏ sequence numbers
- ❏ UDP
- ❏ connectionless

1. List the two protocols at the Transport layer.

   _____

   _____

2. List two important characteristics of each protocol.

   _____

   _____

3. What is the name of the process that TCP uses to set up a connection?

   _____

4. What does TCP at the destination host send back to the sending host after receiving data?

   _____

5. How long will UDP on the sending host wait for an acknowledgment before sending more data?

   _____

6. When UDP is used, what is responsible for the guarantee of packet delivery?

   _____

7. What is the benefit of UDP?

   _____

8. What is the benefit of TCP?

_____

9. Which RFC describes TCP?

_____

10. Which RFC describes UDP?

_____

11. Which protocol uses a larger header, TCP or UDP?

_____

12. What is the purpose of a checksum?

_____

Chapter

5

The Application Layer

At the top of the TCP/IP stack is the Application layer. The Application layer contains applications that process requests from other hosts. Ports and sockets are used to receive and send data. To best describe the Application layer, this chapter closely examines the following topics:

 Ports and sockets

 File Transfer Protocol (FTP)

 Hypertext Transfer Protocol (HTTP)

Understanding the Application Layer

The **Application layer** is the part of the TCP/IP where requests for data or services are processed. Applications at this layer are waiting for requests to process and they are all listening at their respective **ports**.

The Application layer is not where your word processor, spreadsheet, or Internet browser application is running. Applications that are running at the Application layer interact with the word processor, spreadsheet, or Internet browser application. Two examples of applications that run at the Application layer are FTP and HTTP. Both are detailed later in this chapter.

Understanding Ports and Sockets

As a packet is moving up through the stack on its way to the Application layer, the Transport layer directs the packet to the appropriate port. A port is a number that the application at the Application layer uses as a send-and-receive address. A port is like a stereo speaker, and applications are set up to listen at a particular speaker. The application puts its ear to the speaker and waits for a request to be passed through it.

Imagine that the application is listening for requests to process. As a request makes its way up the TCP/IP stack, either TCP or UDP at the Transport layer hands the request up to the application. Remember, the application is set up to listen at a specific port number, and TCP or UDP sends the request to the appropriate port based on information in the packet's header.

As a good analogy, imagine a local fast-food restaurant, which is a combination of a popular hamburger franchise and a popular seafood franchise. When I order the Number 1 Value Meal, how do the employees know which Number 1 Value Meal I mean? Do I mean the hamburger or seafood Number 1? What kind of burger or fish is the Number 1?

I specify that I want the hamburger restaurant's Number 1 Value Meal when I place the order. The employee behind the counter documents the order and passes it to the appropriate cook. Both the hamburger and the seafood cooks have a different meaning for *Number 1 Value Meal*, and depending on which cook the order is passed to, I get a burger or fish. Based on it being a Number *1* Value Meal, the cook knows which burger to cook or fish to fry.

Note that when I order a Number 1 Value Meal, instead of saying the name of the burger, fries, and soda, I just say "Hamburger Number 1." The employee at the counter then knows which cook to pass my order to so that it can be processed. Similarly, rather than specify the name of an application to get passed to, the packet specifies the port number to get passed to.

TCP and UDP have use of 65,536 ports each. A packet, for example, may specify that it is bound for TCP port 80. TCP port 80 is the standard port for Web servers to listen for HTTP requests. As another example, a packet may specify that it is bound for UDP port 69, which is the standard for TFTP requests. The Internet layer passed this packet to either TCP or UDP and now TCP or UDP at the Transport layer passes the packet to the appropriate port where the application is listening for requests.

socket
IP address : TCP or UDP : port number.

Think of this port information forming a funnel through the TCP/IP stack. As soon as a packet is delivered to a particular IP address, it is passed up through the stack to make sure it is addressed to the host that received it. Then it is passed up to TCP or UDP and then to the appropriate port so that the application at the Application layer can process the request. This funnel is called a **socket**.

A socket combines three pieces of information: the IP address, TCP or UDP, and the port number. The TCP or UDP indicates which protocol is to be used. A socket is written like this:

    131.107.2.200:TCP:80 or 131.107.2.200:UDP:69

The illustration below shows the TCP/IP protocol stack with 65,536 TCP ports and 65,536 UDP ports at the Application layer. Notice that as a packet moves up the stack, IP will direct the packet to the either a TCP port or a UDP port. The applications are listening at their appropriate ports so that when data arrives, it can be processed accurately.

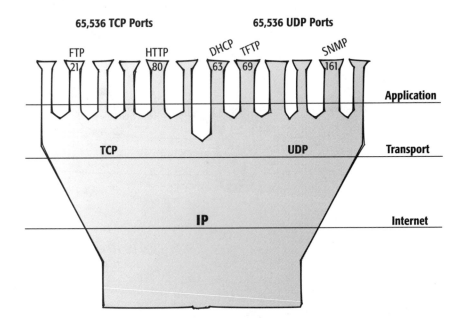

Well-Known Ports

Well-known ports are port numbers that the **Internet Assigned Number Authority (IANA)** has reserved for specific applications to use. For example:

Port	Reserved For
TCP:80	HTTP
TCP:21	FTP
TCP:20	FTP-Data
UDP:69	Trivial File Transfer Protocol (TFTP)
UDP:161	Simple Network Management Protocol (SNMP)

The port numbers between 1 and 1,024 are considered well-known port numbers and are reserved for specified applications, just as 911 and 411 are reserved and well-known telephone numbers. Port numbers between 1,025 and 65,536 have no specified use. Programmers use these ports for new applications they are writing. Well-known ports were originally documented in RFC 1060 and were updated in RFC 1700.

The illustration below shows Harry the Host sending a request to Wally the Web Server, who is listening to requests from a few different ports. Harry sends a request to TCP port 80, requesting that Wally send him a Web page.

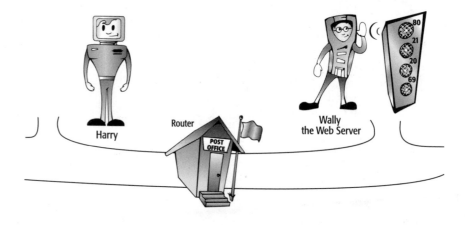

File Transfer Protocol (FTP)

File Transfer Protocol (FTP) is the protocol that defines how a file can be transferred from one host to another. For a file to be transferred from one host to another, the FTP on the initiating host creates the request for a file, and FTP on the FTP server processes the requests for a file. A programmer who would like to learn all of the idiosyncrasies of FTP should read RFC 959.

Two hosts are involved in an FTP session. One host requests a file, and the other host has a copy of the file and transfers a copy to the requesting host. Files can be transferred in either a text or **binary format**.

The host that is requesting the service is called a client and the host that provides the service is called a server. These two hosts establish a client/server relationship, which is simply one host making requests of another.

The requesting host uses an application to request the file. The application may be a word processor, an **FTP command line utility**, or an **FTP command interpreter**. The FTP command line utility enables a host to connect to an **FTP server** without using a fancy interface by having the user simply enter FTP commands at the command line. FTP connects to the FTP server, and the user is requested to log in. The user must supply a username and a password. In the screen capture below, a connection was made to an FTP server at `ftp.microsoft.com`. In this FTP session, the user logged in with the account name `ftp` and no password.

```
C:\>ftp ftp.microsoft.com
Connected to ftp.microsoft.com.
220 CPMSFTFTPA04 Microsoft FTP Service (Version 5.0).
User (ftp.microsoft.com:(none)): ftp
331 Anonymous access allowed, send identity (e-mail name) as password.
Password:
230-This is FTP.MICROSOFT.COM. Please see the dirmap.txt file for more information.
230 Anonymous user logged in.
ftp>
```

TIP

Most FTP sites will allow an **anonymous** user to log in with no password. When prompted for a username, you can type **anonymous**. However, because *anonymous* is so difficult to spell, you might want to log in by typing **ftp** as your anonymous username. Although no password is required, using your e-mail address as a password is considered "good FTP etiquette" when using the anonymous account.

File Transfer Protocol (FTP)
An application used to transfer files from one host to another and to store the files on the requesting host.

binary format
A compressed file format.

FTP command line utility
A non-mouse and non-fancy interface used to access an FTP server.

FTP command interpreter
A nice looking, easy-to-use application used to access an FTP server.

FTP server
Server on which an FTP server application is running to transfer files out to clients.

anonymous
Account set up so that anyone can access files on an FTP server without a secret password.

How FTP Works

The first packet that is sent from the requesting host to the FTP server is a TCP/IP packet requesting to set up a connection. In this example, the packet was sent to TCP port 21 on the FTP server. The requesting host chose a non-well-known port to listen for the reply. In this case, the requesting host chose 1177 as the return port and will be listening for a response sent to that port number. In the next screen capture, the first TCP/IP packet is shown as the requesting host makes a request from the source port of 1177 to destination port of 21.

```
Frame Src MAC Addr              Dst MAC Addr           Protocol Description
2356  Harry's Default Gateway HARRY                    FTP      Resp. to Port 1177, '230 Anonymous user logged i▲
2357  HARRY                   Harry's Default Gateway  TCP      .A...., len:     0, seq:    2218581-2218581, ack:1
◄                                                                                                              ►▼

⊕FRAME: Base frame properties
⊕ETHERNET: ETYPE = 0x0800 : Protocol = IP:  DOD Internet Protocol
⊕IP: ID = 0xC104; Proto = TCP; Len: 40
▬TCP: .A...., len:     0, seq:    2218581-2218581, ack:1654872938, win: 8516, src: 1177 dst:   21 (FTP)
   TCP: Source Port = 0x0499
   TCP: Destination Port = FTP [control]
   TCP: Sequence Number = 2218581 (0x21DA55)
   TCP: Acknowledgement Number = 1654872938 (0x62A35B6A)
   TCP: Data Offset = 20 (0x14)
   TCP: Reserved = 0 (0x0000)
   ⊕TCP: Flags = 0x10 : .A....
   TCP: Window = 8516 (0x2144)
   TCP: Checksum = 0x6CA1
   TCP: Urgent Pointer = 0 (0x0)
```

The FTP application was listening at port 21. Upon receiving the request, the application sent back an **FTP/TCP/IP** packet to set up the connection and ask that the client send back the username to log in. In this return packet, the FTP server is the source, and the FTP client is the destination. The FTP server sends this reply to port 1177, where the FTP client said it would be listening. In the FTP header that the FTP server built, the FTP server is passing FTP information to the FTP client.

Notice in the screen capture that the source port labeled src: is set to port 1177. Harry, the requesting host, has decided that the FTP server should send data back to this port.

The following screen capture shows the next packet in the sequence, where the FTP server replies to the FTP client.

```
Frame Src MAC Addr              Dst MAC Addr           Protocol Description
2355  HARRY                   Harry's Default Gateway  TCP      .A...., len:     0, seq:    2218581-2218581, ack:1▲
2356  Harry's Default Gateway HARRY                    FTP      Resp. to Port 1177, '230 Anonymous user logged i
◄                                                                                                              ►▼

⊕FRAME: Base frame properties
⊕ETHERNET: ETYPE = 0x0800 : Protocol = IP:  DOD Internet Protocol
⊕IP: ID = 0xBE4A; Proto = TCP; Len: 71
⊕TCP: .AP..., len:    31, seq:1654872907-1654872937, ack:    2218581, win:17503, src:   21 (FTP) dst: 1177
   ▬FTP: Resp. to Port 1177, '230 Anonymous user logged in.'
     FTP: FTP Error Return Code = 230
     FTP: FTP Command Arg1 = Anonymous
     FTP: FTP Data: Number of data bytes remaining = 18 (0x0012)
```

This dialog continues as the FTP server responds to the FTP client's requests. The client will be able to see a list of files that are available and request either one or more server files be transferred.

The command-line FTP client application requires that the user know the FTP commands and how to use them. Another way that the user can connect to an FTP server—without knowing how to use the commands—is to use an FTP command interpreter. Several of these interpreter applications are available on the Internet; some are shareware and some can be downloaded and used for a trial period. An example of one that can be downloaded for a 30-day trial before you buy it is **CuteFTP**. CuteFTP has an easy-to-learn and easy-to-use interface. This client application interprets the user's clicks, translates them to FTP commands, and passes those commands to the FTP server. Another example of an FTP command interpreter available on the Internet is FTP Voyager.

CuteFTP

An easy-to-use FTP command interpreter application that turns your mouse clicks into FTP commands.

TIP

For FTP to work, the server must be running an FTP server application, and the client must be using an FTP client application.

Hypertext Transfer Protocol (HTTP)

Hypertext Transfer Protocol (HTTP)

An application used to transfer files from one host to another and to display the files at the requesting host.

Web server

Server on which an HTTP server application is running that users can surf to and request files be transferred and displayed.

Web browser application

A client application used for surfing the Web. Examples are Netscape Navigator and Microsoft Internet Explorer.

Uniform Resource Locator (URL)

The address of the Web site that the user is surfing to.

Hypertext Transfer Protocol (HTTP) is a set of rules for exchanging files on the Internet. This is the protocol that your Web browser uses when surfing the Internet. Unlike FTP, HTTP is designed so that very little user intervention is required. HTTP transfers preformatted files that are displayed in their browser instead of just saved to disk. The HTTP application runs on a **Web server** and listens for requests, and then responds by sending files back to the requestor. A Web server is a server that has the HTTP service application running on it. HTTP listens at a TCP port, usually port 80 for requests, and then transfers the requested file back to the requestor. The requesting host displays the file in a **Web browser application**.

The client makes the HTTP request by issuing a command to their Web browser. The command is initiated by typing a **Uniform Resource Locator (URL)**, (such as www.sybex.com) in the address line of the Web browser or by clicking a **hyperlink** on a page that is being displayed by the Web browser. The Web browser formats the client's request into an **HTTP/TCP/IP** request packet with a destination port of 80.

At the Web server, the HTTP application is listening at port 80 for any requests. After the packet is received, the appropriate file is retrieved and packaged for delivery to the client. The packets leave the Web server, and upon arrival at the client, the Web browser decodes the **Hypertext Markup Language (HTML)** file and displays it onscreen with the proper formatting.

So, let's look at what is really happening when you connect to a Web site:

1. You open your Web browser and type in the URL www.sybex.com.

2. Your Web browser creates the TCP/IP packet and sends it to a Web server somewhere on the Internet. In other words, little ol' you makes a request of a big Web server to set up a connection.

3. The Web server hears your request at port 80 and sends back a packet to you that says, "Okay, I'll set up a connection with you."

4. Now that you have a connection with the Web server, you request that the Web server send you its default page.

5. The Web server receives your response and gets the file that you requested. The file is put into one or more packets, depending on how big the file is, and it is sent to you.

74

6. Your Web browser receives the packets and sends back an acknowledgement that they were received. If the Web server does not get an acknowledgement from you, the packet is re-sent.

7. Your Web browser displays the information that you requested on your screen as the packets are received.

Below is a screen capture of Harry communicating with a Web server. Harry sends a GET request to port 80. The Web server is listening at port 80 and will answer Harry's GET request with a response that you can see in the next frame.

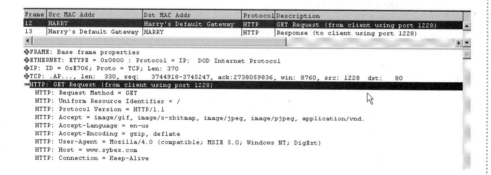

Several applications run at the Application layer. You have looked at FTP and HTTP as examples of how applications operate. Some other common applications that run at the Application layer include Simple Network Management Protocol (SNMP), Telnet, Simple Mail Transfer Protocol (SMTP), and Trivial File Transfer Protocol (TFTP).

hyperlink
Underlined word on a Web site that links to another document on that Web server or possibly another.

HTTP/TCP/IP
A packet with an HTTP header on top of a TCP header on top of an IP header.

Hypertext Markup Language (HTML)
The file format of Web pages housed on a Web server that can be displayed in a useful format by a Web browser.

Review Questions

Terms to Know
- ❏ Application layer
- ❏ ports
- ❏ socket
- ❏ well-known ports
- ❏ IANA
- ❏ FTP
- ❏ binary format
- ❏ FTP command line utility
- ❏ FTP command interpreter
- ❏ FTP server

1. Where do applications listen for requests?

2. How many ports are there?

3. Which are the well-known ports?

4. Describe how FTP works.

5. Describe how HTTP works.

6. List some TCP/IP applications other than FTP and HTTP that may be running at the Application layer.

7. Why do the screen captures in this chapter show that Harry the Host is communicating with his default gateway instead of the actual FTP server or Web server?

8. Can a server be both an FTP server and a Web server?

9. Why would an administrator change the HTTP port on the Web server to a port number other than 80?

_____

10. Which agency controls the well-known port assignments?

_____

11. What is the standard HTTP port?

_____

12. What are the three pieces of information that make up a socket?

_____

_____

_____

13. What is an FTP command line interpreter?

_____

Chapter
6

IP Addressing

This chapter covers Internet Protocol (IP) addresses. You will learn what an IP address is, how to distinguish valid from invalid IP addresses, and how all the available IP addresses are divided into categories called classes.

In this discussion of IP addresses, you will learn about the following:

  Binary and decimal numbering systems

  Binary-to-decimal and decimal-to-binary conversions

  The five classes of IP addresses

What Is IP Addressing?

Every host on a TCP/IP network needs to have a unique address, similar to you needing a unique address for your house. With this unique address, it is possible to send data from host to host. Every packet contains addressing information in the header, and the IP address in the header is used to route packets. If several people on your street had the same address, the post office would have a difficult time sorting mail. For a similar reason, IP addresses are unique on each network.

IP addressing is simply configuring each TCP/IP host with a valid IP address. For access to the Internet, a host must have an IP address that identifies not only the host address (like a house number) but also identifies the network address (like a street number). An administrator needs to be aware of proper addressing techniques so that the hosts on the network will function correctly.

binary

The base-2 number system that computers use to represent data. It consists of only two digits: 0 and 1.

decimal

The base-10 number system that people use to represent data. It consists of 10 digits: 0, 1, 2, 3, 4, 5, 6, 7, 8, 9.

Numbering Systems

An IP address uniquely identifies every host on a network. Just as your mailing address uniquely identifies your home, an IP address uniquely identifies a host.

Consider that your mailing address is made up of two parts. Part of it tells the postal carrier what street you live on and part of it tells which house you live in on that street. All addresses on your street include the same street name but have a unique number for each house. IP addresses are similar: They can be broken down into two parts. One part of the IP address represents the network that the host is on, and the other part represents that unique host on that network.

TCP/IP looks at IP addresses in **binary** form, but as humans, we prefer to see IP addresses in **decimal** form. Because the protocol is seeing only binary, working with IP addresses makes more sense when you also look at the IP addresses in binary. To do so, you need to understand the two numbering systems and be able to convert from one to another.

The decimal numbering system uses the digits 0, 1, 2, 3, 4, 5, 6, 7, 8, and 9. In the binary numbering system, the only digits that exist are 0 and 1.

To better understand the binary numbering system, let's take a closer look at the decimal numbering system that you are already familiar with. When you analyze the decimal numbering system, it is clear that the numbers represent a specific value depending on which place, or column, the number is in. For example, the number 27 has a 2 in the tens column and a 7 in the ones column. The resulting value is $(2 \times 10) + (7 \times 1)$.

As you scan across a decimal number, the value of the digit in each column increases from right to left. The value of the digit in the rightmost column results from multiplying the number by 1. The value of the digit in the next column to the left is found by multiplying the number by 10, the next column to the left by 100, and the next by 1,000. The value of the columns continues to increase by a factor of 10 as you move to the left. After you have found the value of each of the columns, you add the values together to obtain the value of the overall number.

You increase numbers in the decimal and binary systems in the same way. In either system, you continue to increase the rightmost digit by 1 until you reach the highest value in the numbering system (that is, until you reach 9 in the decimal system or until you reach 1 in the binary system). After you have reached the highest value, add 1 to the digit immediately to the left and start the rightmost digit from the lowest value again.

For example: In the decimal number 321, 1 is the rightmost digit. To increase 321 incrementally, add 1 to the rightmost digit to get 322. Continue increasing the rightmost digit by 1 until the rightmost digit holds the highest value: 329. Now increase the digit to the left and start the rightmost digit over from the lowest value: 330. After the highest digit is reached in the rightmost column, increase the digit in the next left column by 1. Then begin again, increasing the rightmost digit starting from 0.

NOTE

The octal and hexadecimal numbering systems are also used often in the computer industry. Octal is base-8 and hexadecimal is base-16.

Reviewing Binary and Decimal Numbering Systems

In the chart of decimal numbers below, notice that each number is represented by four digits. In the left column of the chart, the number 0000 is increased by one until the value of 0009 is reached. At this point, the ones place has reached the highest value of the numbering system so the digit in the tens place is increased, and the value in the ones place begins again from 0010. Each of the chart's columns shows the four-digit number being increased incrementally by 1 until the 9 is reached.

Each group of three columns represents a point in the decimal numbering system where increasing the rightmost value causes the next column to be increased.

0000	0010	0020	...	0090	0100	0110	...	0990	1000	1010
0001	0011	0021		0091	0101	0111		0991	1001	1011
0002	0012	0022		0092	0102	0112		0992	1002	1012
0003	0013	0023		0093	0103	0113		0993	1003	1013
0004	0014	0024		0094	0104	0114		0994	1004	1014
0005	0015	0025		0095	0105	0115		0995	1005	1015
0006	0016	0026		0096	0106	0116		0996	1006	1016
0007	0017	0027		0097	0107	0117		0997	1007	1017
0008	0018	0028		0098	0108	0118		0998	1008	1018
0009	0019	0029		0099	0109	0119		0999	1009	1019

The binary numbering system works the same way except that you can use only 1s and 0s. Therefore, every time that you increase by an increment of 1, you have reached the highest value in the binary numbering system. The following chart shows four binary digits being increased by 1.

0000	1000
0001	1001
0010	1010
0011	1011
0100	1100
0101	1101
0110	1110
0111	1111

Converting Binary Numbers to Decimal

TCP/IP always uses binary IP addresses. But people tend to use decimal IP addresses because they can more easily work with this familiar form. Converting binary to decimal and decimal to binary is an important skill enabling network administrators to know the exact values that TCP/IP uses.

 TEST IT OUT: CONVERT FROM BINARY TO DECIMAL

To convert binary to decimal, first examine the binary digits. For each column that has a 1, note its decimal value, and then add those values together to get the decimal equivalent. The decimal values for each column remain constant:

- ◇ The rightmost column has a decimal value of 1.
- ◇ The second column from the right has a decimal value of 2.
- ◇ The third column from the right has a decimal value of 4.
- ◇ The fourth column from the right has a decimal value of 8.

So, for example, in the binary number 0011, you have 1s in two columns. You know that the rightmost column has the decimal value of 1, and the second column from the right has the decimal value of 2. Add 1 and 2 and you get 3. Therefore, the decimal equivalent of 0011 is 3.

Now try the following examples:

1. Convert the binary number 0001.

   The decimal equation for the conversion is $0 + 0 + 0 + 1$

   $= 1$ decimal

2. Convert the binary number 0110.

   The decimal equation for the conversion is $0 + 4 + 2 + 0$

   $= 6$ decimal

3. Convert the binary number 1110.

   The decimal equation for the conversion is $8 + 4 + 2 + 0$

   $= 14$ decimal

4. Convert the binary number 1111.

   The decimal equation for the conversion is $8 + 4 + 2 + 1$

   $= 15$ decimal

Each of these columns represents a bit (*binary digit*). The greatest decimal number that can be represented by 4 bits is 15.

Converting Decimal Numbers to Binary

Several simple methods can be used to convert decimal numbers to binary. Find one that you are comfortable with, practice it, and you'll get the hang of it. Presented in this section are a few methods that you might find useful.

Using the Bit Value Method

One method of converting a decimal number to binary is the opposite of converting binary to decimal. First, you find the binary position with the greatest decimal value that is still less than the number that you are converting. Give a value of 1 for that binary position, subtract the bit value from the original decimal number, and repeat the process for the remainder.

TEST IT OUT: CONVERT FROM DECIMAL TO BINARY

To convert the decimal value 9 to binary by using the bit value method, start with a binary chart like the following:

x	x	x	x
8	4	2	1

You can see that the binary position with the greatest decimal value that is still less than 9 is the 8-bit. So you put a 1 in the 8-bit, subtract the bit value (8) from the original number (9), and you have a remainder of 1.

1	x	x	x =	8, and 9 − 8 leaves a remainder of 1
8	4	2	1	

You repeat the process with the remainder: The largest binary position that has a value less than 1 is the 1-bit. Put a 1 in the 1-bit. Because you have no remainder, the rest of the bits are 0s and you are finished.

1	0	0	1 =	9, and 9 − 9 leaves a remainder of 0
8	4	2	1	

So, the decimal value 9 is 1001 in binary.

Now, try these examples:

1. Convert the decimal value 6 to binary.

	x	x	x	x
	8	4	2	1
Result:	0	1	1	0 = 6 (0 + 4 + 2 + 0)

TEST IT OUT: CONVERT FROM DECIMAL TO BINARY (cont.)

2. Convert the decimal value 11 to binary.

X	X	X	X
8	4	2	1

Result: 1   0   1   1 =   11 (8 + 0 + 2 + 1)

3. Convert the decimal value 3 to binary.

X	X	X	X
8	4	2	1

Result: 0   0   1   1 =   3 (0 + 0 + 2 + 1)

4. Convert the decimal value 15 to binary.

X	X	X	X
8	4	2	1

Result: 1   1   1   1 =   15 (8 + 4 + 2 + 1)

5. Convert the decimal value 8 to binary.

X	X	X	X
8	4	2	1

Result: 1   0   0   0 =   8 (8 + 0 + 0 + 0)

6. Convert the decimal value 9 to binary.

X	X	X	X
8	4	2	1

Result: 1   0   0   1 =   9 (8 + 0 + 0 + 1)

7. Convert the decimal value 5 to binary.

X	X	X	X
8	4	2	1

Result: 0   1   0   1 =   5 (0 + 4 + 0 + 1)

8. Convert the decimal value 13 to binary.

X	X	X	X
8	4	2	1

Result: 1   1   0   1 =   13 (8 + 4 + 0 + 1)

Using the Division Method

Another method of converting decimal numbers to binary is called the division method. The division method uses a series of simple divide-by-2 problems to complete the conversion. Every time you divide by 2, the remainder will be either 1 or 0. It is important to list the remainders (whether a 1 or a 0) in an orderly fashion because the binary result will be comprised of these remainders.

The process is as follows:

1. Divide the decimal number by 2 and write the remainder, 1 or 0.
2. Divide the quotient (answer) by 2 and write that remainder, 1 or 0.
3. Repeat steps 1 and 2 until the quotient is 0.
4. Write the remainders in reverse order for the binary equivalent.

 TEST IT OUT: CONVERT FROM DECIMAL TO BINARY USING THE DIVISION METHOD

Follow this example step-by-step and then try using the division method to complete the next conversion problems. To convert the decimal value 6 to binary:

1. Divide 6 by 2 (6/2 = 3 with a remainder of 0). Write 0 as the first remainder.
2. Divide the quotient, 3, by 2. (3/2 = 1 remainder of 1). Write 1 as the second remainder.
3. Divide the quotient, 1, by 2. (1/2 = 0 remainder of 1). Write 1 as the third remainder. The quotient is now 0 so you don't have to repeat the previous steps.
4. Note that the remainders are 011. Reverse them to get the binary number 110.

Now try the following examples:

1. Convert the decimal value 11 to binary.

   11/2 = 5 remainder of 1

   5/2 = 2 remainder of 1

   2/2 = 1 remainder of 0

   1/2 = 0 remainder of 1

   Result: 1011

TEST IT OUT: CONVERT FROM DECIMAL TO BINARY USING THE DIVISION METHOD (cont.)

2. Convert the decimal value 15 to binary.

   $15/2 = 7$ remainder of 1

   $7/2 = 3$ remainder of 1

   $3/2 = 1$ remainder of 1

   $1/2 = 0$ remainder of 1

   Result: 1111

3. Convert the decimal value 4 to binary.

   $4/2 = 2$ remainder of 0

   $2/2 = 1$ remainder of 0

   $1/2 = 0$ remainder of 1

   Result 100

4. Convert the decimal value 10 to binary.

   $10/2 = 5$ remainder of 0

   $5/2 = 2$ remainder of 1

   $2/2 = 1$ remainder of 0

   $1/2 = 0$ remainder of 1

   Result 1010

5. Convert the decimal value 7 to binary.

   $7/2 = 3$ remainder of 1

   $3/2 = 1$ remainder of 1

   $1/2 = 0$ remainder of 1

   Result 111

Using a Calculator

One other method of converting either decimal to binary or binary to decimal is to use a calculator. It is important that you understand the math behind converting numbers between the numbering systems, but most administrators end up using a calculator because it is quicker and easier to avoid mistakes.

The most common calculator is the electronic calculator that is installed with all the Microsoft desktop operating systems. The calculator has not changed much from Windows 95, 98, or NT. You can access the calculator by clicking Start ➢ Programs ➢ Accessories ➢ Calculator. A screen shot of the calculator is shown below.

TIP

Be sure the calculator is in the Scientific mode by clicking View ➢ Scientific.

After you are sure the calculator is in Scientific view, notice the row of radio buttons on the upper-left side. The Dec button puts the calculator into decimal mode, and the Bin button puts the calculator into binary mode. To do any conversions, type in the number that you would like to convert, then click the radio button that is not selected. The number displayed is the converted number.

WARNING

When using a calculator to convert decimal numbers to binary, pay close attention to leading 0s getting dropped. For example, the decimal number 7 is displayed as 111 on a binary calculator. But when working with IP addresses, you'll generally want to use 4 or 8 bits. The number 7 expressed with 4 bits is 0111 and with 8 bits is 0000 0111. A calculator does not display the leading 0s because they are considered insignificant.

IP Addresses

TCP/IP addresses are based on 32-bit addresses. But rather than working with 32 ones and zeros, people use decimals to represent IP addresses—specifically, they use four decimal numbers separated by periods. These four decimal numbers represent the 32 binary digits separated into four equal parts called octets. An **octet** is 8 bits.

An IP address expressed in decimal is referred to as **dotted decimal notation** because it has four decimal numbers, each separated by a period, or a dot. As I've stated, each of the four decimal numbers represents 8 binary digits, or bits. In the preceding conversion examples, you looked only at 4-bit binary numbers. In 8-bit numbers, the decimal values of the bits continue increasing from right to left:

- ◆ The fifth bit has a decimal value of 16.
- ◆ The sixth bit has a decimal value of 32.
- ◆ The seventh bit has a decimal value of 64.
- ◆ The eighth bit has a decimal value of 128.

128	64	32	16	8	4	2	1
X	X	X	X	X	X	X	X

So, for example, the binary number 0101 0101 is equal to the decimal 85:

$$0 + 64 + 0 + 16 + 0 + 4 + 0 + 1 = 85$$

The binary number 1001 0101 is equal to the decimal 145:

$$128 + 0 + 0 + 16 + 0 + 4 + 0 + 1 = 145$$

The binary number 1111 1111 is equal to the decimal 255:

$$128 + 64 + 32 + 16 + 8 + 4 + 2 + 1 = 255$$

octet
Eight bits of data.

dotted decimal notation
An IP address presented as four decimal numbers, each separated by a period, or dot.

The highest decimal number that an octet can contain is 255. The decimal number 256 cannot be represented with 8 bits; therefore, no IP address has a number greater then 255 in any octet.

TCP/IP uses all 32 bits; therefore, it is important when you look at the four decimal numbers to understand that there are really 32 bits that TCP/IP is using. For example, the IP address 131.107.2.200 can be translated into the following binary octets:

131	=	1000 0011
107	=	0110 1011
2	=	0000 0010
200	=	1100 1000

Therefore, TCP/IP will see 131.107.2.200 as this:

10000011011010110000001011001000

To humans, seeing all 32 bits is a little overwhelming, so obviously using the decimal equivalent is easier. When looking at the binary, most people separate each set of 4 bits so that all the 1s and 0s don't run together.

For example, the IP address 209.132.95.62 would be:

209	=	1101 0001
132	=	1000 0100
95	=	0101 1111
62	=	0011 1110

TCP/IP will see 209.132.95.62 as this:

1101 0001 1000 0100 0101 1111 0011 1110

Some sample IP addresses are:

15.231.25.115

1.26.251.32

221.26.0.1

209.132.95.3

IP Address Classes

IP addresses are divided into five classes: Class A, Class B, Class C, Class D, and Class E. All addresses are placed in a particular class based on the decimal values of their first octets. In the first octet, an IP address can start with a decimal value between 1 and 255.

The system of class addresses has been set up to help ensure assignment of unique IP addresses. Let's take a look at how these classes are divided and who gets the IP addresses in each category.

Class A Addresses

Class A addresses have first octets with a decimal number between 1 and 127. For example:

> 1.x.y.z
>
> 10.x.y.z
>
> 27.x.y.z
>
> 102.x.y.z

In binary, a Class A address always starts with 0 as the leftmost bit. For example:

1.x.y.z	=	0000 0001.x.y.z
10.x.y.z	=	0000 1010.x.y.z
27.x.y.z	=	0001 1011.x.y.z
102.x.y.z	=	0110 0110.x.y.z
127.x.y.z	=	0111 1111.x.y.z

Notice that 127 has a 1 in every bit of the octet except the first bit. The next higher binary value will put a 1 in the leftmost bit, and the resulting address will not be a Class A. Therefore, 127.x.y.z is the highest Class A address.

Class A addresses use the first octet to represent the unique network address and leave three octets to develop unique host addresses on that network. Because there is a 0 in the first bit, the following 7 bits in the first octet are used to distinguish the network from all other networks, and 24 bits are used by each host to make itself unique on the network. An important rule to note here is that a network address cannot have all 0s.

This means that there are only 127 Class A networks available. At first glance, it seems obvious that there are 127 networks, but the following equation proves the number:

$$2^7 - 1 = 127$$

where 2 is the number of possible values that each bit can contain (a 1 or a 0), 7 is the number of bits used, and 1 is the address where all 7 bits are 0 (you cannot have a network address of all 0s).

On each of those 127 networks, each address uses the other 24 bits to make itself unique. All possible combinations of these 24 bits make up the number of unique host IP addresses that can be on each of those 127 networks. There are 16,777,214 possible unique IP addresses on each of the 127 Class A networks. Similar to the rule that the network portion of the address cannot be all 0s, the host portion of the address cannot be all 0s and it cannot be all 1s. A host portion with all 1s refers to an IP broadcast address, which you learn about in a later chapter, and the host portion with all 0s is a reference to the network. Therefore, the equation for the number of hosts on each Class A network is:

$$2^{24} - 2 = 16,777,214$$

You subtract 2 because addresses with all 0s and all 1s are invalid.

Of the 127 Class A networks available, one address was reserved for testing: The network address 127.*x.y.z* was reserved as a **loopback** address. No host can ever use 127-dot-anything as its address because it has been reserved for diagnostic purposes. When testing a TCP/IP installation, 127-dot-anything refers to that TCP/IP installation. Therefore, for example, as a network administrator is testing a TCP/IP installation, testing 127.0.0.1 refers to the host that is being tested.

Addresses Reserved for Private Use

Certain addresses have been set aside by the InterNIC and reserved for private use only. If you would like to use TCP/IP on your internal network (intranet), and not use the Internet, the following addresses are suggested:

Class A   10.0.0.0 through 10.255.255.255

Class B   172.16.0.0 through 172.31.255.255

Class C   192.168.0.0 through 192.168.255.255

Routers on the Internet will not route data from or to these addresses; they are for internal, private use only. To use these addresses on an intranet and have access to the Internet, you must use a **proxy server** or **Network Address Translation (NAT)**.

---

loopback
An address that is used for diagnostic purposes, to test the TCP/IP stack of a TCP/IP host.

---

proxy server
An application that relays TCP/IP traffic from one network to another while changing the IP address of the sending host.

Network Address Translation (NAT)
An application that translates the IP address of the sending host to another IP address while relaying the TCP/IP data to another network.

Class B Addresses

Class B addresses have first octets with a decimal number between 128 and 191. For example:

128.*x*.*y*.*z*

151.*x*.*y*.*z*

165.*x*.*y*.*z*

191.*x*.*y*.*z*

In binary, a Class B address always starts with 10 as the 2 leftmost bits. For example:

128.*x*.*y*.*z* =   1000 0000.*x*.*y*.*z*

151.*x*.*y*.*z* =   1001 0111.*x*.*y*.*z*

165.*x*.*y*.*z* =   1010 0101.*x*.*y*.*z*

191.*x*.*y*.*z* =   1011 1111.*x*.*y*.*z*

Notice that 191 has a 1 in every bit of the octet except the second leftmost bit. The next higher binary value will put a 1 in the second leftmost bit, and the resulting address will not be a Class B. Therefore, 191.*x.y.z* is the highest Class B address.

Class B addresses use the first two octets to represent the unique network address and leave only two octets to develop unique host addresses on that network. Because there is a 10 in the first 2 bits, the following 6 bits in the first octet and all 8 bits in the second octet are used to distinguish this network from all other networks. Sixteen bits are used by each host to make itself unique on the network. The equation that proves the number of Class B networks is:

$$2^{14} = 16,384$$

This means that there are 16,384 Class B networks available. On each of these 16,384 networks, each address uses the other 16 bits to make itself unique. All possible combinations of these 16 bits make up the number of unique host IP addresses that can be on each of those 16,384 networks. There are 65,534 possible unique IP addresses on each of the 16,384 Class B networks:

$$2^{16} - 2 = 65,534$$

Class C Addresses

The Class C addresses have first octets with a decimal number between 192 and 223. For example:

192.*x*.*y*.*z*

200.*x*.*y*.*z*

210.*x*.*y*.*z*

223.*x*.*y*.*z*

In binary, a Class C address always starts with 110 as the 3 leftmost bits. For example:

192.*x*.*y*.*z* = 11000000.*x*.*y*.*z*

200.*x*.*y*.*z* = 11001000.*x*.*y*.*z*

210.*x*.*y*.*z* = 11010010.*x*.*y*.*z*

223.*x*.*y*.*z* = 1101 1111.*x*.*y*.*z*

Notice that 223 has a 1 in every bit of the octet except the third leftmost bit. The next higher binary value will put a 1 in the third leftmost bit, and the resulting address will not be a Class C. Therefore, 223.*x.y.z* is the highest Class C address.

Class C addresses use the first three octets to represent the unique network address and leave only one octet to develop unique host addresses on that network. Because the first 3 bits in the first octet are 110, the network portion of a Class C address includes the remaining 5 bits in the first octet, all 8 bits in the second octet, and all 8 bits in the third octet, for a total of 21 bits. That leaves only 8 bits to be used by each host to make itself unique on this network.

The equation for Class C networks is:

$$2^{21} = 2,097,152$$

This means that there are 2,097,152 Class C networks available. On each of these 2,097,152 networks, each address uses the other 8 bits to make itself unique. All possible combinations of these 8 bits make up the number of unique host IP addresses that can be on each of those 2,097,152 networks. There are 254 possible unique IP addresses on each of the 2,097,152 Class C networks:

$$2^{8} - 2 = 254$$

Class D Addresses

Class D addresses have decimal values between 224 and 239 in the first octet. In the first octet, the first 4 bits are 1110.

Class A, B, and C are the only address classes that are available for TCP/IP host IP addresses. In contrast, no one host can have a Class D address. These addresses are called **multicast** addresses, and they are invalid for any workstation or host to use.

The purpose of a multicast address is to enable a server somewhere to send data to a Class D address that no one host has so that several hosts can listen to that address at the same time. When you are watching TV on the Internet or listening to the radio on the Internet, your computer is listening to a Class D address. No server is sending data directly to your workstation; instead, a server is sending data to the multicast address. Any host can use software to listen for data at that address, and many hosts can be listening at once.

Class E Addresses

The last class of addresses is Class E. Class E addresses range from 240–255 in the first octet, and the 4 leftmost bits are 1111.

Class E addresses are reserved addresses and are invalid host addresses. They are used for experimental purposes by the IETF.

Classless Inter-Domain Routing (CIDR)

Classless Inter-Domain Routing (CIDR) is an IP addressing scheme that was developed after the class system of A, B, C, D, and E. The traditional class system considers an IP address as four octets with the network portion of the address highlighted by a subnet mask. The standard network portion is the first octet, the first two octets, or the first three octets. CIDR addressing still represents IP addresses in the traditional dotted decimal notation, but highlights the network portion with a slash followed by a number. For example:

```
192.168.3.15/26

172.21.165.1/19
```

The number after the slash is the number of bits that represent the network portion of the IP address. CIDR was developed to increase the efficiency of address allocation and to alleviate overloaded Internet routers. Using CIDR addressing, fewer and shorter addresses/routes need to be entered into the routing tables.

multicast

A communication between a single sender and multiple receivers on a network. No one host can have this address, but several can receive data by listening to it.

Classless Inter-Domain Routing (CIDR)

An IP addressing scheme that uses a slash followed by a number to highlight the network portion of an address instead of using a subnet mask.

IP Address Class Summary

It is important to understand the overall scheme of addresses. Then, as you make decisions about the TCP/IP addressing scheme for your network, you will use a network address that enables you to address all the hosts on the network and that allows room for growth.

To summarize the rules and equations for Class A, B, and C addressing:

- A host ID cannot be all 0s.
- A host ID cannot be all 1s.
- To determine the number of networks that can be created, use the formula 2^N where N is the number of bits in the network portion of the address.
- To determine the number of hosts that can be created, use the formula $2^N - 2$ where N is the number of bits in the host portion of the address.

Following is a chart summarizing the classes of addresses:

Class	Range	Leftmost Bits	# of Network Bits	# of Networks	# of Host Bits	# of Hosts
A	1–127	0	8	126	24	16,777,214
B	128–191	10	16	16,384	16	65,534
C	192–223	110	24	2,097,152	8	254
D	224–239	1110	INVALID			
E	240–255	1111	INVALID			

Review Questions

Terms to Know
- ❏ binary
- ❏ decimal
- ❏ octet
- ❏ dotted decimal notation
- ❏ loopback
- ❏ proxy server
- ❏ NAT
- ❏ multicast
- ❏ CIDR

1. Convert the following binary numbers to their decimal equivalents:

   a. 1100 0011

   b. 1010 0101

   c. 1001 1011

   d. 1110 0111

   _____

   _____

   _____

   _____

2. Convert the following decimal numbers to their binary equivalents:

   a. 10

   b. 57

   c. 127

   d. 255

   _____

   _____

   _____

   _____

3. What is the range of first octet addresses for the following classes?

   a. Class A

   b. Class B

   c. Class C

   _____

   _____

   _____

4. What is a Class D address used for?

_____

5. How many hosts can be on a Class C network?

_____

6. How many Class B networks are there?

_____

7. How many hosts can be on a Class A network?

_____

8. What does a host address with all 1s represent?

_____

9. What does a host address with all 0s represent?

_____

10. When is a host address of all 0s or all 1s invalid?

_____

11. What is the equation used to find the number of hosts that a network can have?

_____

Chapter

7

Addressing
IP Hosts

In this chapter, you are going to look at the different ways of assigning IP addresses to each host. There are two methods of assigning IP addresses: manual configuration and automatic configuration. In this chapter, you will learn about:

 Installing TCP/IP

 Assigning IP addresses

 Obtaining an IP address from a DHCP server

 Renewing IP addresses

 Reserving IP addresses

 Setting the Lease Duration

 Setting DHCP scopes and options

Installing and Assigning IP Addresses

Because every host has to have a unique IP address, somebody needs to assign an IP address to each host. Other optional pieces of configuration information might also need to be assigned to a host, such as a default gateway, a Domain Name System (DNS) server, a Windows Internet Naming Service (WINS) server, and many other options.

Two methods are used to assign IP addresses: manual configuration and automatic configuration. Both are discussed in this section.

There are several operating systems and procedures for installing and configuring an IP address. The instructions and screen captures in this section will guide you through installing and manually configuring TCP/IP in several of the most popular operating systems: Windows XP, 2000, NT, and 95/98.

Manual IP Address Configuration

An administrator with only a few hosts on a network may determine that the best method of assigning IP addresses is to do so manually. An administrator who has 10 hosts on a network, for example, might sit in front of each of the 10 hosts and input the IP address, subnet mask, and possibly some other optional addresses. This may be the preferred method because there are only a few hosts to address.

However, an administrator with 254 hosts on a network would have to type in all the information at each of the 254 hosts. While inputting this information 254 times, chances are the administrator would make a couple of typos here and there. Those typos might be difficult to troubleshoot. An administrator with 2,540 hosts would have a lot more typing to do and probably would make a lot more typos and face a lot of extra troubleshooting.

Therefore, manually configuring IP addresses is efficient for only a few hosts. To assign IP addresses to the majority of their hosts, however, most administrators choose to use Dynamic Host Configuration Protocol (DHCP), which is discussed in this section.

Installing TCP/IP on Windows XP

During the installation of Windows XP, TCP/IP is installed automatically. There is no option to remove it; therefore, there is no option to install it. All that can be done with TCP/IP in Windows XP is to modify and configure its settings. If any new network cards or devices are added to a machine that has XP installed, the operating system will install TCP/IP as it is being configured.

Manually Assigning an IP Address for Windows XP

To manually configure an IP address on a Windows XP client, take the following steps:

1. Click Start ➢ Control Panel. Control Panel will be in either Classic view or Category view.

   If Control Panel is in Classic view, double-click the Network Connections icon.

If Control Panel is in Category view, click Network and Internet Connections.

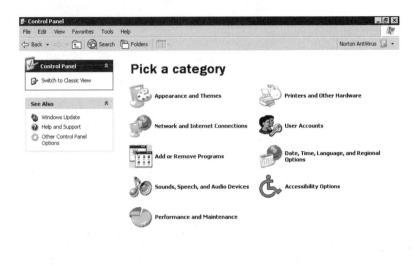

Then choose Network Connections.

2. Right-click the connection that is being modified, and choose Properties. (Notice that when you click the connection, XP displays the details of the connection in the left margin.)

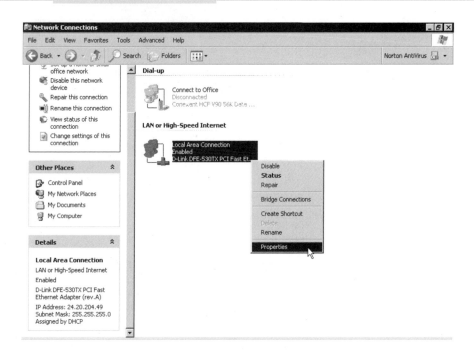

3. On the Local Area Connection Properties page, choose Internet Protocol (TCP/IP) and click Properties.

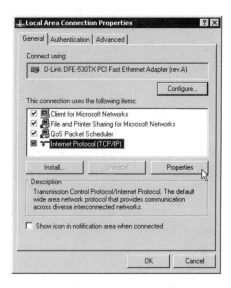

4. In the Internet Protocol (TCP/IP) Properties dialog box, click the radio button that is labeled Use the Following IP Address. Type in the IP address and the subnet mask for this host. If the network that this host is on connects with another network, type in the default gateway.

> **NOTE**
>
> When you click the radio button labeled Use the Following IP Address, the radio button labeled Use the Following DNS Server Addresses is selected automatically.

5. Type the address of a DNS server for this host to use. On this page, you have the choice of entering two DNS server addresses, so that if the first doesn't respond, this host will consult the second. Then click OK. Windows XP does not always require a reboot at this point. If prompted to reboot, however, TCP/IP will not function properly until the host has been rebooted.

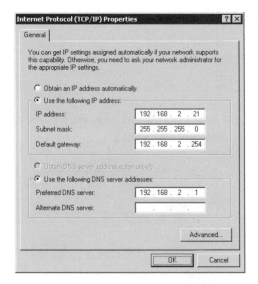

Installing TCP/IP on Windows 2000

To install TCP/IP in Windows 2000, follow these steps:

1. Access the network and dial-up connection settings by first clicking Start ➢ Settings ➢ Control Panel, and then double-clicking Network and Dial-Up Connections. Or, on the Windows 2000 Desktop, right-click My Network Places and then click Properties. Either way, the following Network and Dial-Up Connections window appears. An icon will be available for every component that Windows 2000 can use to connect to other devices. Right-click the connection on which to install TCP/IP.

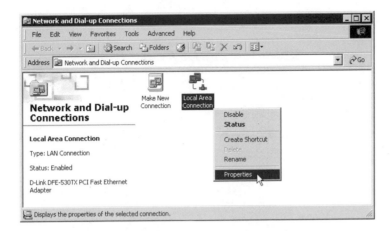

2. TCP/IP will not be listed as already installed. Click Install.

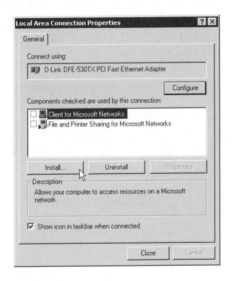

3. Choose Protocol and then Add.

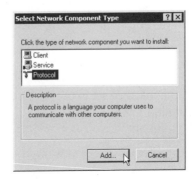

4. Choose Internet Protocol (TCP/IP) and click OK.

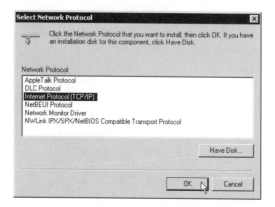

5. Be patient while TCP/IP is being installed; it may take several seconds after you've clicked OK before anything appears to be happening. Once TCP/IP is installed and listed on the General tab in the Local Area Connection Properties dialog box, click Close.

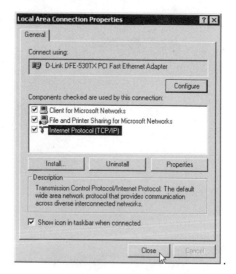

NOTE

Windows 95/98 is installed set to use DHCP. After rebooting, you can modify the configuration if desired.

Manually Assigning an IP Address for Windows 2000

To manually assign an IP address for a Windows 2000 host, take the following steps:

1. Access the network and dial-up connection settings by clicking Start ➤ Settings ➤ Control Panel, and then double-clicking Network and Dial-Up Connections. Or, on the Windows 2000 Desktop, right-click My Network Places and then click Properties. Either way, the Network and Dial-Up Connections window appears. An icon will be available for every component that Windows 2000 can use to connect to other devices. Right-click the connection on which to configure TCP/IP, and choose Properties.

2. In the Local Area Connection Properties dialog box, highlight Internet Protocol (TCP/IP) and choose Properties. The Internet Protocol (TCP/IP) Properties dialog box will appear. By default, TCP/IP is set to Obtain an IP Address Automatically.

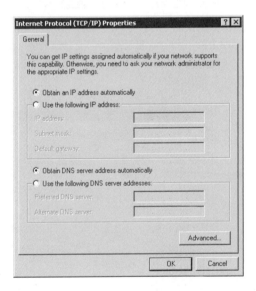

3. In the Internet Protocol (TCP/IP) Properties dialog box, click the radio button that is labeled Use the Following IP Address. Type in the IP address and the subnet mask for this host. If the network that this host is on connects with another network, type in the default gateway.

NOTE

When you click the radio button labeled Use the Following IP Address, the radio button labeled Use the Following DNS Server Addresses is selected automatically.

4. Type the address of a DNS server for this host to use. On this page, you have the choice of entering two DNS server addresses, so that if the first doesn't respond, this host will consult the second. Then click OK. Windows 2000 does not always require a reboot at this point. If prompted to reboot, however, TCP/IP will not function properly until the host has been rebooted. (Please refer to the graphic on page 106.)

Installing TCP/IP on Windows NT

To install TCP/IP on Windows NT, follow these steps:

1. Access the network settings by clicking Start ➤ Settings ➤ Control Panel and then double-clicking Network. Or, on the Windows NT Desktop, right-click Network Neighborhood and then click Properties. The following dialog box appears.

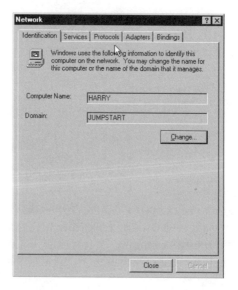

2. Begin adding TCP/IP by clicking the Protocols tab and then clicking the Add button.

3. In the Select Network Protocol dialog box that appears next, choose the TCP/IP Protocol option. Then click OK, as shown below.

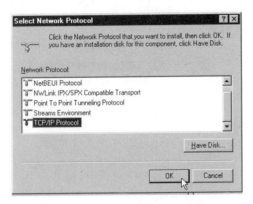

4. In the TCP/IP Setup dialog, choose to use DHCP or to manually assign an IP address by clicking Yes or No. If you choose No, you are prompted later to fill in all TCP/IP information. If you choose Yes, a DHCP server will supply all TCP/IP configuration information.

5. In the Windows NT Setup dialog shown below, supply a path to the Windows NT system files. System files are needed to complete the protocol installation. Depending on your installation, the system files may already be on the hard drive, or you may need the NT installation CD. Click Continue.

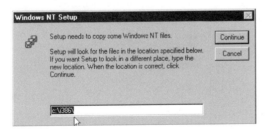

6. Several files are copied, and the installation stops at the Network Settings page. Click Close. More files are copied, and then you are prompted to type the IP address information if you chose No in step 4. Reboot if you are prompted to.

Manually Assigning an IP Address for Windows NT

To manually assign an IP address for Windows NT, take the following steps:

1. Access the network settings by clicking Start ➤ Settings ➤ Control Panel and then double-clicking Network. Or, on the Windows NT Desktop, right-click Network Neighborhood and then click Properties. The following dialog box appears.

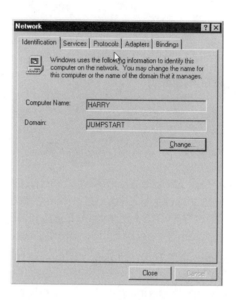

2. Access the TCP/IP properties by clicking the Protocols tab, the TCP/IP option, and then the Properties button, as shown below.

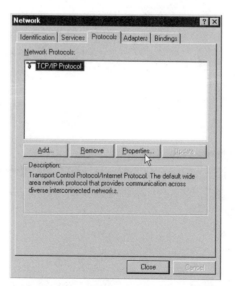

3. You are now viewing the Microsoft TCP/IP Properties dialog box shown below. This is where you can choose either to put in the address manually or obtain an address from a DHCP server. Choose to enter the IP address manually by clicking the radio button labeled Specify an IP Address.

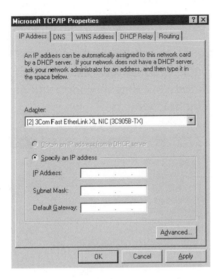

4. Enter the configuration information: the IP address, the subnet mask, and the default gateway. The default subnet mask will appear after the IP address is supplied; you must overwrite it if you want to modify it. Although the default gateway is an optional parameter, it is usually configured. You need to specify a default gateway if this host will be sending data to a host on another network.

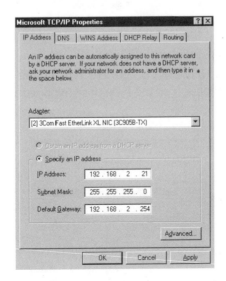

5. Save the configuration by clicking OK on the TCP/IP Properties page and then clicking OK on the Network Protocols page. Reboot if prompted.

Installing TCP/IP on Windows 95/98

To install TCP/IP for Windows 95/98, take the following steps:

1. Access the Network settings by clicking Start ➣ Settings ➣ Control Panel and double-clicking Network. Or, on the Windows 95/98 Desktop, right-click Network Neighborhood and then click Properties. The following dialog box appears.

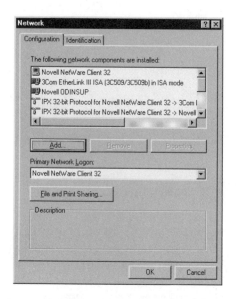

2. Begin adding the TCP/IP protocol by ensuring that you are on the Configuration page and then clicking Add.

3. In the Select Network Component Type dialog box shown below, select the Protocol option as the type of network component to install. Then click Add.

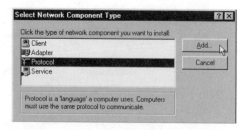

4. On the Select Network Protocol page, select the TCP/IP protocol: On the Manufacturers side of the screen, click Microsoft, and on the Network Protocols side of the screen, click TCP/IP. Then click OK.

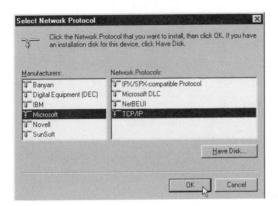

5. To complete the installation, click OK and then reboot.

NOTE

Windows 95/98 is installed set to use DHCP. After rebooting, you can modify the configuration if desired.

Manually Assigning an IP Address for Windows 95/98

To manually assign an IP address for Windows 95/98, take the following steps:

1. Access the network settings by clicking Start ➤ Settings ➤ Control Panel and then double-clicking Network. Or, on the Windows 95/98 Desktop, right-click Network Neighborhood and click Properties.

2. Access the TCP/IP properties by clicking the Configuration tab. Then scroll to TCP/IP and click that option. Finally, click Properties. If there is more than one TCP/IP line, choose the one that corresponds to the name of the network card in the computer.

DHCP server

A host running a service to lease IP addresses to other hosts. The DHCP server is configured by an administrator with the pool, or scope, of addresses to be leased.

```
Network                                          ? X
 Configuration | Identification |

 The following network components are installed:

   IPX/SPX-compatible Protocol -> Novell ODINSUP
   NetBEUI -> 3Com EtherLink III ISA (3C509/3C509b) in ISA
   NetBEUI -> Novell ODINSUP
   TCP/IP -> 3Com EtherLink III ISA (3C509/3C509b) in ISA
   TCP/IP -> Novell ODINSUP

        Add...          Remove          Properties

 Primary Network Logon:
   Novell NetWare Client 32

        File and Print Sharing...

 Description
   TCP/IP is the protocol you use to connect to the Internet and
   wide-area networks.

                              OK            Cancel
```

3. You are now viewing the TCP/IP Properties dialog box. This is where you can choose either to enter the address manually or obtain an address from a DHCP server. Click the radio button labeled Specify an IP Address to enter the IP address manually.

4. Enter the configuration information: the IP address and the subnet mask.

5. Configure the default gateway by clicking the Gateway tab, typing in the default gateway, and clicking Add. Although the default gateway is an optional parameter, it is usually configured. You need to specify a default gateway if this host will be sending data to a host on another network. Click OK on the Gateway page and again on the Configuration page, and reboot if prompted.

Dynamic Host Configuration Protocol (DHCP)

DHCP is the automatic IP-address giver. In essence, an administrator configures a **DHCP server** with a pool of addresses to lease out to hosts. The administrator may configure the server to lease out addresses to different networks by creating several pools of addresses.

Each pool of addresses contains the information that a TCP/IP host needs to build a TCP/IP stack. The pool is sometimes referred to as a **scope**, or range, of addresses. As a DHCP client is building its TCP/IP stack, it requests an IP address, and the DHCP server looks in the pools of addresses to see whether there are any IP addresses that can be leased out to the network that the host is on.

The client doesn't already have an IP address because the administrator did not type one in. Instead, the administrator determined that the client should get its IP address automatically from a DHCP server. So the client broadcasts a packet out onto the network; the packet says something like, "Hey! Who's the DHCP server?"

After a DHCP server receives a packet indicating that a DHCP client is looking for a DHCP server, the server examines its pools of addresses and possibly offers an IP address to the client. If the DHCP server is not configured with a pool of addresses for the network where the DHCP client is located, the request is ignored.

The DHCP client might receive offers from several DHCP servers. The client selects the first one that it receives and sends back a packet that says, "Yeah, I would like that IP address." That packet goes back to the DHCP server, and the DHCP server responds with a packet that says, "All right, you can have that IP address."

In the following sections, you will examine the four-step process that a DHCP client goes through to obtain an IP address from a DHCP server.

scope
A pool of IP addresses that a DHCP server leases to DHCP clients.

The DHCP Process

The four-step process of DHCP can easily be remembered by using the mnemonic of DORA:

- ⬥ Discover
- ⬥ Offer
- ⬥ Request
- ⬥ Acknowledgment

Obtaining an IP Address from a DHCP Server

DHCP discover

The first step in using DHCP to lease an IP address. A DHCP discover packet is broadcast saying, "Hey, who is a DHCP server?"

There are four steps in getting an IP address from a DHCP server: DHCP discover, DHCP offer, DHCP request, and DHCP acknowledgment.

Let's walk through these steps and examine the packets at each.

DHCP Discover

The first step is the broadcast of a **DHCP discover** packet. As the client is building its TCP/IP stack, it broadcasts a message that says, "Hey! I need a DHCP server!" The client broadcasts this packet so that no configuration is necessary. No administrator needs to type in the address of the DHCP server. Also, the client that is looking for a DHCP server has to broadcast the discover packet so that all hosts on the network will receive it—one of which is hopefully a DHCP server.

In the illustration below, Harry the Host represents a DHCP client. The first thing that Harry needs to do is find a DHCP server. Because Harry doesn't know where one is, nor does he have an address yet, he broadcasts a DHCP discover packet to help find one.

Below is a screen capture of a DHCP discover packet. Inside the packet, the source Ethernet (hardware) address contains the MAC address of the DHCP client that is requesting the address (005004818D42). The IP source address is all 0s (0.0.0.0) because the client does not yet have an IP address. The destination Ethernet (hardware) address is set to FFFFFFFFFFFF, which is the broadcast hardware address, and the IP destination address is set to 255.255.255.255 because it's the broadcast IP address.

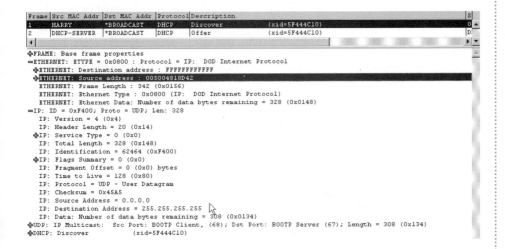

The DHCP client puts its hardware address in the DHCP discover packet because that address distinguishes that client from any other host on the network.

If a DHCP discover packet is broadcast and no DHCP offers are returned, the DHCP client is going to have a problem. The DHCP client needs to have an IP address to use any TCP/IP communications and applications. The DHCP client will send out several DHCP discover packets before showing the user an error message. (The error message usually states that a DHCP server cannot be found.) The DHCP client will try again in about five minutes by sending out another volley of DHCP discover packets. Without an IP address, the user can still use local applications; only the network functionality is unavailable.

DHCP Offer

The DHCP server monitors every incoming packet to check whether or not it is a DHCP discover packet. When a DHCP discover packet is received, the DHCP server examines its pools of IP addresses to see whether any of those addresses correspond to the network that the request is coming from.

If the DHCP server has an available address for the network where the DHCP discover packet originated, the server creates a **DHCP offer** packet. The DHCP offer packet includes the IP address that the server is offering to the client. Also included in this packet is the subnet mask, the length of the lease, and a few other parameters.

The server broadcasts the DHCP offer packet back onto the network because the DHCP client does not yet have an IP address that the server could use to send the packet directly to the client. The client will know that the packet is intended for it because the DHCP discover packet included the client's hardware address, and the DHCP offer packet also contains the same address.

The following illustration shows Donna the DHCP Server responding to Harry's DHCP discover packet. Donna broadcasts a DHCP offer packet back to the network so that Harry will receive it.

The following screen capture shows a DHCP offer packet. Notice that the Ethernet destination address is FFFFFFFFFFFF, which is the broadcast hardware address. The Ethernet source address is 005004744FFF, which is the hardware address of the DHCP server.

DHCP offer

The second step in using DHCP to lease an IP address. A DHCP offer packet is broadcast saying, "I'm a DHCP server, how would you like this fine address?"

```
Frame Src MAC Addr  Dst MAC Addr  Protocol Description                              S
1     HARRY         *BROADCAST    DHCP     Discover          (xid=5F444C10)         0
2     DHCP-SERVER   *BROADCAST    DHCP     Offer             (xid=5F444C10)         D

✛FRAME: Base frame properties
➡ETHERNET: ETYPE = 0x0800 : Protocol = IP:  DOD Internet Protocol
  ✛ETHERNET: Destination address : FFFFFFFFFFFF
  ✛ETHERNET: Source address : 005004744FFF
   ETHERNET: Frame Length = 342 (0x0156)
   ETHERNET: Ethernet Type : 0x0800 (IP:  DOD Internet Protocol)
   ETHERNET: Ethernet Data: Number of data bytes remaining = 328 (0x0148)
➡IP: ID = 0x1D8; Proto = UDP; Len: 328
   IP: Version = 4 (0x4)
   IP: Header Length = 20 (0x14)
  ✛IP: Service Type = 0 (0x0)
   IP: Total Length = 328 (0x148)
   IP: Identification = 472 (0x1D8)
  ✛IP: Flags Summary = 0 (0x0)
   IP: Fragment Offset = 0 (0x0) bytes
   IP: Time to Live = 128 (0x80)
   IP: Protocol = UDP - User Datagram
   IP: Checksum = 0x7427
   IP: Source Address = 192.168.2.254
   IP: Destination Address = 255.255.255.255
   IP: Data: Number of data bytes remaining = 308 (0x0134)
✛UDP: IP Multicast:  Src Port: BOOTP Server, (67); Dst Port: BOOTP Client (68); Length = 308 (0x134)
✛DHCP: Offer             (xid=5F444C10)
```

The last line of the screen capture above is not expanded to show the contents of the DHCP offer section. This section includes the IP address that is being offered, as well as other parameters such as the subnet mask and the length of the lease.

Since the DHCP client sent out the DHCP discover packet, the client has been closely monitoring the network, waiting for a DHCP offer.

It's possible that the network administrator has set up more than one DHCP server. Therefore, the DHCP client might receive more than one DHCP offer. If the DHCP client receives more than one offer, the client will take the first offer that is received—it's not like shopping around for the best car you can find. The client doesn't look at the different IP address offers and say, "Hey! Now this IP address looks really nice. It's got power windows, power brakes, and a really good lease length on it." The client will request an IP address from the first offer that it receives.

DHCP Request

After the DHCP client receives a DHCP offer, the client sends back a **DHCP request** packet. This packet lets the DHCP server know that the offer is being accepted.

The DHCP client broadcasts the DHCP request packet onto the network. This packet is broadcast for a couple of reasons. First, the client still does not have a valid lease on the address, which means the DHCP client still does not have a valid IP address needed to address a packet for direct delivery. The lease deal is

DHCP request
The third step in using DHCP to lease a new IP address and the first step in renewing an IP address lease. A DHCP request packet is broadcast for new IP address leases and sent directly to the DHCP server for renewals. The packet says, "Yes, I would like to have this IP address."

invalid because it has not yet been completed—no driving the car until all the papers are signed.

Second, several DHCP servers might have broadcast DHCP offers after receiving the DHCP discover packet. When the DHCP servers sent out the offers, any IP addresses offered were marked as reserved and would not be offered to any other host. By broadcasting the DHCP request, the client enables all DHCP servers to hear the request and then examine their reserved addresses to see whether any were offered to the client's hardware address. If a DHCP request comes from a hardware address that is in the DHCP server's reserved pool, and the request is not for the IP address that this DHCP server offered, the DHCP server's offer is considered denied. The DHCP server can put that IP address back into the pool and offer it to another client.

The following illustration shows Harry the Host requesting the IP address that Donna offered. Harry must broadcast the DHCP request packet because he still doesn't have a bona fide and confirmed IP address.

The following screen capture shows the Ethernet portion of the DHCP request packet. The Ethernet destination address is FFFFFFFFFFFF because that is the broadcast hardware address. The Ethernet source address is 005004818D42, which is the hardware address of the DHCP client.

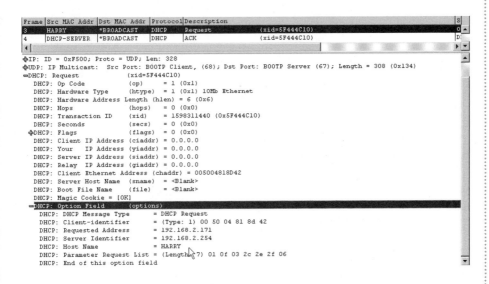

The following screen capture shows the remainder of the DHCP request packet. In the DHCP portion of the packet, the client's Ethernet address is listed again. In the DHCP Option Field, the DHCP requested address is listed, which in this packet is 192.168.2.171. The DHCP server's address is also listed, which is 192.168.2.254. As the packet is broadcast, the DHCP server with the address 192.168.2.254 will know that the DHCP client is requesting the offered IP address. All other DHCP servers that had offered an IP address to the client with the hardware address of 005004818D42 will put the IP address offered back into the pool of available addresses.

DHCP Acknowledgment

Now the deal is almost done. A DHCP client was looking for a DHCP server to lease an IP address from, and a DHCP server heard the discover packet and sent an offer. The offer was received, and a request to use that address was made. Now all that needs to be done is to sign the lease papers and the deal is closed.

The DHCP server receives the DHCP request and prepares a packet to close the deal. This packet is called a **DHCP acknowledgment (ack)** packet. Like the other packets, this one is also broadcast because the DHCP client still does not have a valid IP address. The DHCP ack packet simply says, "I received your request for the IP address that I offered you, and yes, you can have that address. By the way, here are all the options that come with that address."

The following illustration shows the final packet in the DHCP sequence. Donna broadcasts a DCHP ack, which is the acknowledgment packet. After Harry receives this, he knows that the deal is done and he has a valid lease on his new IP address.

DHCP acknowledgment (ack)

The final step in using DHCP to lease a new IP address or to renew an IP address lease. A DHCP ack is broadcast for new IP address leases and sent directly to the DHCP client for renewals. The packet says, "It's a done deal! You can have this IP address, and here are some extra parameters that you can have."

The next screen capture shows the Ethernet portion of the DHCP ack packet. The Ethernet destination address is FFFFFFFFFFFF, which is the broadcast hardware address, and the Ethernet source address is 005004744FFF, which is the hardware address of the DHCP server.

The DHCP portion of the DHCP ack packet contains information about the IP address and the lease parameters. The following screen capture shows the DHCP portion with all the DHCP options. After the DHCP client receives this acknowledgment, then the client has an IP address. Now that the client has a valid lease on an IP address, the client finishes building its TCP/IP stack.

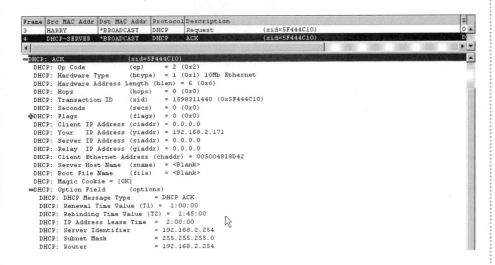

DHCP Leases

Because IP addresses are leased from the DHCP server, the DHCP client must renew the lease on the address at a specified time. If the lease were to expire, the host would cease to be able to communicate using TCP/IP.

time to live (TTL)
The amount of time that the lease on an IP address is valid.

When half of the **time to live (TTL)** value has expired, the DHCP client will send a DHCP request to the DHCP server asking for a new lease. For example, if the IP address is leased for 24 hours, after 12 hours the DHCP client will send a DHCP request directly to the DHCP server. The DHCP request is not broadcast this time because the DHCP client has a valid IP address and a valid lease, and the client knows the IP address of the DHCP server. Notice in the previous DHCP acknowledgment packet that an option field specifies an IP address lease time. This is the way that the DHCP server informs the client of the length of the lease. The length of lease was also specified in the offer packet.

In the next screen capture, a DHCP client is sending a DHCP request to renew the lease on an IP address. In the Ethernet portion of the DHCP request packet, both the Ethernet destination and source addresses are filled in with the appropriate hardware addresses. This is not a broadcast. In the IP portion of the DHCP request, the IP addresses of the client and of the server are filled in. Including the server's IP address enables the packet to be routed to the correct network (and therefore the DHCP client does not have to broadcast the request).

The DHCP server receives the DHCP request and sends back a DHCP ack. This packet is sent directly to the client requesting the IP address. The DHCP ack

126

includes all the options and a new TTL. The following screen capture shows the DHCP ack with the DHCP parameters that are being sent back to the client.

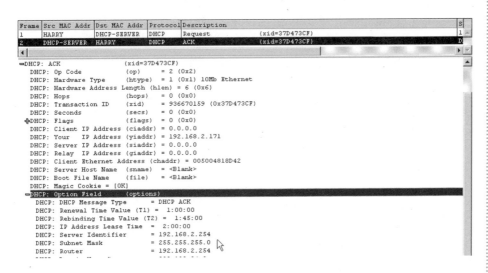

```
Frame Src MAC Addr  Dst MAC Addr  Protocol Description                              S
1      HARRY         DHCP-SERVER   DHCP     Request      (xid=37D473CF)             1
2      DHCP-SERVER   HARRY         DHCP     ACK          (xid=37D473CF)             D

⇒DHCP: ACK                    (xid=37D473CF)
    DHCP: Op Code                 (op)      = 2 (0x2)
    DHCP: Hardware Type           (htype)   = 1 (0x1) 10Mb Ethernet
    DHCP: Hardware Address Length (hlen) = 6 (0x6)
    DHCP: Hops                    (hops)    = 0 (0x0)
    DHCP: Transaction ID          (xid)     = 936670159 (0x37D473CF)
    DHCP: Seconds                 (secs)    = 0 (0x0)
 ⊕DHCP: Flags                     (flags)   = 0 (0x0)
    DHCP: Client IP Address (ciaddr) = 0.0.0.0
    DHCP: Your   IP Address (yiaddr) = 192.168.2.171
    DHCP: Server IP Address (siaddr) = 0.0.0.0
    DHCP: Relay  IP Address (giaddr) = 0.0.0.0
    DHCP: Client Ethernet Address (chaddr) = 005004818D42
    DHCP: Server Host Name   (sname)  = <Blank>
    DHCP: Boot File Name      (file)  = <Blank>
    DHCP: Magic Cookie = [OK]
 ⇒DHCP: Option Field      (options)
    DHCP: DHCP Message Type        = DHCP ACK
    DHCP: Renewal Time Value (T1) =  1:00:00
    DHCP: Rebinding Time Value (T2) =  1:45:00
    DHCP: IP Address Lease Time   =  2:00:00
    DHCP: Server Identifier       = 192.168.2.254
    DHCP: Subnet Mask             = 255.255.255.0
    DHCP: Router                  = 192.168.2.254
```

The process of renewing the IP address lease after only half of the TTL keeps the DHCP clients coming back often, and well before the expiration time. If there are any problems renewing the address, plenty of time remains to rectify them. For example, if the DHCP client sends a DHCP request after half of the TTL and the DHCP server does not respond, it is not yet a problem because the client still has a valid lease.

If $7/8$ of the TTL has expired, and the client has not successfully renewed the lease, the DHCP client will broadcast a DHCP request so that any DHCP server can respond with a DHCP ack. A DHCP server may also respond with a DHCP nack (negative acknowledgment). A DHCP nack says that the client cannot use that IP address any longer. If the DHCP client receives a DHCP nack or the TTL expires, the client will cease using any TCP/IP communication. If the user is working with locally installed applications and is not using any networked applications, the user can continue working. If the user is using networked applications when the lease expires, those applications will terminate.

DHCP IP Address Renewal

When a DHCP client is restarted and still has a valid lease on its IP address, a DHCP request containing the leased IP address is broadcast onto the network. The DHCP server sends a DHCP ack to the client, which renews the lease on the

IP address. If the DHCP client does not get a DHCP ack and the TTL has not expired, the client will continue to use the IP address. Another DHCP server on the network may send a DHCP nack, which will cause the DHCP client to cease using that IP address and start all over again by broadcasting a DHCP discover packet.

When a DHCP client shuts down, it does not release the IP address that it has leased. There are times when an administrator would like a DHCP client to release the IP address back to the DHCP server, however. This may be because the administrator is troubleshooting or because the DHCP client will not need an IP address anymore, for example, when it's leaving the network. Most implementations of the DHCP client software allow the user to release the IP address at any time.

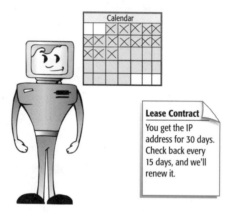

NOTE

Recent implementations of Microsoft's TCP/IP include a special feature called Automatic Private IP Addressing (APIPA), which generates an IP address for a DHCP-configured host that cannot obtain a lease from a DHCP server. APIPA randomly generates an address from the Microsoft-reserved IP address range of 169.254.0.1–169.254.255.254, and broadcasts an ARP request to make sure that no other host on the network has generated the same address. Using this address, the host can communicate with other hosts on the network that are also using an APIPA-generated address.

Reserving DHCP IP Addresses

A DHCP server randomly assigns IP addresses to clients on the network. But a network administrator might prefer some hosts to always have the same IP addresses. These hosts can use a manually assigned IP address. A manual configuration requires the administrator either to type in the IP address configuration information or to make a reservation.

An IP address reservation is set at the DHCP server. The administrator sets up a reservation for the host by entering the host's hardware address and the IP address into a reservation list. Whenever a DHCP request is received, the DHCP server sees the hardware address and matches it to the IP address that has been reserved for it. The DHCP offer that is sent back out will include the reserved IP address.

Some examples of hosts that an administrator will want to always have the same IP addresses are:

Servers   Applications may be mapped to use a particular IP address.

Printers   Hosts may be configured to print to a printer with a particular address.

Routers   Hosts are configured with an address for their router (default gateway).

An administrator might also need to reserve IP addresses when the number of addresses for a network is limited. If an administrator has 254 valid IP addresses and 300 hosts on the network, there could be a problem: If all hosts need an IP address at the same time, some will fail to get one and therefore will not be able to communicate on the network. Probably not all the hosts will be turned on and using an IP address at the same time. So, chances are that this scheme will work fine, but the administrator will want to make sure that the CEO always gets an IP address. To do so, the administrator should get the hardware address of the CEO's workstation and reserve one IP address on the DHCP server for the CEO's computer. Then the CEO is always guaranteed an IP address. The administrator had better be sure to type in the hardware address correctly or the CEO will never get the IP address that has been reserved.

Setting the Lease Duration

Setting the length of the TTL is up to the administrator. A long TTL means that the DHCP clients will not have to renew their IP addresses for a long time. It also means that the IP addresses will not be available to any other host for a long time.

Let's say that a user from our New York office is visiting the San Diego office and has a DHCP-enabled laptop. When the user plugs into the network in San Diego, the laptop broadcasts a DHCP discover. A DHCP server responds and a lease is consummated with the laptop. If the lease is for 30 days, the DHCP server will not lease that address to any other DHCP client for that time period.

If the laptop leaves the San Diego network later that same day, the DHCP server does not know that the laptop has left and doesn't need the IP address anymore. The IP address is gone for 30 days even though it is not being used; the DHCP server will not return it to the available pool of addresses until the lease has expired. Meanwhile, the DHCP clients on the San Diego network have one less IP address to use.

If the administrator had set the TTL to 24 hours, the IP address would be available the next day to be leased to another DHCP client. However, every 12 hours all the DHCP clients would be renewing their leases. This would cause some added network traffic that might be unnecessary.

Many Internet Service Providers (ISPs) use DHCP with a short TTL. A TTL of two hours will cause the DHCP clients to renew their lease every hour, but IP addresses are returned to the available pool more frequently. Therefore, the ISP can have fewer IP addresses than clients because they will not all be in use at the same time and are reused within two hours.

When IP addresses are at a premium and there aren't many available in the pool, an administrator should set a short TTL. This way, leases are expiring sooner, and the DHCP server will have the address back sooner to re-lease. An administrator should also set a short lease when the options are undergoing frequent changes (for example, when the address of the DNS server, WINS server, or default gateway is going to change). A shorter TTL requires the DHCP clients to renew their leases more often, and their associated options can be updated then. However, if the pool is rich with addresses and a tremendous amount of unused addresses are in the pool, an administrator can set the TTL for much longer.

Setting DHCP Scopes and Options

An administrator must configure the DHCP server with the appropriate scopes, or pools, of addresses and DHCP options. After the server is set up correctly, DHCP clients will begin getting IP addresses, and no further setup is required.

As stated earlier in this chapter, the range of IP addresses is referred to as a scope of addresses. Besides the IP address, the scope includes the subnet mask, a TTL, and possibly other options such as a default gateway. As DHCP discover packets are received, the DHCP server randomly offers IP addresses starting from the lower end of the scope.

The administrator needs to enter the scope options. The options include any addressing information that should be included with the IP address. Some common options included with an address from a DHCP server are:

- ◇ IP address of one or more DNS servers
- ◇ IP address of the WINS server
- ◇ IP address of the default gateway

If the administrator has manually assigned an IP address, it must be excluded from the scope of addresses. For example, if the administrator has manually configured a server with the IP address of 192.168.2.5, it is important that the DHCP server not offer that address to any DHCP clients. If the DHCP server has been set up to offer addresses in the range of 192.168.2.1 through 192.168.2.150, then the administrator must make an **exclusion** for the address 192.168.2.5.

A DHCP option that is set for all scopes that a DHCP server services is called a **global option**. A DHCP option that is set for just one scope is called a **scope option**. If any options are set for just one particular address, that is done as part of the reservation for that IP address.

One of the benefits of DHCP is that the DHCP clients come back to renew the leases on their addresses. If any option needs to be changed, an administrator has to change it only at the server, and when the DHCP clients come back to renew their leases, all the new options get sent out with the DHCP ack. The administrator has to manually update those options at the hosts if their IP address was manually configured.

exclusion
An IP address that falls into a range of addresses to be leased, but that has been set by an administrator not to be leased.

global option
A parameter that is set at the DHCP server and that applies to all scopes of IP addresses that this DHCP server serves.

scope option
A parameter that is set at the DHCP server that applies to only one scope of IP addresses.

Review Questions

Terms to Know
- ❏ DHCP server
- ❏ scope
- ❏ DHCP discover
- ❏ DHCP offer
- ❏ DHCP request
- ❏ DHCP ack
- ❏ TTL
- ❏ exclusion
- ❏ global option
- ❏ scope option

1. What are two ways to assign IP addresses to hosts?

_____

_____

2. What are the four steps of using DHCP?

_____

_____

_____

_____

3. Which of the four steps uses a broadcast packet?

_____

_____

_____

_____

4. What information is included in a discover packet?

_____

5. What information is included in an offer packet?

_____

6. Why would an administrator use a reservation?

_____

7. When should an administrator use DHCP instead of manually configuring IP addresses?

_____

8. When does a DHCP client renew the lease of an address?

_____

9. When a DHCP offer is sent on the network, how does the client know which host the packet is intended for?

_____

10. List some hosts for which a network administrator should consider using manually assigned IP addresses.

_____

Chapter
8

Introduction to
Subnet Masks

Subnet masks are one of the most interesting aspects of TCP/IP. Subnet masks point out to IP which bits of the 32-bit IP address refer to the network. A good network administrator understands how to determine and use subnet masks.

In this chapter, you will examine the following topics:

 What is a subnet mask?

 Two parts of a subnet mask

 Determining if the destination is local or remote

 Standard subnet masks

What Is a Subnet Mask?

A **subnet mask** is a number that looks like an IP address. It shows TCP/IP how many bits are used for the network portion of the IP address by covering up, or "masking," the IP address's network portion. As you learned in Chapter 6, an IP address is made up of two parts: the network portion and the host portion.

For every outgoing packet, IP has to determine whether the destination host is on the same **local network** or on a **remote network**. If the destination is local, then IP uses an ARP broadcast to find out the hardware address of the destination host. If the destination host is not on the local network, then ARP broadcasts a request for the hardware address of the router. Therefore, IP sends packets that are bound for a remote network directly to the router, which is also known as the default gateway. The router then sends the packet to the next network on its journey to the correct destination network.

Just as the telephone system uses an area code to determine whether a number is local or long distance, TCP/IP uses the subnet mask to determine whether the destination of a packet is a host on the local network or a host on a remote network. In the same way that every U.S. telephone number must have an area code, every IP address must have a subnet mask.

If, for example, your telephone number is (619) 555-1212, and you call someone whose telephone number is (619) 345-1111, it is a local call. You know that because you can look at the numbers between the parentheses and see that they have the same value. If, on the other hand, your number is (619) 555-1212 and you call someone whose number is (213) 888-8146, it's a long distance call. You know that because the numbers inside of the parentheses are different. You can think of the subnet mask as the area code in the parentheses of a telephone number. Just as an area code determines a phone call's destination, a subnet mask tells IP how many bits to look at when determining if the destination IP address is local or remote.

The following graphic shows Harry calling Amber. Since Amber has a different area code, the phone call will have to go through the router. When Harry calls Sally, however, it is a local call and does not need to go through the router.

When determining if the packet is bound for the local network or a remote network, IP compares the network portion of the sender's IP address with the same number of bits from the destination's IP address. If the bit values are exactly the same, the packet's destination is determined to be local. If there are any differences in the bit values, the packet's destination is determined to be remote.

subnet mask

A 32-bit address that looks like an IP address but actually points out to IP which part of the IP address is the network portion.

local network

Hosts that are on the same side of a router are considered to be on the same local network. Two hosts on the same local network have the exact same bit values in the network portion of their IP addresses.

remote network

Hosts that have a router separating them are considered to be on a remote network from each other. Two hosts on remote networks have different bit values in the network portion of their IP addresses.

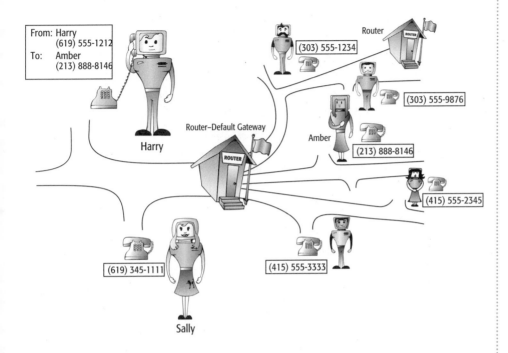

From: Harry
     (619) 555-1212
To: Amber
     (213) 888-8146

Router

(303) 555-1234

(303) 555-9876

Router–Default Gateway

Amber

(213) 888-8146

Harry

(415) 555-2345

(619) 345-1111

(415) 555-3333

Sally

To know how many bits to compare, IP evaluates the subnet mask of the sending host. In the subnet mask, there is a series of 1s, and then the rest of the bits are set to 0. When IP evaluates the subnet mask, it is looking specifically for the answer to the question, "How many bits are set to 1?" Once IP determines how many bits are set to 1, it knows how many bits of the source host's IP address and the destination host's IP address will be compared.

You can think of the number of bits that are set to 1 in the subnet mask as the number of digits inside the parentheses in a telephone number—if that number could change (in other words, if it's variable). If, for example, a telephone number has 10 digits, imagine if the parentheses include 4, 5, or 6 digits. You would then evaluate the number to be local or long distance based on the digits that are in the parentheses. If there are 8 bits set to 1 in the subnet mask, IP will compare the first 8 bits of the host with the first 8 bits of the destination. If there are 16 bits in the subnet mask that are set to 1, IP will compare the first 16 bits of host and destination.

A subnet mask is a required element of every IP address. When you want to type in the IP address for a host, the only two required elements are the IP address itself and the subnet mask. Likewise, when you want to call someone, it is required that you know the correct area code for the phone number. You then compare the first three characters of your phone number (your area code) with the first three characters of their phone number (their area code). If the area codes are the same, you don't need to dial the area code, nor do you have to pay for a long distance call, because it is a local call. If the area code is not the same, however, you'll have to dial their area code so that the telephone system can route your call to their city.

You'll see over the next several pages that IP looks at everything in binary. Subnet masks and routing will become clearer if you think about the IP addresses and subnet masks in binary, so begin now to think of IP addresses and subnet masks as 32 bits. When thinking in binary, do not pay attention to the periods that we use in the decimal representation. IP does not pay attention to the periods; neither should we. Just consider the addresses as 32 1s and 0s.

subnet goggles

A fictional set of goggles that IP wears when looking at an IP address to determine whether an address is local or remote. The goggles "light up" the network and subnet bits with 1s as the bit values in the subnet mask.

Impress Your Friends with a New Party Trick

In this trick, you will count to 15 in binary with just 4 fingers. Let four of your fingers represent 4 bits. Your thumb represents the 1's place; your index finger represents the 2's place; your middle finger, the 4's place; and your ring finger the 8's place.

Start by making a fist for a binary 0, and then say out loud, "Zero." Then raise your thumb (1) and say out loud, "One." Put your thumb back into your fist, raise your index finger (2), and say out loud, "Two." Now raise both your thumb and your index finger. This represents a decimal value of 2 + 1, so say out loud, "Three." Put your thumb and your index finger back into your fist and raise your middle finger (4). This finger represents the 4's place. Apologize for the gesture, and say, "Four." Raise your middle finger and thumb (4 + 1) and say, "Five." Now put your thumb back, raise your middle finger and index finger (4 + 2), and say, "Six." Raise your middle finger, index finger, and thumb (4 + 2 + 1) and say, "Seven." Continue counting all the way up to 15 with just 4 fingers. For added fun, use 4 fingers on your other hand and you have a whole octet! You can also count all the way to 255 with just 8 fingers.

Network and Host

Applying a subnet mask is like looking through a set of "**subnet goggles**." Imagine wearing a set of goggles as you look at an IP address; you see all 32 bits, each in its own slot. When you ask the question, "How many bits are used for the network portion of this IP address?" the subnet mask lights up the slots that are in the network portion of the address.

Through subnet goggles, 255.0.0.0 looks like this:

    NNNN NNNN.HHHH HHHH.HHHH HHHH.HHHH HHHH

The goggles light up the first 8 bits as the network portion (**N**), and the remaining 24 bits are used for the host portion (H).

Through subnet goggles, 255.255.0.0 look like this:

NNNN NNNN.NNNN NNNN.HHHH HHHH.HHHH HHHH

The goggles light up the first 16 bits as the network portion.

The subnet mask simply provides a means to light up the correct slots so that IP can figure out the number of bits used for the network portion of the address. After IP figures this out, it can compare the address to that of another host to determine whether that host is local or remote. Using our telephone number and area code example, we can say that the subnet goggles are illuminating the area code of a telephone number. With subnet masks, the subnet goggles are illuminating the network portion of the source and destination IP addresses.

Identifying a Local or Remote Network

With every packet that is sent across a network, the big question is: Is the destination address local or remote? The destination is local if the network portion of the source's IP address is the same as that of the destination's IP address.

If any bits of the network portions differ from each other, then the destination is remote. This is similar to figuring out whether someone lives on the same street as you do. If you look at the person's street name and it is the same as yours, the person lives on the same street as you do. If any part of the street name is different, the person is remote to your street.

But, as stated earlier, before IP can figure out whether the destination address is remote, IP has to determine how many bits are in the network portion of the source IP address. IP uses the subnet mask to determine which bits of the IP address represent the network portion of the address.

The subnet mask is 32 bits long, but you use **dotted decimal notation** to represent it, just as you do with an IP address. A subnet mask, in binary, is made up of several contiguous 1s, which represent the network portion of the address, and then the rest of the bits are 0s. When determining how many of the 32 bits are in the network portion of an IP address, IP looks at the subnet mask for the contiguous 1s.

When you look at a subnet mask in binary, imagine that the 1s represent the beginning and end of an area code. The number of bits set to 1 in the subnet mask is the number of bits that will be compared to determine if the destination is local or remote. This is similar to evaluating two telephone numbers by comparing the values that are inside the parentheses. The 1s in the subnet mask will act like the number of digits within the parentheses in an area code; these are the only values that are compared to determine if the destination is local or remote. When someone gives you their telephone number, you can tell if it is a long distance number just by looking at the digits in the parentheses. Likewise, the subnet mask's only purpose is to determine how many bits are used to identify if the destination host of every packet is local or remote.

For example, if the first 16 bits are set to 1, then IP compares the first 16 bits of the source IP address with the first 16 bits of the destination IP address. If these 16 bits are exactly the same, the destination host is local; if any of the bits are different, the destination host is remote. If the first 24 bits are set to 1, then IP compares the first 24 bits of the source IP address with the first 24 bits of the destination IP address. If these 24 bits are exactly the same, the destination host is local; if any of the bits are different, the destination host is remote.

It is called a subnet "mask" for a good reason: It indicates or "masks" the network bits. Think of it as a shadow covering up some of the bits. The subnet mask shows us how big the shadow, or mask, is.

Finding a Local Address

A subnet mask of 255.0.0.0 in decimal converts to this binary number:

    1111 1111.0000 0000.0000 0000.0000 0000

This binary number tells IP that the first 8 bits are used in the network portion of the address and the last 24 bits are used in the host portion of the address.

For example, if the source IP address is 10.1.2.3 with a subnet mask of 255.0.0.0, and the destination address is 10.3.4.5, then IP examines the addresses like this:

	Decimal	Binary
Subnet Mask	255.0.0.0	1111 1111.0000 0000.0000 0000.0000 0000
Source	10.1.2.3	0000 1010.0000 0001.0000 0010.0000 0011
Destination	10.3.4.5	0000 1010.0000 0011.0000 0100.0000 0101
RESULT		Same = Local

dotted decimal notation

The decimal representation of an IP address or subnet mask. Four decimal numbers separated by periods (or dots) is the preferred way to represent an address or mask.

Based on the subnet mask having the first 8 bits set to 1, IP compares the first 8 bits of the source to the first 8 bits of the destination. In this case, the first 8 bits of both addresses are the same, so the destination is local. Knowing that the destination host has a local address, IP can broadcast an ARP to get the hardware address.

Finding a Remote Address

In another example, if the source IP address is 10.1.2.3 with a subnet mask of 255.0.0.0, and the destination address is 11.3.4.5, then IP examines the addresses like this:

	Decimal	Binary
Subnet Mask	255.0.0.0	1111 1111.0000 0000.0000 0000.0000 0000
Source	10.1.2.3	0000 1010.0000 0001.0000 0010.0000 0011
Destination	11.3.4.5	0000 1011.0000 0011.0000 0100.0000 0101
RESULT		Different = Remote

Based on the subnet mask having the first 8 bits set to 1, IP compares the first 8 bits of the source to the first 8 bits of the destination. In this case, the first 8 bits of both addresses are *not* the same, so the destination is remote. Knowing that the destination host has a remote address, IP cannot broadcast an ARP to get the hardware address because a router will stop the broadcast. Instead, IP broadcasts an ARP for the router, which is where IP must send the packet to move it off of the local network and on its way to the remote network.

In another example, suppose that the source address is 176.16.2.3 and the destination address is 176.16.4.5. If I ask you the question, "Is the destination local or remote?" the answer you should give is "I don't know; I don't have enough information." Without the subnet mask, you can only guess if the destination is local or remote. So, I'll tell you what the subnet mask is: 255.255.0.0.

Now you can answer that the destination is local because we are going to evaluate the first 16 bits of both the source and the destination. Just by looking at the first 2 octets (16 bits), it's obvious that these addresses are on the same network. There is no difference between any of those 16 bits. It doesn't even matter if we change the source address to 176.16.200.200; they are still on the same network because the first 16 bits did not change.

But what if I change the subnet mask to 255.255.255.0? Now IP needs to compare the first 24 bits. Just by looking at the first 3 octets, you can tell that the destination is on a remote network. It should be simple to see that there is a difference in the first 24 bits.

Standard Subnet Masks

In Chapter 6, you looked at the five classes of IP addresses. For each class of address, there is a standard, or default, subnet mask. Each is discussed in the following sections.

standard subnet mask

Also called a default subnet mask. Class A = 255.0.0.0, Class B = 255.255.0.0, and Class C = 255.255.255.0.

Class A Addresses

The **standard subnet mask** for a Class A address is 255.0.0.0. This tells IP that the first 8 bits are used for the network portion of the IP address, and the remaining 24 bits are used for the host portion. IP looks at the 32 bits and uses the subnet mask to mask out the network portion of the address:

NNNN NNNN.HHHH HHHH.HHHH HHHH.HHHH HHHH

Because 24 bits are left for the host portion of the address, there are almost 17 million unique host IP addresses for each Class A network address.

Class B Addresses

A Class B address has a standard subnet mask of 255.255.0.0. This mask tells IP that the first 16 bits are used for the network portion of the address, and the remaining 16 bits are used for the host portion:

NNNN NNNN.NNNN NNNN.HHHH HHHH.HHHH HHHH

The 16 bits that are used for the host portion of the address can uniquely address more than 16,000 hosts on each Class B network.

Class C Addresses

A Class C address has a standard subnet mask of 255.255.255.0, which masks out the first 24 bits as the network portion and leaves the remaining 8 bits for the host portion:

NNNN NNNN.NNNN NNNN.NNNN NNNN.HHHH HHHH

The 8 bits used for the host portion can uniquely address 254 hosts on each of the Class C networks.

In summary:

Class	Standard Mask (Decimal)	Standard Mask (Binary)
A	**255**.0.0.0	1111 1111.0000 0000.0000 0000.0000 0000
B	**255.255**.0.0	1111 1111.1111 1111.0000 0000.0000 0000
C	**255.255.255**.0	1111 1111.1111 1111.1111 1111.0000 0000

You can remember the standard masks this way:

> 1 octet = Class A (1st letter in the alphabet)
>
> 2 octets = Class B (2nd letter in the alphabet)
>
> 3 octets = Class C (3rd letter in the alphabet)

In most cases, however, using the standard subnet mask is not the optimal solution for designing a TCP/IP addressing plan. Most implementations use a variation of the standard subnet mask called a custom subnet mask, which is explained in Chapter 9.

The following screen capture shows a custom subnet mask being used. Because the IP address has "10" in the first octet, this is a Class A address, and the standard subnet mask is 255.0.0.0. However, the administrator has defined a custom subnet mask of 255.255.255.240, which enables him to create more networks with fewer hosts on each network.

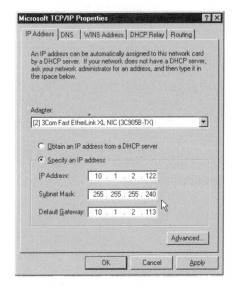

Review Questions

1. An IP address is really made up of two portions. What are they?

   _____

2. What is IP trying to determine when the subnet mask is examined?

   _____

3. When IP evaluates the IP addresses of the source host and the destination host, on which portion does IP focus?

   _____

4. True or False: The subnet mask is an optional part of the IP address.

   _____

5. What is the standard subnet mask for a Class A address?

   _____

6. If a source IP address is 10.1.2.3 and the destination address is 10.3.4.5, are these two hosts on the same network?

   _____

7. What is the standard subnet mask for a Class B address?

   _____

8. If a source IP address is 176.16.2.3 with a subnet mask of 255.255.0.0, and the destination address is 176.16.4.5, are these two hosts on the same network? List the network and the host value of each.

   Source address:

   Network:_____ Host:_____

   Destination address:

   Network:_____ Host:_____

9. If a source IP address is 176.16.2.3 with a subnet mask of 255.255.255.0, and the destination address is 176.16.4.5, are these two hosts on the same network? List the network and the host value of each.

    Source address:

    Network:_____ Host:_____

    Destination address:

    Network:_____ Host:_____

10. What is the standard subnet mask for a Class C address?

_____

11. If a source IP address is 192.168.1.3 with a subnet mask of 255.255.255.0, and the destination address is 192.168.2.3, are these two hosts on the same network? List the network and the host value of each.

    Source address:

    Network:_____ Host:_____

    Destination address:

    Network:_____ Host:_____

12. If an IP address is 192.168.1.37 with a subnet mask of 255.255.255.0, what is the value of the host portion?

_____

13. If an IP address is 176.16.1.37 with a subnet mask of 255.255.0.0, what is the value of the host portion?

_____

14. If a source IP address is 10.1.2.3 with a subnet mask of 255.255.255.0, and the destination address is 10.1.3.4, are these two hosts on the same network? List the network and the host value of each.

    Source address:

    Network:_____ Host:_____

    Destination address:

    Network:_____ Host:_____

Chapter

9

Using Custom Subnet Masks

A network is divided into two subnets by using a router. The router looks at every packet, compares the destination address to its routing table, and determines which subnet to forward the packet on to. A router is at the edge of every network, connecting it to other networks.

Most medium to large companies would like to be able to create several subnets within their company's network. As soon as they begin adding routers, however, they're going to need a new network IP address on each side of the router so that the router will know which subnet to send it to.

As a network administrator, you will need to understand how to create custom subnet masks so that you can put routers into your network and create subnets without paying for several network addresses.

In this chapter, you will examine:

 Custom subnet masks

 How to create additional networks

 Rules for valid IP addresses

Custom Subnet Masks

On most networks, the network administrator uses an IP addressing scheme that includes a **custom subnet mask**. Because the routers that are in the physical Local Area Network (LAN) define each network, a network administrator must use a different network address for each side of a router. When a router is used to create smaller networks, the smaller network is called a **subnet**.

A Class A address can have close to 17 million hosts on a network. However, no network has 17 million hosts on one side of a router; it would not be physically possible. A large network is divided into several smaller networks by routers, and every time that a router is used, a new network address is required. Rather than obtain a new network address for each network, the network administrator can *create* more network addresses by using a custom subnet mask.

custom subnet mask
A non-standard subnet mask used by a network administrator to make more efficient use of a network address by creating more subnets.

subnet
A smaller network created by dividing a larger network.

A Custom Subnet Mask Analogy

Let's say that I win the lottery and suddenly have more money than I know what to do with. So the first thing I do is buy a huge new house. This enormous home has 50 bedrooms, 50 bathrooms, and 50 kitchens. This is a pretty big house for a family of four, so pretty soon we figure out that it is just too big. A better use of this house would be to subdivide it into apartments. I decide to put up a few walls and make 50 smaller homes, each with a bedroom, bathroom, and kitchen. To make the most efficient use of this huge home, I will have 50 families live in the apartments. This is a similar idea to subnetting an IP address.

The concept of a custom subnet mask is simple: Use the subnet mask to "take" some bits for the network portion of the IP address and use fewer bits for the host portion.

For example, a standard Class A subnet mask is 255.0.0.0, which uses 8 bits to mask the network portion of the IP address. If an administrator is using a Class A address with this mask, then only 8 bits can be used for the network portion of the address, and those 8 bits are already set by which address is being used. In this scheme, 24 bits are left for the host portion, which means almost 17 million unique host addresses.

```
255.0.0.0 =
1111 1111.0000 0000.0000 0000.0000
NNNN NNNN.HHHH HHHH.HHHH HHHH.HHHH HHHH
```

A subnet mask of 255.255.0.0 masks 16 bits of the IP address for the network portion and leaves 16 bits for the host portion. If the administrator is using the same Class A address as before, but with a custom subnet mask of 255.255.0.0, then IP will use 16 bits as the network portion of the IP address. In this scheme, 8 bits mask the Class A network address portion that was assigned as the network address. The first 8 bits are the standard portion of the mask, the second 8 bits mask the subnet portion (**S**), and 16 bits are still left for unique host addresses.

255.255.0.0 =

1111 1111.1111 1111.0000 0000.0000 0000

NNNN NNNN.SSSS SSSS.HHHH HHHH.HHHH HHHH

The following screen capture shows the display of the IP Subnet Calculator available from WildPackets, Inc., a company that conducts network analysis in the areas of consulting, training, and value-added software. The IP Subnet Calculator figures out the correct subnet mask, network addresses, and valid host IP addresses based on the parameters that you supply. Notice that 6 subnet bits are requested. The Subnet Mask field in the center portion of the calculator shows that the subnet mask is 255.255.255.252. A couple of fields below that, the Subnet Bit Map field shows the significance of every bit in the subnet mask. The significance of each bit is displayed as either:

- ◆ n   for network
- ◆ s   for subnet
- ◆ h   for host

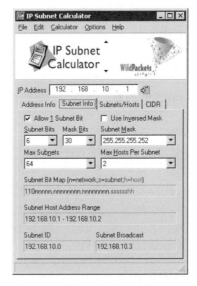

Creating Additional Networks

With a custom subnet mask, the administrator still cannot change the first 8 bits, which represent the assigned IP network address, but now can use the next 8 bits to create more networks. This scheme still leaves 16 bits for the host portion of the address. Using the 8 **subnet bits**, an administrator can create 254 subnets; and using the remaining 16 host bits, an administrator can address 65,534 hosts on each network.

subnet bits

Bits used in the subnet mask to extend the number of bits available for the network portion of the IP address.

To create the 254 subnets, simply use every binary variation of the 8 subnet bits. For example:

Decimal	Binary
255.255.0.0	1111 1111.1111 1111.0000 0000.0000 0000
Subnet Goggles	NNNN NNNN.SSSS SSSS.HHHH HHHH.HHHH HHHH
10.1.0.0	0000 1010.0000 0001.HHHH HHHH.HHHH HHHH
10.2.0.0	0000 1010.0000 0010.HHHH HHHH.HHHH HHHH
10.3.0.0	0000 1010.0000 0011.HHHH HHHH.HHHH HHHH
10.4.0.0	0000 1010.0000 0100.HHHH HHHH.HHHH HHHH
10.5.0.0	0000 1010.0000 0101.HHHH HHHH.HHHH HHHH
10.6.0.0	0000 1010.0000 0110.HHHH HHHH.HHHH HHHH
10.7.0.0	0000 1010.0000 0111.HHHH HHHH.HHHH HHHH

Notice in the table above that the 8 network (**N**) bits stay the same while the 8 subnet (**S**) bits are incrementing. This is how to create several unique networks. I've taken some bits from the host (H) portion of the address and given them to the network/subnet portion. In doing this, I am now able to create more networks that have fewer hosts on each of the networks. On each of these networks, 16 bits are still left for the host portion of the address, which can make up the 65,534 unique host addresses.

Subnetting Rules

If an administrator has a Class A address and needs to create more than 254 networks, then the appropriate subnet mask will extend to the next octet. An administrator needs to determine the number of networks to be addressed and the maximum number of hosts to be addressed on those networks, and then create the proper subnet mask. Sometimes the subnet mask will use an entire octet and sometimes it won't. An administrator can use any number of subnet bits to create the correct subnet mask.

However, there are some rules to subnetting:

- The subnet bits in the IP address cannot be all 1s.
- The subnet bits in the IP address cannot be all 0s.
- The host bits in the IP address cannot be all 1s.

    When all of the host bits are set to 1, the IP address becomes a **broadcast** address. This means that every host on that network will accept the packet for further processing. No host can have a broadcast IP address because it is like a community mailbox address.

- The host bits in the IP address cannot be all 0s.

    When all of the host bits are set to 0, the IP address refers to the network and not to any of the hosts. An address with all 0s in the host portion of the address is invalid, and no host can use it.

These rules are easy to follow when using the subnet goggles. Always check out binary IP addresses with the subnet goggles and confirm that neither the Ss nor the Hs are all 1s or all 0s.

NOTE

RFC 1878 describes a means of subnet addressing that allows for all 1s and all 0s in the subnet bits. Most hardware and software do not support RFC 1878 addressing; check the documentation of the hardware or software that you are using.

Creating a Custom Subnet Mask

The easiest way to create valid subnet masks is to use a **subnet calculator**, like the one mentioned earlier. Several subnet calculators are available for free on the Internet. To be able to create subnet masks without a subnet calculator is a skill. This skill is useful for certification tests that don't allow calculators. Network administrators also need this skill to set up, troubleshoot, and understand their TCP/IP addressing scheme.

TIP

Appendix D references the companion website for this book. At this website, you will find links for downloading some free subnet calculators.

---

broadcast
A packet that is intended to go to all hosts on a network. Routers will generally stop broadcasts from moving on to another network.

subnet calculator
A software calculator that figures out subnet masks, valid networks, number of hosts, and host ranges. Several are available for download from the Internet.

In lieu of using a subnet calculator, an administrator can determine the custom subnet mask by using a simple procedure. The procedure presented in this section is relatively popular and easily understandable. I have found that the more examples I do, the closer I get to mastering this procedure.

First get out some paper and a pencil; you'll find that what seems at first difficult will be easy after several repetitions. There are only six steps to follow in creating a custom subnet mask:

1. Determine how many subnets are needed.
2. Determine the maximum number of hosts on each network.
3. Determine the subnet mask.
4. Determine the valid network addresses.
5. Determine the range of valid host IP addresses on each subnet.
6. Confirm that you met the requirements for the number of networks and maximum number of hosts.

Each of the steps is outlined in the following sections.

Determining How Many Subnets Are Needed

The first step is to determine how many unique subnets are going to be required. A unique subnet address is required on each side of a router where there is not another router on that segment. For example, look at these networks:

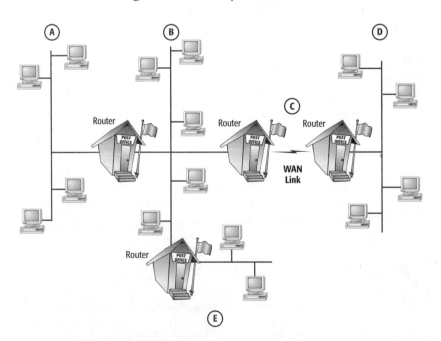

In this example, five unique subnet addresses are required—each on its own side of a router. Notice that although network B connects to three routers, only one network address is required. Also notice that a unique subnet address is needed for a Wide Area Network (WAN) connection. A **WAN connection** consists of two routers that connect two segments of a WAN.

WAN connection
A connection between two LANs (Local Area Networks) is a WAN (Wide Area Network) connection.

Determining the Maximum Number of Hosts on Each Network

The second step in figuring out the subnet mask is to find the maximum number of hosts on any of the subnets. For example, if your network has 10 workstations and a router, you'll need 11 host addresses. If your network has 1,000 workstations, 150 TCP/IP printers, and 8 routers, you'll need to plan for 1,158 host addresses on that network. Remember to count the interface to the router as a host.

For the networks illustrated in the previous example, the following number of host IP addresses is required on each network:

Network	Number of Hosts
A	5
B	8
C	2
D	5
E	3

This table shows that the most host addresses needed on any network is 8 on Network B.

Determining the Subnet Mask

In this step, you first determine the number of bits you need to take from the host portion of the address to use in the subnet portion; you then determine the correct subnet mask. You can use either of two methods to figure out how many bits are needed:

Method 1: Calculate

Method 2: Memorize/use a chart

Both are explained in the following sections.

Method 1: Calculate

To calculate the number of bits needed to create the proper subnet mask:

1. Add 1 to the number of subnets you need. If you need 8, figure that you need 9. If you need 30, figure 31. If you need 900, figure 901.

2. Convert this decimal number to binary.

Decimal	Binary
9	1001
31	11111
901	11 1000 0101

3. Determine the number of subnet bits that you need: This number is the same as the number of bits that it takes to form the binary number.

Binary	# of Bits
1001	4
11111	5
11 1000 0101	10

4. Add this number to the network portion of the standard subnet mask.

# of Bits	Class A Binary Subnet Mask and Subnet Goggles
4	1111 1111.1111 0000.0000 0000.0000 0000
	NNNN NNNN.SSSS HHHH.HHHH HHHH.HHHH HHHH
5	1111 1111.1111 1000.0000 0000.0000 0000
	NNNN NNNN.SSSS SHHH.HHHH HHHH.HHHH HHHH
11	1111 1111.1111 1111.1110 0000.0000 0000
	NNNN NNNN.SSSS SSSS.SSSH HHHH.HHHH HHHH

Converted into decimal, these subnet masks are:

# of Bits	Decimal Subnet Mask
4	255.240.0.0
5	255.248.0.0
11	255.255.224.0

Using Custom Subnet Masks

Method 2: Memorize/Use Chart

You can use the following table to determine the correct subnet mask:

Max # of Networks Needed	Mask for Subnetted Octet
2	192
3–6	224
7–14	240
15–30	248
31–62	252
63–126	254
127–254	255

contiguous bits
One bit following another.

Knowing that you will always use **contiguous bits** in the subnet mask, there are only eight possible subnet masks:

# of Bits	Subnetted Octet in Binary	Subnet Mask
1	1000 0000	128
2	1100 0000	192
3	1110 0000	224
4	1111 0000	240
5	1111 1000	248
6	1111 1100	252
7	1111 1110	254
8	1111 1111	255

If you are subnetting more than 8 bits, the first 8 bits will be set to all 1s, or decimal 255, and the subnetted octet will use this same chart with the remainder of the subnet bits.

Consider this subnet mask:

    255.192.0.0 = in binary,

    1111 1111.1100 0000.0000 0000.0000 0000

There are 2 subnet bits. This means that IP will look at 10 bits (8 network and 2 subnet) to determine whether another host is local or remote. The number of networks that can be created with this subnet mask is determined by the number of unique combinations that these 2 bits can form in the IP address. All possible combinations of these 2 bits are:

00

01

10

11

According to the subnetting rules that you looked at earlier, however, the subnet bits cannot be all 1s or all 0s. Therefore, only two networks can be created with a subnet mask of 255.192.0.0.

Now consider this subnet mask:

255.128.0.0 = in binary,

1111 1111.1000 0000.0000 0000.0000 0000

This subnet mask isn't going to work out because there is only 1 subnet bit. The possible combinations of the 1 bit to create unique subnets are:

0

1

Both of these are invalid, because the first is all 0s and the second is all 1s.

Finally, consider the next possible subnet mask:

255.224.0.0 = in binary,

1111 1111.1110 0000.0000 0000.0000 0000

Now you have 3 subnet bits to work with. The possible combinations of these 3 bits to create unique subnets are:

000

001

010

011

100

101

110

111

This list shows eight unique combinations; however, you have to discard the first and last because of the subnetting rules. This leaves you with six unique subnet addresses.

Determining the Valid Network Addresses

All hosts on each network have to use the same network address, and each network must use a unique network address. The next step in determining an IP addressing scheme is to determine the valid network addresses based on the subnet mask that you decided to use. For every subnet mask, only certain network addresses are valid. In this step, you determine the first valid network address, and then from that you determine the next valid network addresses.

There is a simple way to determine the valid network addresses for a given subnet mask. For example, 192 in binary is 1100 0000. The decimal value of the rightmost bit that is a 1 is 64. Therefore, the first network address is 64, and the next network address is 128.

TIP

The decimal value of the subnet mask's rightmost bit that is a 1 is the first network address and the incremental value.

The following chart illustrates this point:

	128	64	32	16	8	4	2	1
SNM = 192	1	1	0	0	0	0	0	0

The next chart continues this illustration. Note the rightmost bit in each subnet mask that is set to 1 (this bit is bold). The rightmost bit in each number corresponds to a decimal value at the top of the chart; this decimal value is the first network number and the incremental value. In this chart's first example, 224 in binary is 1110 0000. The decimal value of the rightmost bit that is a 1 is 32. Therefore, the first network address is 32.

	128	64	32	16	8	4	2	1
SNM = 224	1	1	**1**	0	0	0	0	0
SNM = 240	1	1	1	**1**	0	0	0	0
SNM = 248	1	1	1	1	**1**	0	0	0
SNM = 252	1	1	1	1	1	**1**	0	0
SNM = 254	1	1	1	1	1	1	**1**	0
SNM = 255	1	1	1	1	1	1	1	**1**

For example, say that with the address 131.107.0.0, you would like to create four networks. Following the steps you learned earlier:

1. Add 1 to the number of subnets you need: $4 + 1 = 5$.

2. Convert 5 to binary: 101.

3. Because 101 has 3 bits, you need 3 bits for the subnet mask. The subnet mask is 255.255.224.0.

4. The rightmost bit set to 1 in 224 has a decimal value of 32. This is the
    - first network number.

Therefore, to create four subnets from 131.107.0.0, you use a subnet mask of 255.255.224.0, and the four networks will be:

131.107.32.0

131.107.64.0

131.107.96.0

131.107.128.0

Why are some network addresses invalid? What about the 131.107.31.0 network? Let's look at the math:

The subnet mask 255.255.224.0 in binary is the following:

1111 1111.1111 1111.1110 0000.0000 0000

Using subnet goggles, you have this:

NNNN NNNN.NNNN NNNN.*SSS*H HHHH.HHHH HHHH

131.107.31.0 = **1000 0011.0110 1011.***000*1 1111.0000 0000

Notice that the subnet bits in the IP address are set to all 0s. This goes against the subnetting rules; therefore, 131.107.31.0 with a subnet mask of 255.255.224.0 is invalid. In this example, this rule applies to all numbers less than 32 in the third octet.

Determining the Range of Valid Host IP Addresses

Only certain addresses will be valid on each of the networks that is created. Therefore, you have to determine the valid IP addresses for each network. In the IP addressing scheme, you must also list the range of valid IP addresses. Finding the range of IP addresses is simple when using the subnet goggles. Simply apply the subnet mask and identify the valid addresses that can be created with the remaining bits. For example, the subnet mask 255.255.224.0 in binary is

1111 1111.1111 1111.1110 0000.0000 0000

Using subnet goggles, you see:

NNNN NNNN. NNNN NNNN.*SSS*H HHHH.HHHH HHHH

131.107.32.0 = **1000 0011. 0110 1011.***0010* 0000.0000 0000

The valid, unique host IP addresses on this network are going to be formed from every combination of the last 13 bits. Remember that IP uses the subnet goggles and does not look at the periods.

You start with the first address:

131.107.32.0 = **1000 0011. 0110 1011.** *001*0 0000.0000 0000

This is invalid because it has all 0s in the host.

And then you increase the value of the hosts:

131.107.32.1 = **1000 0011. 0110 1011.** *001*0 0000.0000 0001

131.107.32.2 = **1000 0011. 0110 1011.** *001*0 0000.0000 0010

131.107.32.3 = **1000 0011. 0110 1011.** *001*0 0000.0000 0011

Continue increasing the value of the hosts, and jump ahead to consider:

131.107.32.255 = **1000 0011. 0110 1011.** *001*0 0000.1111 1111

Is this a valid host IP address? Yes, IP looks at all 13 host bits to see if the host bits are all 1s or all 0s (0000011111111). It can be tricky, but just use the goggles and ignore the periods.

The next IP address in the network can be figured out by again incrementing the 13 host bits by 1, which gives you:

131.107.33.0 = **1000 0011. 0110 1011.** *001*0 0001.0000 0000

Is this a valid host IP address? Yes, don't forget that IP looks at all 13 host bits (0000100000000), and this address does not have all 1s nor all 0s. So, 131.107.33.0 is a valid host IP address on the 131.107.32.0 network!

Let's continue incrementing the 13 host bits by 1:

131.107.33.1 = **1000 0011. 0110 1011.** *001*0 0001.0000 0001

131.107.33.2 = **1000 0011. 0110 1011.** *001*0 0001.0000 0010

131.107.33.3 = **1000 0011. 0110 1011.** *001*0 0001.0000 0011

Continue to increment the 13 host bits and soon you'll run up to:

131.107.33.255 = **1000 0011. 0110 1011.** *0010* 0001.1111 1111

Is this a valid host IP address? Absolutely. Look at all 13 host bits (0000111111111). Are they all 1s or all 0s? No, so this is a valid host IP address on the 131.107.32.0 network. Notice that the 3 subnet bits have not changed.

Continue incrementing the 13 host bits by 1 until you get to:

131.107.63.254 = **1000 0011. 0110 1011.** *0011* 1111.1111 1110

This is still a valid host IP address on the 131.107.32.0 network. Look at all 13 host bits (1111111111110). Then increment by 1 and get:

131.107.63.255 = **1000 0011. 0110 1011.** *0011* 1111.1111 1111

Is this a valid host IP address? No, it's not. Look at the 13 host bits (1111111111111). Having all 1s is invalid.

From this exercise, you can conclude that the range of valid host IP addresses on the 131.107.32.0 network with a subnet mask of 255.255.224.0 is 131.107.32.1–131.107.63.254.

The next network starts when you increment the 3 subnet bits. The next network is going to be:

131.107.64.0 = **1000 0011. 0110 1011.** *010*0 0000.0000 0000

Now you go through the whole range of unique combinations of the 13 host bits. The range of valid host IP addresses for the 131.107.64.0 network with a subnet mask of 255.255.224.0 is 131.107.64.1–131.107.95.254.

To summarize the example of creating four networks from 131.107.0.0: The subnet mask is 255.255.224.0. The valid networks and host IP address ranges are:

Network	Range of IP Addresses
131.107.32.0	131.107.32.1–131.107.63.254
131.107.64.0	131.107.64.1–131.107.95.254
131.107.96.0	131.107.96.1–131.107.127.254
131.107.128.0	131.107.128.1–131.107.159.254

TEST IT OUT: PUTTING IT ALL TOGETHER, CLASS A

In the following exercise, you will be guided through the process of solving a subnetting problem for a Class A address.

Problem:

Create 1,101 subnets with the Class A address of 10.0.0.0 and find:

1. The subnet mask
2. The first three valid network numbers
3. The range of host IP addresses on those three networks
4. The last valid network and range of IP addresses

Solution:

1. Determine the subnet mask:

    Add 1 to the number of subnets needed: 1,101 + 1 = 1,102

    Determine how many bits are needed for the binary equivalent of the decimal 1,102

    10001001101 is the binary representation of 1,102 =

    11 bits are needed in the subnet mask

    Standard Class A uses 8 bits + 11 bits = 19 bits needed in subnet mask

    NNNN NNNN.**SSSS SSSS.SSS**H HHHH.HHHH HHHH

    Subnet mask = 255.255.224.0

2. Determine the first three valid networks:

    The rightmost subnet bit that equals 1 has a decimal value of 32; therefore, 32 is the first network address and the incremental value.

    First network = 10.0.32.0

    0000 1010.**0000 0000.001**0 0000.0000 0000

    Second network = 10.0.64.0

    0000 1010.**0000 0000.010**0 0000.0000 0000

    Third network = 10.0.96.0

    0000 1010.**0000 0000.011**0 0000.0000 0000

TEST IT OUT: PUTTING IT ALL TOGETHER, CLASS A (cont.)

3. Determine the range of hosts on those three networks:

For 10.0.32.0 = 10.0.32.1−10.0.63.254

0000 1010.0000 0000.0010 **0000.0000 0001**

0000 1010.0000 0000.0011 **1111.1111 1110**

For 10.0.64.0 = 10.0.64.1−10.0.95.254

0000 1010.0000 0000.0100 **0000.0000 0001**

0000 1010.0000 0000.0101 **1111.1111 1110**

For 10.0.96.0 = 10.0.96.1−10.0.127.254

0000 1010.0000 0000.0110 **0000.0000 0001**

0000 1010.0000 0000.0111 **1111.1111 1110**

4. Determine the last valid network and range of addresses:

NNNN NNNN.*SSSS SSSS.SSS*H HHHH.HHHH HHHH

0000 1010.**1111 1111.110**H HHHH.HHHH HHHH

The last network = 10.255.192.0

Range of hosts are:

0000 1010.1111 1111.1100 **0000.0000 0001** = 10.255.192.1

0000 1010.1111 1111.1101 **1111.1111 1110** = 10.255.223.254

In summary:

1. Subnet mask: 255.255.224.0

2. First three valid networks:

10.0.32.0

10.0.64.0

10.0.96.0

3. Range of host IP addresses:

For 10.0.32.0, 10.0.32.1−10.0.63.254

For 10.0.64.0, 10.0.64.1−10.0.95.254

For 10.0.96.0, 10.0.96.1−10.0.127.254

4. Last valid network and host IP address range:

10.255.192.0 and 10.255.192.1−10.255.223.254

TEST IT OUT: PUTTING IT ALL TOGETHER, CLASS B

In the following exercise, you will be guided through the process of solving a subnetting problem for a Class B address.

Problem:

Create 315 subnets with the Class B address of 172.20.0.0 and find:

1. The subnet mask
2. The first three valid network numbers
3. The range of host IP addresses on those three networks
4. The last valid network and range of IP addresses

Solution:

1. Determine the subnet mask:

   Add 1 to the number of subnets needed: 315 + 1 = 316

   Determine how many bits are needed for the binary equivalent of the decimal 316

   100111100 is the binary representation of 316 =

   9 bits are needed in the subnet mask

   Standard Class B uses 16 bits + 9 bits = 25 bits needed in subnet mask

   NNNN NNNN.NNNN NNNN.*SSSS SSSS*.S HHH HHHH

   Subnet mask = 255.255.255.128

2. Determine the first three valid networks:

   The rightmost subnet bit that equals 1 has a decimal value of 128; therefore, 128 is the first network address and the incremental value.

   First network = 172.20.0.128

   1010 1100.0001 0100.**0000 0000.1**000 0000

   Second network = 172.20.1.0

   1010 1100.0001 0100.**0000 0001.0**000 0000

   Third network = 172.20.1.128

   1010 1100.0001 0100.**0000 0001.1**000 0000

TEST IT OUT: PUTTING IT ALL TOGETHER, CLASS B (cont.)

3. Determine the range of hosts on those three networks:

For 172.20.0.128 = 172.20.0.129–172.20.0.254

1010 1100.0001 0100.0000 0000.**1000 0001**

1010 1100.0001 0100.0000 0000.**1111 1110**

For 172.20.1.0 = 172.20.1.1–172.20.1.254

1010 1100.0001 0100.0000 0001.**0000 0001**

1010 1100.0001 0100.0000 0001.**0111 1110**

For 172.20.1.128 = 172.20.1.129–172.20.1.254

1010 1100.0001 0100.0000 0001.**1000 0001**

1010 1100.0001 0100.0000 0001.**1111 1110**

4. Determine the last valid network and range of addresses:

NNNN NNNN.NNNN NNNN.*SSSS SSSS*.**S**HHH HHHH

1010 1100.0001 0100.**1111 1111.0**HHH HHHH

The last network = 172.20.255.0

Range of hosts are:

1010 1100.0001 0100.1111 1111.0**000 0001** = 172.20.255.1

1010 1100.0001 0100.1111 1111.0**111 1110** = 172.20.255.254

In summary, the answers are:

1. Subnet mask: 255.255.255.128

2. First three valid networks:

    172.20.0.128

    172.20.1.0

    172.20.1.128

3. Range of host IP addresses:

    For 172.20.0.128, 172.20.0.129–172.20.0.254

    For 172.20.1.0, 172.20.1.1–172.20.1.254

    For 172.20.1.128, 172.20.1.129–172.20.1.254

4. Last valid network and host IP address range:

    172.20.255.0 and 172.20.255.1–172.20.255.254

Valid Hosts for Class C Addresses

Finding the range of valid hosts with a Class C address is the same process, except that there are so few host bits available that some of the addresses may seem strange. The network portions look like real IP addresses, and the range of valid addresses is as obvious as in the previous examples.

Let's consider the address 192.168.2.0. Say, for example, that you need 11 networks from this address. You'd take the following steps to find the range of valid hosts:

1. Add 1 to the number of subnets you need: $11 + 1 = 12$.

2. Convert the result to binary: 1100.

3. Because 1100 has 4 bits, you need 4 bits in the subnet mask:

   1111 0000 = 240

   Subnet mask 255.255.255.240 =

   1111 1111.1111 1111.1111 1111.1111 0000

   Using subnet goggles:

   NNNN NNNN.NNNN NNNN.NNNN NNNN.*SSSS* HHHH

   The first network address is 192.168.2.16 =

   1100 0000.1010 1000.0000 0010.*0001* 0000

The valid unique host IP addresses on this network are going to be every combination of the last 4 bits. Remember that IP uses the subnet goggles and does not look at the periods.

The first address is invalid because it has all 0s in the host:

192.168.2.16 =
1100 0000.1010 1000.0000 0010.0001 **0000**

The next addresses are:

192.168.2.17 =
1100 0000.1010 1000.0000 0010.0001 **0001**

192.168.2.18 =
1100 0000.1010 1000.0000 0010.0001 **0010**

192.168.2.19 =
1100 0000.1010 1000.0000 0010.0001 **0011**

192.168.2.20 =

1100 0000.1010 1000.0000 0010.0001 **0100**

Continue increasing the value of the hosts, and jump ahead to consider:

192.168.2.29 =

1100 0000.1010 1000.0000 0010.0001 **1101**

192.168.2.30 =

1100 0000.1010 1000.0000 0010.0001 **1110**

192.168.2.31 =

1100 0000.1010 1000.0000 0010.0001 **1111**

This last address is invalid because it has all 1s in the host portion.

So the first network and range of addresses are:

192.168.2.16 with an IP address range of 192.168.2.17–192.168.2.30

Some of the next networks and their address ranges are:

192.168.2.32 with an IP address range of 192.168.2.33–192.168.2.46

192.168.2.48 with an IP address range of 192.168.2.49–192.168.2.62

192.168.2.64 with an IP address range of 192.168.2.65–192.168.2.78

Using this scheme, 14 subnets can be built, of which you need only 11.

TIP

To find valid hosts for a Class C network: Find the first network address, and the first valid IP address on that network is one more than the network address. The last valid IP address on that network is the *next* network address minus 2.

To determine the last valid network that can be created with the address of 192.168.2.0 and a subnet mask of 255.255.255.240, let's look at the numbers in their binary representations.

192.168.2.225 = 1100 0000.1010 1000.0000 0010.*1110* **0000**

With an IP address range of

192.168.2.225 = 1100 0000.1010 1000.0000 0010.*1110* **0001**

through

$192.168.2.238 = 1100\ 0000.1010\ 1000.0000\ 0010.\mathit{1110}\ \boldsymbol{\mathit{1110}}$

The IP address 192.168.2.239 would be invalid because it is the broadcast address on the 192.168.2.224 network:

$192.168.2.239 = 1100\ 0000.1010\ 1000.0000\ 0010.\mathit{1110}\ \boldsymbol{\mathit{1111}}$

If you were to try to create one more network by incrementing the subnet bits by one, you would have:

$192.168.2.240 = 1100\ 0000.1010\ 1000.0000\ 0010.\mathit{1111}\ \boldsymbol{\mathit{0000}}$

Notice that the subnet bits are all 1, thus making this an invalid network address. Always consider the binary representation when determining the validity of addresses.

TEST IT OUT: PUTTING IT ALL TOGETHER, CLASS C

In the following exercise, you will be guided through the process of solving a subnetting problem for a Class C address.

Problem:

Create 12 subnets with the Class C address of 192.168.2.0 and find:

1. The subnet mask
2. The first three valid network numbers
3. The range of host IP addresses on those three networks
4. The last valid network and range of IP addresses

Solution:

1. Determine the subnet mask:

   Add 1 to the number of subnets needed: $12 + 1 = 13$

   Determine how many bits are needed for the binary equivalent of the decimal 13

   1101 is the binary representation of $13 =$

   4 bits are needed in the subnet mask

   Standard Class C uses 24 bits + 4 bits = 28 bits needed in subnet mask

   NNNN NNNN.NNNN NNNN.NNNN NNNN.*SSSS* HHHH

   Subnet mask = 255.255.255.240

TEST IT OUT: PUTTING IT ALL TOGETHER, CLASS C (cont.)

2. Determine the first three valid networks:

The rightmost subnet bit that equals 1 has a decimal value of 16; therefore, 16 is the first network address and the incremental value.

First network = 192.168.2.16

1100 0000 . 1010 1000 . 0000 0010 . **0001** 0000

Second network = 192.168.2.32

1100 0000 . 1010 1000 . 0000 0010 . **0010** 0000

Third network = 192.168.2.48

1100 0000 . 1010 1000 . 0000 0010 . **0011** 0000

3. Determine the range of hosts on those three networks:

For 192.168.2.16 = 192.168.2.17−192.168.2.30

1100 0000 . 1010 1000 . 0000 0010 . 0001 **0001**

1100 0000 . 1010 1000 . 0000 0010 . 0001 **1110**

For 192.168.2.32 = 192.168.2.33−192.168.2.46

1100 0000 . 1010 1000 . 0000 0010 . 0010 **0001**

1100 0000 . 1010 1000 . 0000 0010 . 0010 **1110**

For 192.168.2.48 = 192.168.2.49−192.168.2.62

1100 0000 . 1010 1000 . 0000 0010 . 0011 **0001**

1100 0000 . 1010 1000 . 0000 0010 . 0011 **1110**

4. Determine the last valid network and range of addresses:

NNNN NNNN . NNNN NNNN . NNNN NNNN . *SSSS* HHHH

1100 0000 . 1010 1000 . 0000 0010 . **1110** HHHH

The last network = 192.168.2.224

Range of hosts are:

1100 0000 . 1010 1000 . 0000 0010 . 1110 **0001** = 192.168.2.225

1100 0000 . 1010 1000 . 0000 0010 . 1110 **1110** = 192.168.2.238

In summary:

1. Subnet mask: 255.255.255.240

2. First three valid networks:

192.168.2.16

192.168.2.32

192.168.2.48

TEST IT OUT: PUTTING IT ALL TOGETHER, CLASS C (cont.)

3. Range of host IP addresses:

For 192.168.2.16 = 192.168.2.17–192.168.2.30

For 192.168.2.32 = 192.168.2.33–192.168.2.46

For 192.168.2.48 = 192.168.2.49–192.168.2.62

4. Last valid network and host IP address range:

192.168.2.224 and 192.168.2.225–192.168.2.238

$2^N - 2$

Equation used to figure out the number of subnets and hosts per subnet that can be created with a subnet mask. N is the number of bits that you are using for the subnet portion or the host portion of the address.

Calculating the Number of Networks and Hosts

Now let's look at some of the interesting math solutions of subnetting.

1. To solve for how many networks you can create, use the equation:

$(2^N) - 2$ where N is the number of subnet bits

For example: A Class B address with a subnet mask of 255.255.240.0 will create $(2^4) - 2 = 14$ networks.

TIP

When using the calculator program that is installed with Windows to solve an exponential equation, click the View option and choose Scientific. Type **2**, click the x^y button, type **4** (or however many subnet bits), type **-**, type **2**.

2. To solve for how many host IP addresses are on each network, use the same equation:

$(2^N) - 2$ where N is the number of host bits

For example: A Class B address with a subnet mask of 255.255.252.0 will allow $(2^{10}) - 2 = 1022$ hosts on each network.

3. To figure out the range of IP addresses on each network, use this two-part equation:

The first part, or start of the range = (the network address + 1)

The second part, or end of the range =

For Class A, B: (the next network address − 1)

For Class C: (the next network address − 2)

For example, for the network 131.107.2.0 with a subnet mask of 255.255.255.0, the range of IP addresses is 131.107.2.1–131.107.2.254 because:

(the network address + 1) = 131.107.2.1

through

(the next network address, which is 131.107.3.0 − 1) = 131.107.2.254

 TEST IT OUT: NUMBER OF NETWORKS AND HOSTS

In the following exercise, you will determine the number of networks and hosts given a Class A address and a subnet mask.

Problem:

With the Class A address of 10.0.0.0 and a subnet mask of 255.255.224.0, find:

1. How many subnets can be created?
2. How many hosts on each subnet?

Solution:

1. To determine how many subnets can be created:

    Determine how many bits are set to 1 in the custom subnet mask

    255.255.224.0 has 11 bits set to 1 in the custom portion

    (Standard Class A has 8 bits set to 1)

    Use the $2^N - 2$ equation where $N = 11$

    $2^{11} - 2 = 2{,}046$

    2,046 unique subnets can be created

2. To determine how many hosts can be on each of those 2,046 subnets:

    Determine how many bits are set to 0 in the subnet mask

    255.255.224.0 has 13 bits set to 0

    Use the $2^N - 2$ equation where $N = 13$

    $2^{13} - 2 = 8{,}190$

    8,190 unique hosts can be addressed on each of the 2,046 subnets

Class A Subnet Masks

The table below summarizes all of the Class A subnet masks, the number of valid networks, and the number of hosts on each network.

Subnet Mask	# of Unique Valid Networks	# of Hosts On Each Network
255.0.0.0	1—standard subnet mask	16,777,214
255.128.0.0	Invalid—only 1 bit for subnet portion	—
255.192.0.0	2	4,194,302
255.224.0.0	6	2,097,150
255.240.0.0	14	1,048,574
255.248.0.0	30	524,286
255.252.0.0	62	262,142
255.254.0.0	126	131,070
255.255.0.0	254	65,534
255.255.128.0	510	32,766
255.255.192.0	1,022	16,382
255.255.224.0	2,046	8,190
255.255.240.0	4,094	4,094
255.255.248.0	8,190	2,046
255.255.252.0	16,382	1,022
255.255.254.0	32,766	510
255.255.255.0	65,534	254
255.255.255.128	131,070	126
255.255.255.192	262,142	62
255.255.255.224	524,286	30
255.255.255.240	1,048,574	14
255.255.255.248	2,097,150	6
255.255.255.252	4,194,302	2
255.255.255.254	Invalid—only 1 bit left for host portion	—
255.255.255.255	Invalid—no bits left for host portion	—

You can memorize this table, or just use the equation $(2^N) - 2$ to figure out any of the entries. The variable N in the equation is the number of subnet bits or the number of host bits.

Class B Subnet Masks

The table below summarizes all of the Class B subnet masks and the number of networks and hosts.

Subnet Mask	# of Unique Valid Networks	# of Hosts On Each Network
255.255.0.0	1—standard subnet mask	65,534
255.255.128.0	Invalid—only 1 bit for subnet portion	–
255.255.192.0	2	16,382
255.255.224.0	6	8,190
255.255.240.0	14	4,094
255.255.248.0	30	2,046
255.255.252.0	62	1,022
255.255.254.0	126	510
255.255.255.0	254	254
255.255.255.128	510	126
255.255.255.192	1,022	62
255.255.255.224	2,046	30
255.255.255.240	4,094	14
255.255.255.248	8,190	6
255.255.255.252	16,382	2
255.255.255.254	Invalid—only 1 bit left for host portion	–
255.255.255.255	Invalid—no bits left for host portion	–

Class C Subnet Masks

This table summarizes the Class C subnet masks and the number of networks and hosts.

Subnet Mask	# of Unique Valid Networks	# of Hosts On Each Network
255.255.255.0	1—standard subnet mask	254
255.255.255.128	Invalid—only 1 bit for subnet portion	—
255.255.255.192	2	62
255.255.255.224	6	30
255.255.255.240	14	14
255.255.255.248	30	6
255.255.255.252	62	2
255.255.255.254	Invalid—only 1 bit left for host portion	—
255.255.255.255	Invalid—no bits left for host portion	—

Review Questions

Terms to Know
- ❏ custom subnet mask
- ❏ subnet
- ❏ subnet bits
- ❏ broadcast
- ❏ subnet calculator
- ❏ WAN connection
- ❏ contiguous bits
- ❏ 2^{N-2}

1. You need to create 652 networks with the Class B address 150.150.0.0.
   a. What is the subnet mask?
   b. List the first three valid network numbers.
   c. List the range of host IP addresses on those three networks.
   d. List the last valid network and range of IP addresses.
   e. How many subnets does this solution allow?
   f. How many host addresses can be on each subnet?

   _____

   _____

   _____

   _____

   _____

2. You need to create 506 networks with the Class B address 151.151.0.0.
   a. What is the subnet mask?
   b. List the first three valid network numbers.
   c. List the range of host IP addresses on those three networks.
   d. List the last valid network and range of IP addresses.
   e. How many subnets does this solution allow?
   f. How many host addresses can be on each subnet?

   _____

   _____

   _____

   _____

3. You need to create 223 networks with the Class B address 152.152.0.0.

   a. What is the subnet mask?

   b. List the first three valid network numbers.

   c. List the range of host IP addresses on those three networks.

   d. List the last valid network and range of IP addresses.

   e. How many subnets does this solution allow?

   f. How many host addresses can be on each subnet?

   _____

   _____

   _____

   _____

   _____

4. You need to create 12 networks with the Class C address 200.200.200.0.

   a. What is the subnet mask?

   b. List the first three valid network numbers.

   c. List the range of host IP addresses on those three networks.

   d. List the last valid network and range of IP addresses.

   e. How many subnets does this solution allow?

   f. How many host addresses can be on each subnet?

   _____

   _____

   _____

   _____

   _____

5. You need to create five networks with the Class C address 201.201.201.0.

    a. What is the subnet mask?

    b. List the first three valid network numbers.

    c. List the range of host IP addresses on those three networks.

    d. List the last valid network and range of IP addresses.

    e. How many subnets does this solution allow?

    f. How many host addresses can be on each subnet?

_____

_____

_____

_____

_____

6. You need to create 110 networks with the Class C address 202.202.202.0. What is the subnet mask?

_____

7. You need to create 140,000 networks with the Class A address 10.0.0.0. What is the subnet mask?

_____

8. You need to create 54 networks with the Class B address 155.155.0.0. What is the subnet mask?

_____

9. You need to create 110 networks with the Class B address 131.107.0.0. What is the subnet mask?

_____

10. You need to create 425 networks with the Class A address 15.0.0.0. What is the subnet mask?

_____

11. Using the subnet mask of 255.255.0.0 and the Class A address of 10.0.0.0,

    a. How many unique networks can be created?

    b. How many host IP addresses can be on each network?

_____

_____

Chapter

10

Supernetting
and CIDR

IP address allocation has undergone some changes and modifications over the last 20 years. As Internet architects looked at ways to extend the life of the IP-addressing system and responsibly administer any remaining public network addresses, some interesting and useful addressing schemes have been developed.

Two addressing schemes that delve a bit deeper into subnetting are supernetting and Classless Inter-Domain Routing (CIDR). These addressing schemes are used in large TCP/IP networks that have many subnets to make routing simpler and more manageable. Understanding subnets and subnet masks is critical to understanding these addressing schemes, and understanding these addressing schemes will give you a better and more simplistic understanding of subnetting.

In this chapter, you will learn about:

 Address allocation

 Supernetting

 CIDR

IP Address Allocation

The Internet has grown at a rate that no one anticipated. The designers of this network could not have possibly foreseen this kind of growth—a growth that has been described as exponential and explosive—and this is obvious in some of the initial assessments and decisions about address allocations that the designers made. Some people have compared the address allocation structure with the initial **PC DOS** operating systems; these early systems were written to never use more than a whopping 640K of RAM. In both of these cases, the pioneers of these fields could not have forecasted the unbelievable expansion of the systems they were designing.

The initial decision was made to use an IP address of 32 bits. Within those 32 bits, a portion of that address referred to the network on which the host belonged, and the other portion of the address referred to its unique host address on that network. A major question that the designers of the Internet were faced with was, "How should the addresses be allocated?" The decision was therefore made to use a **classful addressing system**.

Limitations of the Classful System

By separating the pool of addresses into five distinct classes, allocating these addresses should be pretty simple. First, within these five classes, Class D and Class E would be reserved for purposes other than host addresses. Therefore, companies needing IP addresses would receive Class A, Class B, or Class C addresses based on the number of hosts that needed to be addressed.

In Chapter 6, you learned that in the classful addressing system:

> Class A yields 126 networks with 16,777,214 hosts each.
>
> Class B yields 16,382 networks with 65,534 hosts each.
>
> Class C yields 2,097,152 networks with only 254 hosts each.

An element of this address allocation system that limited its scalability was the strictness of using an explicit 8, 16, or 24 bits to represent the network portion of the address. A company with fewer than 254 hosts would obviously need the smallest class of address possible, a Class C. If that network had only 100 hosts, 154 addresses were wasted. Therefore, many Class C host addresses have never been used. In a similar situation, a company with 5,000 hosts was given a Class B. This wasted over 60,000 host addresses, because a Class B can address up to 65,534 hosts.

PC DOS

PC operating system used with early PCs that could only address up to 640K of RAM. This limitation led to severe issues, as more RAM was needed.

classful addressing system

System of assigning IP network addresses in which addresses are allotted in well-defined blocks. The blocks of addresses in the classful system are Class A, B, C, D, and E.

The Trouble with Class B

Class B address allocation was where the Internet faced its greatest challenge. In May 1992, 49 of the 126 Class A networks had already been allocated—that meant that 38 percent of these addresses were already gone. Furthermore, 45 percent of the Class B networks had been allocated, or 7,354 of the 16,382. The Internet designers projected that at the rate the Internet was growing and network numbers were being assigned, all Class B addresses would be gone within 15 months. (Class Cs were not yet an issue, since only 2 percent or 44,014 of the 2,097,152 networks had been allocated.)

The Internet Assigned Numbers Authority (IANA) decided to hold on to Class B addresses a little tighter, so they created a new set of criteria to make sure that a company would effectively use a Class B before the IANA assigned it to them. The new guidelines to get a Class B included that the organization applying for the Class B must submit a subnetting plan and a document justifying the need for a Class B. The company had to submit an engineering plan to detail the deployment of addresses. The plan needed to include a 24-month forecast of the network and its anticipated growth. If it was possible for the company to manage their network effectively with several Class Cs, the application was rejected. All other requests were subject to the following Class C assignments.

If a company needed fewer than...	The Class C assignment would be...
256 addresses	1 Class C network
512 addresses	2 contiguous Class C networks
1,024 addresses	4 contiguous Class C networks
2,048 addresses	8 contiguous Class C networks
4,096 addresses	16 contiguous Class C networks
8,192 addresses	32 contiguous Class C networks
16,384 addresses	64 contiguous Class C networks

With this plan, the Class B addresses were no longer allocated in a reckless manner. The Internet, however, still faced some pretty significant addressing issues. The two major challenges were:

- ◊ Class B addresses would eventually be exhausted, even with the tighter control of Class B allocation.

- ◊ Internet routing tables were getting too large, which affected delivery, reliability, etc.

Internet routing tables

Tables that are maintained by Internet authorities and Internet Service Providers (ISPs) that provide the information for routing packets on the Internet.

Because Class B addresses would eventually run out, the focus shifted to the second issue. This issue was growing into a big problem, especially with the assignment of contiguous Class C network addresses.

Internet Routing Tables

Internet routing tables contain network addresses and the best route to get to that network. They list the network number, the subnet mask, and the route to take to get to that network. For example, a routing table may contain the following routes:

Network	Subnet Mask	Route
192.168.0.0	255.255.255.0	192.168.0.1
192.168.1.0	255.255.255.0	192.168.1.1
176.16.0.0	255.255.0.0	176.16.0.1
10.1.0.0	255.255.0.0	10.1.0.1

This routing table contains only four routes. Imagine how huge a table would be that contains thousands of routes!

As these routing tables grew in size, two methods of compacting the routing tables were created: supernetting and CIDR. Both of these techniques made routing tables smaller and routing entries more efficient.

Supernetting

Supernetting is used in routing tables to compact contiguous Class C networks. Suppose that a company needs to address 1,024 hosts. The table from earlier in this chapter states that a company this size does not need a Class B; instead it requires four contiguous Class C addresses. This will conserve the Class B addresses; however, it will tax the Internet routing tables.

The company is assigned the four contiguous Class C addresses of 192.168.0.0 through 192.168.3.0, and it sets up its router to the Internet with the address of 192.168.0.1. The routes in the ISP routing table will contain the following:

Network	Subnet Mask	Route
192.168.0.0	255.255.255.0	192.168.0.1
192.168.1.0	255.255.255.0	192.168.0.1
192.168.2.0	255.255.255.0	192.168.0.1
192.168.3.0	255.255.255.0	192.168.0.1

Notice that all of the routes point to the same IP address of 192.168.0.1. These routes therefore seem redundant. The subnet mask tells IP at the router to examine 24 bits of every packet to determine the route that each packet will take. IP then examines 24 bits of the destination address of each packet and finds that the only difference in any of these four routes is in the third octet (specifically the 23rd and 24th bit):

Network	Third Octet
192.168.0.0	0000 0000
192.168.1.0	0000 0001
192.168.2.0	0000 0010
192.168.3.0	0000 0011

Any packet that is bound for any of these contiguous networks has the same first 22 bits; the only difference is in the 23rd and 24th bits. Since all of the networks are routed to the same IP address, supernetting can tell IP to look at only 22 bits. Using supernetting, the same routing table would include only one route instead of four.

Network	Subnet Mask	Route
192.168.0.0	255.255.252.0	192.168.0.1

Now if a packet is bound for 192.168.1.12, 192.168.2.115, 192.168.3.5, or 192.168.0.10, the subnet mask of 255.255.252.0 tells IP to look only at the first 22 bits. All of these addresses have the same first 22 bits:

Destination	First 22 Bits	Last 10 Bits
192.168.1.12	1100 0000. 1010 1000.0000 00	01.0000 1100
192.168.2.115	1100 0000. 1010 1000.0000 00	10.0111 0011
192.168.3.5	1100 0000. 1010 1000.0000 00	11.0000 0101
192.168.0.10	1100 0000. 1010 1000.0000 00	00.0000 1010

By supernetting the network in the routing table, the routes to this company's Class C addresses are reduced to just one entry.

In another example, suppose that a company needs 4,096 host addresses. Rather than using a Class B address, the company would use 16 contiguous Class C addresses. Without a supernetted route, the routing table contains the following 16 routes:

Network	Subnet Mask	Route
192.168.0.0	255.255.255.0	192.168.0.1
192.168.1.0	255.255.255.0	192.168.0.1
192.168.2.0	255.255.255.0	192.168.0.1
192.168.3.0	255.255.255.0	192.168.0.1
192.168.4.0	255.255.255.0	192.168.0.1
192.168.5.0	255.255.255.0	192.168.0.1
192.168.6.0	255.255.255.0	192.168.0.1
192.168.7.0	255.255.255.0	192.168.0.1
192.168.8.0	255.255.255.0	192.168.0.1
192.168.9.0	255.255.255.0	192.168.0.1
192.168.10.0	255.255.255.0	192.168.0.1
192.168.11.0	255.255.255.0	192.168.0.1
192.168.12.0	255.255.255.0	192.168.0.1

Supernetting and CIDR

Network	Subnet Mask	Route
192.168.13.0	255.255.255.0	192.168.0.1
192.168.14.0	255.255.255.0	192.168.0.1
192.168.15.0	255.255.255.0	192.168.0.1

Using a supernetted route, the entries in the routing table can be reduced to one route:

Network	Subnet Mask	Route
192.168.0.0	255.255.240.0	192.168.0.1

To create the right **supernetted subnet mask**, an administrator must look at the binary and determine the last bit where all of the networks are the same. This number depends on how many contiguous Class C addresses are being subnetted. Below is a simple table showing the correct supernetted subnet mask that should be used:

# of Networks Being Supernetted	Mask
2	255.255.254.0
4	255.255.252.0
8	255.255.248.0
16	255.255.240.0
32	255.255.224.0
64	255.255.192.0
128	255.255.128.0
256	255.255.0.0
512	255.254.0.0
1024	255.252.0.0
2048	255.248.0.0
4096	255.240.0.0
8192	255.224.0.0
16384	255.192.0.0
32768	255.128.0.0

supernetted subnet mask
A subnet mask that uses a supernet notation.

Classless Inter-Domain Routing (CIDR)

From Chapter 8, you know that subnet masks use a dotted decimal notation to describe to IP how many bits represent the network portion of the address. Very simply stated, CIDR addresses replace the subnet mask and state the number of bits that IP should use to determine the network portion of an IP address. For example, a subnet mask of 255.255.255.0 tells IP that 24 bits determine the network portion of the address, so CIDR simply uses the notation of /24. In other examples, instead of 255.255.0.0, CIDR uses a /16 notation, and a subnet mask of 255.255.255.240 is replaced with /28.

From earlier in this chapter, you know about the two serious challenges facing address allocation on the Internet. The first is the depletion of Class B networks, and the second is the large routing tables. CIDR is a mechanism to temporarily assist in alleviating both issues.

A great deal of space can be saved in a routing table by using CIDR notation instead of the traditional subnet mask dotted decimal notation. For example, if you replace 255.255.240.0 with /20, space is saved and the exact same information is conveyed. When you multiply this saved space by the number of routes in a routing table, which could be thousands, a tremendous amount of space is saved.

Another enormous benefit of using CIDR is the flexibility in assigning network addresses. Instead of using the "classful" system of addressing, CIDR uses a "classless" system. There is no default mask with CIDR. A network address can be allocated with any number of bits representing the network portion of the address. CIDR addresses can be allocated based on the number of hosts; using this addressing system can suit a company better than using the classful system, which can waste addresses. Table 10.1 lists the appropriate CIDR notation for different networks.

Table 10.1: Summary of CIDR Address Notation

CIDR Notation	# of Hosts	# of Class Cs
/27	32	1/8
/26	64	1/4
/25	128	1/2
/24	256	1
/23	512	2
/22	1024	4
/21	2048	8
/20	4096	16
/19	8192	32
/18	16384	64
/17	32768	128
/16	65536	256 (1 Class B)
/15	131072	512
/14	262144	1024
/13	524288	2048

As you've already learned in this chapter, two major issues faced the growing Internet: the depletion of Class B addresses and the large routing tables. Supernetting and CIDR are two initiatives that have assisted in the impact of these major issues. As you'll see in Chapter 15, the next version of TCP/IP is currently being deployed. The address allocation scheme has undergone intense scrutiny so the issues that faced this version of IP will be avoided in the future.

Review Questions

Terms to Know

❏ CIDR
❏ classful addressing system
❏ Internet routing tables
❏ PC DOS
❏ supernetted subnet mask
❏ supernetting

1. List the two major problems that have challenged the growth of the Internet.

2. Rather than assigning a company one Class B, what did the IANA begin doing?

3. If your company is assigned the four contiguous Class C addresses of 192.168.0.0–192.168.3.0, what is the supernet mask?

4. If your company is assigned the 16 contiguous Class C addresses of 192.168.0.0–192.168.15.0, what is the supernet mask?

5. If you use the supernet mask 255.255.248.0, how many bits is IP going to examine?

6. Instead of having 48 entries in a routing table, how many entries would there be if you use a supernet mask?

7. What is the address 192.168.1.0 with a subnet mask of 255.255.255.224 when converted to CIDR notation?

8. What is the address 192.168.1.0 with a subnet mask of 255.255.255.240 when converted to CIDR notation?

9. What is the address 10.0.0.0 with a subnet mask of 255.255.128.0 when converted to CIDR notation?

_____

10. What is the address 176.16.0.0 with a subnet mask of 255.255.128.0 when converted to CIDR notation?

_____

Chapter

11

Name Resolution

Rather than remember IP addresses, humans find it easier to remember names. Administrators give meaningful names to computers—for example, APPSRVR, ROUTERC, or HARRY. On the Internet, Web sites are given easy-to-remember names such as www.sybex.com. In this way, we can remember names of hosts on our network and of Web sites that we would like to visit.

But TCP/IP cannot find or connect to another computer with just words; TCP/IP needs an IP address. Therefore, the names that we use must be resolved to an IP address before TCP/IP can do anything with them. Resolving—or translating—the name to an IP address is called name resolution. After a name is resolved to an IP address, the host can then figure out whether the destination is local or remote and can continue with the communication. This is similar to finding a phone number when all you know is a name.

In this chapter, you will explore two methods of name resolution:

 Host name resolution

 NetBIOS name resolution

Understanding Name Resolution

Name resolution is the process of figuring out the IP address that corresponds to a given name. Because we like to use words for machines, but TCP/IP needs to use IP addresses, we must have a mechanism or method for making the exchange.

For example, the URL for the Sybex Web site is www.sybex.com. This Web site has an IP address of 206.100.29.83. When using a Web browser, it is easier for me to remember www.sybex.com than it is to remember the IP address 206.100.29.83. If I type 206.100.29.83 in my browser, name resolution will not need to take place. I will have already provided the IP address of the Web server that is hosting the Web site that I am trying to connect to. If I use www.sybex.com instead, TCP/IP will need to translate these meaningful words into the IP address.

As an analogy, consider placing a telephone call to a friend. If you want to call a friend and have only his name, the phone call cannot be placed. You need some mechanism to translate his name to a phone number. When translating a friend's name to a telephone number, you have several methods available. You can call the information operator or look in the phone book. Or maybe you have it written down on a piece of paper somewhere, and you just need to find that piece of paper. Which mechanism are you going to use first? Depending on information that you already have, you will use the method that gives you resolution fastest. How many times have you said, "I'll look in this phone book, and if it's not there, I'll call information"?

Similarly, there are several ways to resolve a name to an IP address. Depending on the application that is asking for resolution, the order of these methods that TCP/IP uses is different.

The applications that are going to be asking TCP/IP for resolution fall into two categories. Based on which type of application is asking for resolution, TCP/IP uses either of these two methods:

- ◇ Host name resolution
- ◇ NetBIOS name resolution

Each method has several steps. TCP/IP shuffles the order of the name resolution steps for the same reason that you shuffle the order of resolution steps when trying to translate a friend's name to a phone number: speed and efficiency. TCP/IP uses the steps within each of the two categories of name resolution so that the names are resolved to TCP/IP addresses as quickly as possible.

In the same way, you will try all methods that you can think of to match a friend's phone number before giving up—no matter how ridiculous the methods might be.

If you try to get to the Web site ww.sybex.com (notice the typo), TCP/IP will go through the entire host name resolution process before letting you know that there is an error. Resolving www.sybex.com will usually take a maximum of three steps. Depending on the contents of files, resolution might take fewer steps.

If you were a detective trying to find the phone number of a missing person, you would take steps in a particular order to solve the mystery. The order depends on how you think you would get the best results. Similarly, when resolving a name to an IP address, TCP/IP uses the order of steps that has the best chance of resolving the name quickest.

host name resolution
The process of resolving a host name to an IP address.

What Is Host Name Resolution?

The most common method of resolving common names (such as the host name Harry) to IP addresses is **host name resolution**. Most TCP/IP utilities and programs use this method. Host name resolution has seven steps to resolving an IP address. Before reporting an error, TCP/IP will complete each step.

The steps of host name resolution include:

1. Local host
2. HOSTS file
3. DNS
4. NetBIOS name cache
5. WINS
6. Broadcast
7. LMHOSTS file

> **NOTE**
>
> You will learn about each of these steps later in this chapter.

Some of the common utilities and programs that follow the host name resolution method include Ping, FTP, and Web browsers (HTTP).

What Is NetBIOS Name Resolution?

Some Microsoft network applications are written to an **Application Programming Interface (API)** called **NetBIOS**. This means that the programmers used a common interface to help the applications better communicate with the other computers on the network. These programs are referred to as NetBIOS applications.

Application Programming Interface (API)
A common interface that enables programmers to write programs to a standard specification.

NetBIOS
Network Basic Input Output System; a program that enables applications on different computers to communicate within a local area network.

NetBIOS name resolution
The process of resolving a NetBIOS name to an IP address.

NetBIOS applications use NetBIOS names, which are also called computer names. By default, the NetBIOS name and host name are the same. To better understand this, imagine that you have a friend who owns a company and you want to look up her telephone number. You can look up the name of the company or the name of your friend—both would reference the same number. Depending on who (which application) is looking for her phone number, a different name is being resolved. If your friend uses her name as the name of the company, the two names would be the same—just as the NetBIOS name and the host name are the same.

The NetBIOS name of a Microsoft computer can be viewed and configured by clicking Control Panel ➢ Network ➢Identification. When a NetBIOS application needs resolution from a NetBIOS name to an IP address, TCP/IP uses **NetBIOS name resolution**.

The NetBIOS name resolution method has six steps that TCP/IP follows to resolve a NetBIOS name to a TCP/IP address. If these six steps fail to resolve the NetBIOS name to a TCP/IP address, then an error message is displayed to the user.

The steps of NetBIOS name resolution are:

1. NetBIOS name cache
2. WINS
3. Broadcast
4. LMHOSTS file
5. HOSTS file
6. DNS

NOTE

You will learn about each of these methods in this chapter.

Some applications that use the NetBIOS name resolution method include Windows Explorer, NT Explorer, and Microsoft's Net application (which has the net use and net view commands).

NetBIOS Name Resolution vs. Host Name Resolution

When troubleshooting TCP/IP configuration issues, it is critical to know which method of resolution the application uses. This helps the administrator figure out where resolution is succeeding and failing.

The NetBIOS name resolution and host name resolution methods are basically the same. They include similar steps—but the order that the steps are applied is different. Each method takes a distinct path to resolve names to IP addresses.

The following table lists the order in which the steps are applied in each method.

Host Name Resolution	NetBIOS Name Resolution
Local host (HOSTNAME)	NetBIOS name cache
HOSTS file	WINS
DNS	Broadcast
NetBIOS name cache	LMHOSTS file
WINS	HOSTS file
Broadcast	DNS
LMHOSTS file	

Some of the steps listed in the table are applied only when the computer that is trying to get resolution is using Microsoft's TCP/IP client. Most workstations today have Microsoft's TCP/IP client software installed. There is also a possibility that a TCP/IP client will not be set up to use some of the resolution steps. For example, a client may not be set up to use WINS as a method of resolution. If the client is not set up to use WINS, this step is bypassed.

The orders of resolution are the maps to solving TCP/IP resolution problems. An administrator must be aware of which cycle of resolution to follow when troubleshooting.

Understanding Host Name Resolution

The first category of name resolution to explore is host name resolution. Host name resolution occurs with most TCP/IP utilities and programs. This is the most common method of resolving names to IP addresses.

All TCP/IP hosts have a host name that is configured in the TCP/IP properties of the host. On a Microsoft TCP/IP client, the host name can be viewed and configured by clicking Control Panel ➢ Network ➢Protocol ➢ TCP/IP ➢ DNS. Only Microsoft clients have a NetBIOS name. Remember, the NetBIOS name and the host name are the same by default.

In this section, you will examine each step in the host name resolution process. Let's use the example of pinging www.sybex.com.

The Ping utility is used to confirm that you can use TCP/IP to communicate with another host. The Ping utility uses TCP/IP to send a Ping packet to another host and request that the other host send a response. Before TCP/IP can send a Ping packet, TCP/IP needs an IP address. The TCP/IP stack needs to figure out the IP address of www.sybex.com.

In the illustration below, Harry the Host is going to ping www.sybex.com. Using the Ping utility and a friendly name instead of an IP address will illustrate the need to use host name resolution.

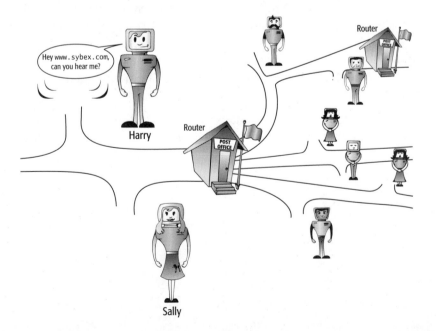

The TCP/IP stack running on the host must resolve the friendly name (www .sybex.com) to an IP address. There are several steps that Harry the host will use to achieve successful resolution. As soon as resolution is successful, the IP address will be passed to the Internet layer of the TCP/IP stack so that IP can determine whether the destination host is local or remote, and communication can commence.

Because Ping falls into the host name resolution category, the steps that the TCP/IP stack running on Harry will follow are:

1. Local host (HOSTNAME)
2. HOSTS file
3. DNS
4. NetBIOS name cache
5. WINS
6. Broadcast
7. LMHOSTS file

Some of these steps refer to Microsoft-specific implementations. Many hosts that today's administrators work with are Microsoft hosts. Any steps that would be skipped by a non-Microsoft host are mentioned as each step is described in the pages that follow.

As you follow the steps involved in host name resolution, keep in mind that all TCP/IP is doing is trying to find the IP address for www.sybex.com. This is similar to trying to find the phone number for somebody when all you have is a name.

As you are learning about host name resolution, also keep in mind the speed with which resolution takes place. You'll be amazed that resolution takes place as fast as it does.

Local Host (HOSTNAME)

The first step in the host name resolution process is to determine whether the local computer (the one that is being used as the source) is also the one that you are trying to reach. This process is known as local host. **Local host** is a method wherein TCP/IP checks to see whether the name of the host that it is on is the same as the host name that it's resolving. Maybe the host that you are sitting at is the host that you are trying to get resolution to. Never overlook the obvious or easiest answer; first check to see whether you are the answer.

In our example, TCP/IP wants to find out whether Harry's name is really www .sybex.com. Harry looks in a mirror to see whether his name is www.sybex.com.

The **HOSTNAME utility** can help answer this question. HOSTNAME is used to discover your host's host name. From a command prompt, type **HOSTNAME** and press Enter. The next line will show you what your host thinks its host name is.

local host

A step in name resolution wherein a host examines its TCP/IP configuration to see whether the name being resolved is its own.

HOSTNAME utility

A simple utility that determines the host name of the computer you are at.

TEST IT OUT: HOSTNAME UTILITY

Here you will use the HOSTNAME utility to find out the name of your local host. Follow these steps:

1. Go to the command prompt by selecting Start ➢ Run, typing **CMD** (Windows NT, 2000, or XP) or **COMMAND** (Windows 95/98), and then pressing Enter.

2. At the command prompt, type **HOSTNAME**, and then press Enter.

3. The screen displays the name of the local computer, as shown below.

```
Microsoft(R) Windows NT(TM)
(C) Copyright 1985-1996 Microsoft Corp.

C:\>HOSTNAME
harry

C:\>
```

Notice that in this example, the name of the local computer is Harry. This host now knows that it is not www.sybex.com; this host's name is Harry.

If TCP/IP realizes that the host name shown by using the HOSTNAME utility is the same as the one that it is trying to get resolution to, the job is done. TCP/IP can use this host's IP address as the destination address.

In most cases, the two host names being compared are different, so TCP/IP moves on to the next step to try to resolve the host name.

 TIP

As an administrator, you can use the HOSTNAME utility as a tool when troubleshooting. To determine the name of a host without having to click through several dialog boxes, you can simply use the HOSTNAME utility.

The *HOSTS* file

The second step that TCP/IP uses to resolve the host name is referred to as the **HOSTS file**. In this step, TCP/IP uses the HOSTS file to try to get resolution.

The HOSTS file is a simple **ASCII text file** that contains host names and IP addresses. The file can contain local and remote names and IP addresses. Because this step occurs so early in the host name resolution process, the file should contain frequently accessed host names and TCP/IP addresses.

The HOSTS file functions in a way that is similar to your personal phone book. You put in names, addresses, and phone numbers of the people that you contact most often. You can enter them anywhere and with any name that makes sense to you. You may put your friend Kevin Sullivan in the Ks because you call him Kevin more often. You may enter Bret Stateham in the Ps because you call him "Pony." You put in their names however you like and can look them up anytime by using the name that you have given to them. If they change their addresses or phone numbers, you can easily update the information.

The illustration below shows Harry looking in a personal phone book. Harry checks his personal phone book early in the resolution process, just like TCP/IP looks in the HOSTS file.

The HOSTS file is named exactly with the word *HOSTS*. There is no file extension and no variation on the name. The location of the HOSTS file depends on the local operating system in use. The following table shows the directory where the HOSTS file is located on the most common local operating systems.

HOSTS file
A file of host names and IP addresses.

ASCII text file
A file that is stored as text only—no fancy characters. It can be edited with any text editor such as Notepad or Edit.

Operating System	Directory
Windows 95, 98	\SYSTEMROOT\SYSTEM
Windows NT, 2000, XP	\SYSTEMROOT\SYSTEM32\DRIVERS\ETC
NetWare	SYS:\ETC
Unix	/etc

alias
A simpler or alternative name for a host.

The HOSTS file contains IP addresses followed by a Tab or space, and then the name that you would like resolution to. For example, to get resolution to www.sybex.com, you would edit the HOSTS file to include the line:

```
206.100.29.83     www.sybex.com
```

parsing
Reading through a file looking for specific data.

This line in your HOSTS file will provide resolution to the Sybex Web site. However, if you would like to include an **alias**, something that would be easier to type or easier to remember than the full URL, just put in whatever alias you would like. When TCP/IP is **parsing** the HOSTS file, as soon as the word that was used in the Web browser is found, resolution is successful.

The following three examples show what this line might look like in the HOSTS file:

```
206.100.29.83     www.sybex.com books
206.100.29.83     books
206.100.29.83     sybex
```

Any of these lines will give resolution to the Sybex Web site by using one of the names listed in the HOSTS file.

As an administrator, you can use the HOSTS file to provide resolution for clients by putting frequently used host names and IP addresses into the file. If the IP address changes for any of the hosts that you typed into the HOSTS file, you must manually edit the file. The HOSTS file can be as large as you like or does not have to exist if you choose not to use it. After the file is in the proper directory and its name is HOSTS, TCP/IP will use that file for host name resolution.

The HOSTS file provides a simple and effective way to resolve the most commonly used host names. To quickly test the HOSTS file, edit it on your home computer by adding one of the lines above with the IP address and a word that references the Sybex Web site. Now you need to enter only one word in your Web browser to get to that Web site.

If TCP/IP has still not successfully resolved the host name, the quest will move to the next step, which is DNS.

Domain Name System (DNS)

Domain Name System (DNS)
Distributed system used on the Internet to resolve host names to IP addresses.

Domain Name System (DNS) is the Internet's mechanism for linking all the host names and IP addresses on the Internet. In other words, DNS is a distributed and linked system of resolving names to IP addresses. The DNS system is similar to an environment in which all telephone information operators are linked together so that your request can get passed to the appropriate operator.

All the URLs that you need to get resolution for on the Internet are in a DNS database somewhere. A DNS database administrator has entered the name and IP address into the database. When you use a browser and request www.sybex.com, *www* refers to a service, and *sybex* refers to the host name. The *.com* refers to the portion of the domain space where this host is found. A URL is a combination of the service, host name, and domain where the host can be found.

A DNS database is like a phone book of host names. All these databases are linked so that when you are trying to get resolution, the DNS server that tries to get resolution for you might get directed from one DNS server to another until you either get resolution or you find out you can't get resolution.

In the graphic below, Harry is calling a long-distance operator to try to get resolution to www.sybex.com, just as TCP/IP will use DNS.

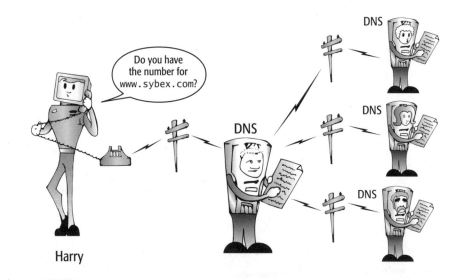

If TCP/IP fails at this point to resolve the address, chances are getting slimmer that resolution will be successful. The next couple of methods refer only to Microsoft TCP/IP clients that are trying to get host name resolution.

NetBIOS Name Cache

The next step in host name resolution is called NetBIOS name cache, which is used by Microsoft's version of TCP/IP. When using a **Microsoft TCP/IP client**, TCP/IP looks in **NetBIOS name cache**. This is a list in the local host's RAM of the recently resolved NetBIOS names to IP addresses. It's possible that the host name that TCP/IP is trying to get resolution for is also the NetBIOS name of a machine that has recently been resolved.

NetBIOS names that are in cache are like phone numbers that are listed on a scratch piece of paper around the telephone. These pieces of scratch paper have names and numbers that you have recently resolved. They are only temporary and may get thrown away soon.

The following illustration shows Harry checking for the www.sybex.com address on scratch pieces of paper, just like TCP/IP will look in the NetBIOS name cache.

NetBIOS names that have been resolved are placed into NetBIOS name cache for a short amount of time. Before TCP/IP continues with other steps toward resolution, Microsoft's TCP/IP client will stop to see whether this host name is also a NetBIOS name that has already been resolved.

If TCP/IP does not get resolution from NetBIOS name cache, the search continues by using WINS.

Microsoft TCP/IP client

Any TCP/IP host that has installed and configured Microsoft's TCP/IP client software. This accounts for most TCP/IP hosts.

NetBIOS name cache

Temporary cache storage for NetBIOS names and IP addresses that have been resolved.

203

Scope ID

A NetBIOS scope ID can be configured as a parameter of a Microsoft TCP/IP host. The scope ID segments a physical network into logical networks. If it is important for two hosts on the same network to use the same NetBIOS name, or for two hosts on the same network to be isolated from each other, the scope ID can be used. It is an optional parameter of a NetBIOS and TCP/IP configuration.

When configuring TCP/IP on a Microsoft host, the scope ID field is seldom used. However, in troubleshooting any TCP/IP issues, the scope ID may become an issue if it is in use. When two hosts have different scope IDs, they cannot use NetBIOS to communicate.

On a TCP/IP network, the NetBIOS names are the unique identifiers used by NetBIOS for name resolution. Therefore, no two hosts can have the same NetBIOS name. The scope ID segments the NetBIOS network into different logical networks. For example, in the scope ID field for the host computers in the accounting department, an administrator might type ACCT. These hosts can be identified as HOST1.ACCT or HOST2.ACCT. In another department, the NetBIOS hosts might have a scope ID of SALES. These hosts can be identified as HOST1.SALES or HOST2.SALES.

In these examples, an administrator has created two logical NetBIOS networks, although they are physically on the same network.

However, hosts with a scope ID of SALES cannot access a host with a scope ID of ACCT. Scope IDs must be the same for NetBIOS communication to occur on the same network. Most administrators leave this field blank.

The following screen capture shows the TCP/IP Properties dialog box where the scope ID is set. You set the scope ID in the Network applet of the Control Panel. You access the scope ID from the Control Panel by clicking Network ➢ TCP/IP Properties ➢ WINS Address.

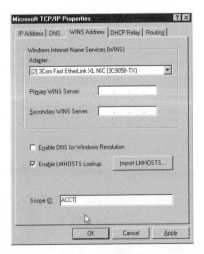

Windows Internet Naming Service (WINS)

The next step in host name resolution is performed only if the host that needs resolution is configured to use **Windows Internet Naming Service (WINS)**. A host that is not configured to use WINS will skip this step. WINS is the implementation of a Microsoft NetBIOS name server.

The WINS server keeps a database of all the NetBIOS names and IP addresses of hosts that either register with this WINS server or have been entered into the database manually by an administrator. The administrator configures Microsoft computers on an internetwork to dynamically register their NetBIOS names with the same WINS server. As machines come online, they register with the central WINS server. Now any time another client needs resolution to that NetBIOS name, they ask the special-purpose information operator—WINS—and the operator either returns a positive response with the IP address or a negative response that that name can't be found.

To continue with the analogy, the WINS server acts as a special-purpose telephone information operator. In the illustration below, Harry is asking the local telephone operator for assistance, just like TCP/IP uses WINS.

Harry

WINS

NOTE

For more information on setting up and using WINS, see Chapter 14.

If TCP/IP still has not resolved the name to an IP address, TCP/IP starts getting anxious and tries an almost last-ditch effort.

Windows Internet Naming Service (WINS)
Microsoft's NetBIOS name server that keeps NetBIOS names and IP addresses in a database and later gives name resolution.

Broadcast

Broadcast is another method of name resolution that a TCP/IP client uses. Sometimes the computer name that you are trying to get resolution to is on the same network that you are. The TCP/IP stack will send out a packet that is addressed to all hosts, requesting a response from the host that it is trying to find. The broadcast will go only as far as the router and will not continue to other networks. Therefore, this is a way for TCP/IP to check the local network for resolution. Any response will include the requested host's IP address.

Consider another analogy: If I want to know the phone number of a restaurant, I could open the front door and yell, "Hey Denny's, if you can hear me, what is your phone number?" It's possible that Denny's will respond, but chances are I just wasted my time. Denny's is probably not on a residential street; Denny's is on a different street and people there probably can't hear me. By broadcasting, I also wasted bandwidth. Everyone in the neighborhood had to hear me yelling. The broadcast disturbs them momentarily until they realize that the broadcast was not for them. Chances of the broadcast succeeding are better if I yell out the front door for the phone number of one of my neighbors. They live close enough to hear my broadcast and would respond. (They might also decide to move if I did this too often.)

After checking for remote networks, host name resolution is finally checking the local network for resolution. In the following graphic, Harry is broadcasting out the door to try to get resolution.

Name Resolution

Broadcasting is an excellent method of name resolution when the computer that you need resolution to is on your local network. If it is not on your local network, the yelling of the broadcast ties up the whole network. The more broadcasts there are on a network, the less **bandwidth** is available for communication. Imagine everyone in your neighborhood constantly broadcasting out their front door to find phone numbers of people and places that don't exist locally. It would just get out of control.

If even after broadcasting TCP/IP cannot get host name resolution, there is one last place to look.

In the screen capture below, notice that Harry sent several DNS queries to his DNS server, through his default gateway. When Harry did not hear back from his DNS server, Harry broadcast three times onto his own network to see if www.sybex.com was on his network.

bandwidth
The amount of data that can move through the cabling.

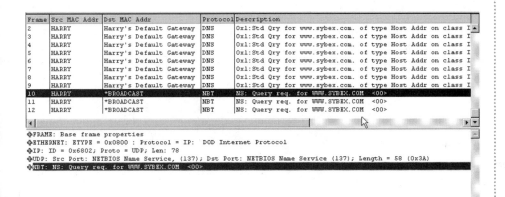

The *LMHOSTS* file

The **LMHOSTS file** is much like the HOSTS file. It is an ASCII text file that has IP addresses, but instead of containing a host name, the LMHOSTS file contains **NetBIOS names**. The LMHOSTS file does not contain any aliases; it can include only the real NetBIOS name of the computer that you would like resolution to.

The LMHOSTS file is used only on Microsoft's TCP/IP clients that are configured to check the LMHOSTS file. If the client is not a Microsoft TCP/IP client or if the client is not configured to check the LMHOSTS file, this step is skipped.

The LMHOSTS file is similar to a special-purpose phone book that you have at home. For example, in addition to a personal phone book at home, I also have a phone book of all the kids in my son's Little League Baseball team. When I need a number for one of the kids from Little League, I look in the special Little League phone book.

In the following graphic, Harry is looking in a smaller, more specialized phone book, just like TCP/IP looks in the LMHOSTS file.

The LMHOSTS file is located in the same directory as the HOSTS file. To locate the proper directory, see the table in the previous HOSTS file section.

LMHOSTS file
A file containing NetBIOS names and IP addresses that is used for name resolution.

NetBIOS names
The name given to a computer that is running a Microsoft operating system.

NOTE

The *LM* in LMHOSTS stands for **LAN Manager**. Because Windows NT has its roots in a product called LAN Manager, several of the configuration files from LAN Manager are still in use. This is one of those files.

The LMHOSTS file is built with the IP addresses and NetBIOS names of remote computers. Following is an example of an LMHOSTS file:

```
131.107.2.200      INSTRUCTOR    #PRE
131.107.5.22       ACCT_SRV      #PRE
131.107.3.19       FS1
```

Some entries in the LMHOSTS file have switches on the end to enhance their use. The first and second lines above, for example, have a **switch** of #PRE. As the computer boots up and TCP/IP is initializing, TCP/IP will look in the LMHOSTS file for any entries that have #PRE. When TCP/IP finds an entry with #PRE, that entry is immediately pre-loaded into NetBIOS name cache and will stay there indefinitely.

When this TCP/IP stack is trying to resolve a NetBIOS name to an IP address, a name in NetBIOS name cache will be immediately resolved. Therefore, the quickest resolution will always take place if the NetBIOS name and IP address are already in NetBIOS name cache.

The #PRE switch is analogous to me writing some names and numbers on a piece of paper that permanently stays by the phone so that I won't have to go digging through any books to find the number.

The **nbtstat** command is used to view the contents of NetBIOS name cache. There are a few important switches used with the nbtstat command that you should know about. The following table explains the most important switches and their functions.

Switch	Function
-c	Lists what is currently in cache
-R	Purges all entries from name cache and reloads entries that are in the LMHOSTS file that have a #PRE
-n	Lists the NetBIOS names that this machine is known by

LAN Manager
A networking product that was the predecessor of Microsoft's Windows NT.

switch
A character or set of characters used to further enhance a command.

nbtstat
A utility used to monitor the names that are in NetBIOS name cache.

TEST IT OUT: EXAMINING NETBIOS NAME CACHE

In this exercise, you will use the `nbtstat` utility to view the NetBIOS name cache. Follow these steps:

1. Go to the command prompt by selecting Start ➢ Run and typing **CMD** (Windows NT, 2000, or XP) or **COMMAND** (Windows 95/98).

2. At the command prompt, type **nbtstat –c** and then press Enter.

3. The screen displays the contents of NetBIOS names and IP addresses that have already been resolved.

Notice in this example that several NetBIOS names have been resolved and are in NetBIOS name cache. TCP/IP examines these for www.sybex.com and will not find it; therefore, name resolution will not be successful at this step.

The `nbtstat` command can also be used to display the NetBIOS names that this host is currently using. For example, examine the following screen capture. By using the `nbstat` command with the –n switch, the local NetBIOS names are displayed.

```
C:\>NBTSTAT -n

Node IpAddress: [192.168.2.21] Scope Id: []

           NetBIOS Local Name Table

   Name               Type         Status
-------------------------------------------------
HARRY          <00>  UNIQUE      Registered
JUMPSTART      <00>  GROUP       Registered
JUMPSTART      <1C>  GROUP       Registered
HARRY          <20>  UNIQUE      Registered
JUMPSTART      <1B>  UNIQUE      Registered
HARRY          <03>  UNIQUE      Registered
JUMPSTART      <1E>  GROUP       Registered
ADMINISTRATOR  <03>  UNIQUE      Registered
INet~Services  <1C>  GROUP       Registered
IS~HARRY.......<00>  UNIQUE      Registered

C:\>
```

NetBIOS name cache looks like this:

```
C:\>nbtstat -c

Node IpAddress: [192.168.2.5] Scope Id: []

           NetBIOS Remote Cache Name Table

   Name              Type      Host Address     Life [sec]
-----------------------------------------------------------
ACCT_SRV      <03>  UNIQUE    192.168.2.107       -1
ACCT_SRV      <00>  UNIQUE    192.168.2.107       -1
ACCT_SRV      <20>  UNIQUE    192.168.2.107       -1
STUDENT_7     <20>  UNIQUE    192.168.2.106      660
STUDENT_6     <20>  UNIQUE    192.168.2.119      600
STUDENT_2     <20>  UNIQUE    192.168.2.101      540

C:\>
```

TEST IT OUT: EXAMINING NETBIOS NAME CACHE (CONT.)

Notice in the screen shot above that the life remaining for these entries in cache varies. As soon as a NetBIOS name is resolved to an IP address, that entry and its IP address are placed into NetBIOS name cache temporarily. The default is 660 seconds, or 11 minutes. That way, if that machine is used again in the next 11 minutes, name resolution does not need to begin again; the name is already resolved to an IP address. The entry for the machine with the NetBIOS name of ACCT_SRV is −1. Because the entry for ACCT_SRV in the LMHOSTS file includes the switch #PRE, as the TCP/IP stack was loading, ACCT_SRV was placed into NetBIOS name cache with an infinite life, which is represented by −1.

As an administrator, you may add an entry to the LMHOSTS file with the #PRE switch and want to test that it is getting pre-loaded into name cache. Instead of rebooting to reinitialize the TCP/IP stack, a nice shortcut is to use the nbtstat command with the −R switch. When you enter the command nbtstat −R, name cache is purged and all the #PRE-loads are Reloaded.

If after all these methods, TCP/IP still cannot resolve the host name to an IP address, an error message is displayed:

```
Microsoft(R) Windows NT(TM)
(C) Copyright 1985-1996 Microsoft Corp.

C:\>ping ww.sybex.com
Bad IP address ww.sybex.com.

C:\>
```

The Host Name Resolution Cycle

You have examined the seven steps that TCP/IP uses to resolve a name to an IP address. This cycle occurs every time a user tries to connect to another host by using a name instead of an IP address.

When the user of a TCP/IP client uses the name of another host to try to connect, TCP/IP cannot connect with just these words. TCP/IP must have an IP address. If the application uses the host name resolution cycle, which most of them do, the TCP/IP stack will try to resolve the name to an IP address through the seven steps explained earlier. The following illustration depicts a summary of the host name resolution methods.

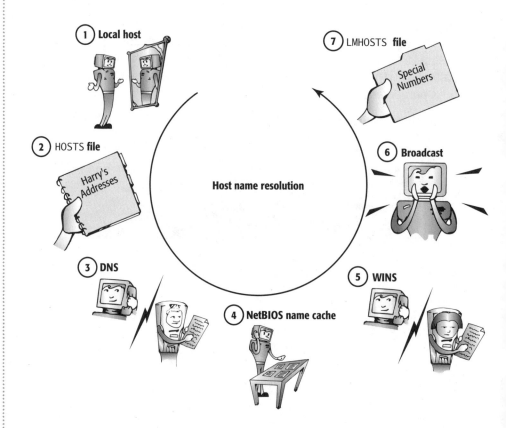

Understanding NetBIOS Name Resolution

shares
A feature of several operating systems that is used to designate local resources that will be accessible across the network.

Because NetBIOS names are used almost exclusively by a few Microsoft products, the NetBIOS name resolution cycle occurs infrequently. An application that uses NetBIOS names follows essentially the same steps that a TCP/IP application does when using host names to try to get resolution. However, the order in which the steps are tried is different.

The sequence that NetBIOS name resolution uses is as follows:

1. NetBIOS name cache
2. WINS
3. Broadcast
4. LMHOSTS file
5. HOSTS file
6. DNS

As an example, instead of Harry trying to ping www.sybex.com, let's have Harry use a Microsoft network application that would cause the NetBIOS name resolution cycle to take place. In this example, the user that is sitting at Harry the Host types in the following command:

```
net view \\instructor
```

This command can be issued when using a Microsoft networked computer, so that the user can view the **shares** that are available on the host with the NetBIOS name instructor. The shares are directories on the machine where the contents are shared.

A Microsoft host has a NetBIOS name of 16 bytes, or characters. The first 15 characters are the name of the host. If the computer name is Harry, then the first 5 characters are completed by the name Harry. If the computer name is Instructor, then the first 10 characters are completed by the name Instructor. The 16th character represents the NetBIOS service that the host is advertising. The characters between the name and the 16th character are padded with special characters, usually spaces.

The NetBIOS Name Resolution Cycle

The following illustration shows a summary of the NetBIOS name resolution methods.

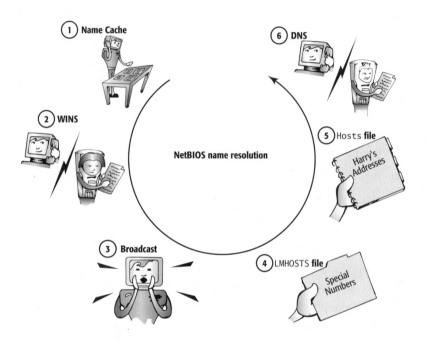

Steps in the cycle occur as follows:

1. Because this application uses NetBIOS names, the first place to look for name resolution is NetBIOS name cache. It's possible that the name has been resolved recently or that it was placed into NetBIOS name cache using the LMHOSTS file.

2. If the NetBIOS name is not in cache, TCP/IP asks the WINS server. If the hosts on this network are set up to use WINS, chances are good that WINS has a listing for the NetBIOS name that this host is trying to get resolution for.

3. If WINS is unsuccessful, or this host is not set up to use a WINS server, TCP/IP broadcasts on the local network to try to get resolution.

4. If the NetBIOS name that is broadcast still does not get resolved, TCP/IP looks in the LMHOSTS file.

5. If the name is not in the LMHOSTS file, maybe it is in the HOSTS file. TCP/IP looks in the HOSTS file next.

6. Finally, if the NetBIOS name is still not resolved, TCP/IP tries DNS.

If any of these methods are successful, the shares on the machine named
instructor are displayed. The following screen capture shows the command
and the successful display:

```
Microsoft(R) Windows NT(TM)
(C) Copyright 1985-1996 Microsoft Corp.

C:\>NET VIEW \\INSTRUCTOR
Shared resources at \\INSTRUCTOR


Share name   Type        Used as   Comment
-------------------------------------------------------------------------
CAP_S00      Disk                  SMS Site S00 CAP 09/28/99
CInfo        Disk
NETLOGON     Disk                  Logon server share
Public       Disk
SMS          Disk
SMS_S00      Disk                  SMS Site S00 09/28/99
SMS_SITE     Disk                  SMS Site S00 09/28/99
SMSLOGON     Disk                  SMS NT logon service
The command completed successfully.


C:\>
```

If none of these methods successfully resolved the NetBIOS name to an IP
address, then an error is displayed for the user. The following screen capture
displays the unsuccessful error message because of the misspelling of *instructor*.

```
Microsoft(R) Windows NT(TM)
(C) Copyright 1985-1996 Microsoft Corp.

C:\>NET VIEW \\INSTRUCTER
System error 53 has occurred.

The network path was not found.

C:\>_
```

Review Questions

Terms to Know
- ❏ name resolution
- ❏ host name resolution
- ❏ API
- ❏ NetBIOS
- ❏ NetBIOS name resolution
- ❏ local host
- ❏ HOSTNAME utility
- ❏ HOSTS file
- ❏ ASCII text file
- ❏ alias
- ❏ parsing

1. What are the two types of name resolution?

_____

_____

2. In the correct order, list the steps of host name resolution.

_____

3. In the correct order, list the methods of NetBIOS name resolution.

_____

4. What is wrong with the following entry in the HOSTS file?

    www.sybex.com   206.100.29.83

_____

5. What would be the fastest way to get host name resolution to www.sybex.com?

_____

6. What would be the fastest way to get NetBIOS name resolution to ACCT_SRV?

_____

7. What directory are the LMHOSTS and HOSTS files stored in on a Windows NT workstation?

_____

8. Can you put an alias in the LMHOSTS file?

_____

9. What file and switch are used to place a NetBIOS name into NetBIOS name cache permanently?

_____

10. Write the command you would type to purge NetBIOS name cache and to reload the LMHOSTS file.

_____

11. Which type of name resolution does FTP use?

_____

12. Which type of name resolution does HTTP use?

_____

13. Which type of name resolution will net view use?

_____

14. What is the utility used to check the local host name?

_____

Terms to Know
- ❑ DNS
- ❑ Microsoft TCP/IP client
- ❑ NetBIOS name cache
- ❑ WINS
- ❑ broadcast
- ❑ bandwidth
- ❑ LMHOSTS file
- ❑ NetBIOS names
- ❑ LAN Manager
- ❑ switch
- ❑ nbtstat
- ❑ shares

Chapter 12

Domain Name System (DNS)

In the preceding chapter, you learned about resolving names to TCP/IP addresses. The top-notch step in resolving host names to TCP/IP addresses is using DNS. The Domain Name System (DNS) is a way to resolve meaningful and easy-to-remember names to IP addresses. Because millions of sites are connected to the Internet, maintaining one central list of the name-to-IP-address relationships across the Internet is unrealistic. The DNS system was designed to coordinate and distribute the resolution load.

The two major tasks that DNS provides are:

◇ IP address resolution to hosts on the Internet, for local hosts

◇ IP address resolution to hosts on the local network, for other hosts on the Internet

In this chapter, you will learn:

 How DNS works

 How a DNS server is set up

 The types of DNS servers

 The types of records in a DNS database

What Is DNS?

Domain Name System (DNS)
A system used to resolve names to IP addresses across the Internet.

HOSTS.TXT
The original file that contained name-to-IP address relationships.

Stanford Research Institute Network Information Center (SRI-NIC)
The site of early Internet growth and host name maintenance.

As you learned in Chapter 11, **Domain Name System (DNS)** is a distributed database of host names and IP addresses on the Internet. If all the hosts on the Internet were in one big database, that database would be enormous and inefficient. But when the Internet was getting started, the initial idea *was* to keep a file with all host names and their IP addresses in a single file.

In the early days of the Internet, the host names of the sites that were connected to the Internet and their IP addresses were kept in a single file called **HOSTS.TXT**. This file was maintained by the **Stanford Research Institute Network Information Center (SRI-NIC)**. As new hosts were added to the growing network, a simple entry was added to the HOSTS.TXT file with the name and IP address of the new host. If you were one of the hosts on the network, you'd dial into the server at SRI-NIC and download the latest version of the HOSTS.TXT file. When you wanted to connect to another host, you could use the host's name, and TCP/IP would examine the HOSTS.TXT file to translate the name to an IP address.

This is a similar idea to the first phone book that was created. There was only one phone book, and as people hooked up their telephones, their names and numbers were added to the phone book. Everyone who had a phone had to keep getting the updated copy of the phone book. Your phone book was good only if you had a recent copy. Likewise, the HOSTS.TXT file was constantly being updated, and your HOSTS.TXT file was good only if you had a recent copy. An entry was added to or removed from the HOSTS.TXT file only a couple of times a week, so you'd need to download the file only that often to have the latest resolution file.

But as the Internet began to grow, this file became unmanageable. The number of updates to the file and the number of hosts that needed to download the file were growing exponentially. The system was becoming a bottleneck in the name resolution process. Several RFCs were written trying to solve the problem (read RFC 849). In November 1987, the Domain Name System was presented as a solution to the bottleneck; it was outlined in RFCs 1034 and 1035.

DNS on the Internet

Rather than keep all the host names and IP addresses in one unmanageable file, DNS distributes the task across the Internet. All the host names on the Internet are divided into different **domains**, or categories. The top-level domains are categories of host names—for example, commercial organizations are in the .com domain, and educational institutions are in the .edu domain. These top-level domains are further divided into second-level domains, and so on. Examples of second-level domains include sybex.com and microsoft.com.

Each top-level domain maintains a database of the second-level domains. The second-level domains maintain the next layer, and so on. An easy way to get a handle on what the Internet looks like is to view a map of the domain name space. **Domain name space** is the term used to reference how the Internet is subdivided. The top of the domain name space is the root. The root of the domain name space is represented by a period (.).

The illustration below shows a portion of the Internet domain name space. The root is at the top of the domain tree and is represented by a period. The top-level domains contain databases that point to DNS servers for the next layer. For example, the .com DNS server contains entries indicating where to find all the .com DNS servers. The Sybex DNS server contains a database with the host names and IP addresses of hosts and services that the Sybex DNS administrator would like others to get resolution to. For example, it might include entries for www, ftp, and any other names that DNS should provide resolution to.

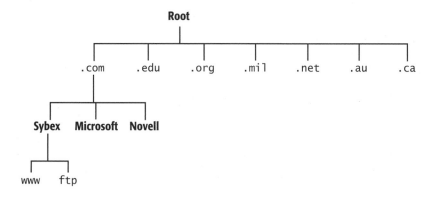

domain
A unique portion of the name space in which an administrator creates an authoritative database of records to give resolution of names within the zone to an IP address.

domain name space
The entire inverted tree of Internet names.

Name Resolution Using DNS

Building a DNS database is similar to building a phone book. When you get a new phone number, you would like people to be able to look up your name in a phone book and get your number. So when you order your phone, you make sure to tell the phone company how you want your name to appear in the phone book. You might also order a second phone line and not want that to be advertised. Your entry appears in a local phone book; putting everyone's name and number in one book would be impossible. Then, if someone wants to resolve your name to a phone number, all they have to do is look in the correct phone book. Because people don't keep a copy of every phone book at home, they don't have access to all phone books, but the information operator does. Information operators can reference all telephone books and resolve names to telephone numbers for a small fee.

resolver
A client that is trying to resolve a host name to an IP address.

DNS provides that special service for its clients on the Internet. When was the last time you saw a commercial advertising the IP address of a Web site? When you sit at a Web browser, rather than type in the IP address of a Web site that you would like to get resolution to, you can type in the name of the Web site and TCP/IP will try to translate that name to an IP address.

When TCP/IP uses DNS as a method of resolution, the host that is trying to get resolution is called a **resolver**. The term *resolver* comes from the Unix world. The resolver sends a message to its DNS server asking for help. The packet says, "Hey, DNS server, can you tell me the IP address for www.sybex.com?"

Imagine, for example, that a user sitting at Harry the Host typed into a Web browser that they'd like to go to www.sybex.com. But with only the words www.sybex.com, Harry cannot get to a Web site. Harry has to have an IP address to send the HTTP request to. He needs to ask Diane, his DNS server, for help.

Querying a DNS Server

Harry knows to ask Diane the DNS Server for resolution help because the administrator who configured Harry's IP address also configured Harry with the IP address of his DNS server. The DNS server can be on the same network or it can be at an ISP. In the illustration below, Harry the Host is the resolver and Diane is the DNS server.

root name servers
Powerful name servers that contain addresses of the top-level name servers.

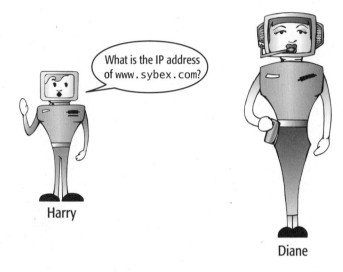

What is the IP address of www.sybex.com?

Harry

Diane

Diane the DNS Server acts as a universal information operator. She receives Harry's request for the IP address of www.sybex.com and first examines what she knows. Diane looks in her database to see whether she can answer Harry's question with no outside assistance. If Diane can answer his question, she'll send the IP address to Harry, and resolution is complete. Harry will then send an HTTP request to the IP address given to him by Diane the DNS Server.

If Diane does not know the answer, she will need to get some outside assistance. She asks a **root name server**. There are 13 root name servers. These are strategically placed name servers that contain the IP addresses of the top-level domain name servers. Every DNS server has the IP addresses of all these root name servers automatically installed to their local database. Therefore, every DNS server can ask any of the 13 root name servers for resolution.

Querying Name Servers

Since Diane the DNS Server has the IP address of the root name servers, she can start the process of name resolution. The first thing that little ol' Diane, a DNS server from some little network that nobody knows about, will do is ask one of these enormous and powerful root name servers if they know the IP address of www.sybex.com. See the illustration below.

cache
Temporary storage of information that is accessed quickly.

The root name servers have IP addresses of the top-level domain name servers. So the root name server responds to Diane and says "No, I don't know www .sybex.com, but I do have the address for .com." The root name server sends back the best information it has.

Now Diane has the address of a .com server. She takes that information and caches it. Diane will keep this information in **cache** as long as was specified by the DNS administrator of the DNS server that provided the information. Diane caches that address of .com because sometime soon she may be asked again for resolution to a URL that is in the .com domain. With the address cached, she won't have to bother the root name server with the same question.

Using the address she obtained, Diane sends a request to the .com name server and asks for resolution to www.sybex.com. The .com name server does not have the IP address of www.sybex.com, but does have the IP address of sybex.com. The .com name server sends a response to Diane that says, "I don't know the IP address of www.sybex.com, but I do know the address of sybex.com."

Domain Name System (DNS)

In the illustration below, Diane the DNS Server sends a request to the .com name server asking for resolution to www.sybex.com. The .com name server responds with the IP address of sybex.com.

.com name server

When Diane the DNS Server receives the response from the .com server, she caches the IP address of sybex.com. Diane then sends a request to the IP address of sybex.com asking for resolution to www.sybex.com.

The DNS server at sybex.com has the address of www.sybex.com. The sybex.com name server responds, "Yes, I do have the IP address for www.sybex.com; here it is." See the illustration below.

sybex.com name server

Completing Resolution

Now that Diane the DNS Server has the IP address for www.sybex.com, she caches the IP address and then sends a packet to Harry. In this response to Harry, Diane sends the IP address of www.sybex.com. Now that Harry has the address, Harry's TCP/IP stack sends an HTTP request to the IP address sent by Diane.

With all these pieces of resolution cached, Diane has part of the work (or possibly all of the work) already completed if another resolver asks her for resolution to anything in .com, or anything at sybex.com, or at www.sybex.com.

The screen capture below shows a packet that is sent from a host named Harry to a DNS server. The packet is a DNS query for www.sybex.com. In the DNS question section of the packet, which is highlighted, you can see the question being asked is "What is the IP address of www.sybex.com?"

recursive query
A question asked with the expectation that the response will be either the complete answer or an error, nothing less.

iterative query
A question asked with the expectation that the best information available will be returned so that more queries can be sent based on that information.

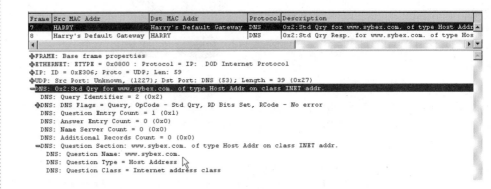

```
Frame  Src MAC Addr             Dst MAC Addr            Protocol Description
7      HARRY                    Harry's Default Gateway DNS      0x2:Std Qry for www.sybex.com. of type Host Addr
8      Harry's Default Gateway  HARRY                   DNS      0x2:Std Qry Resp. for www.sybex.com. of type Hos
```
```
♦FRAME: Base frame properties
♦ETHERNET: ETYPE = 0x0800 : Protocol = IP:  DOD Internet Protocol
♦IP: ID = 0xE306; Proto = UDP; Len: 59
♦UDP: Src Port: Unknown, (1227); Dst Port: DNS (53); Length = 39 (0x27)
➡DNS: 0x2:Std Qry for www.sybex.com. of type Host Addr on class INET addr.
  DNS: Query Identifier = 2 (0x2)
 ♦DNS: DNS Flags = Query, OpCode - Std Qry, RD Bits Set, RCode - No error
  DNS: Question Entry Count = 1 (0x1)
  DNS: Answer Entry Count = 0 (0x0)
  DNS: Name Server Count = 0 (0x0)
  DNS: Additional Records Count = 0 (0x0)
 ➡DNS: Question Section: www.sybex.com. of type Host Addr on class INET addr.
    DNS: Question Name: www.sybex.com.
    DNS: Question Type = Host Address
    DNS: Question Class = Internet address class
```

Understanding Recursive and Iterative Queries

After a query has been sent from the resolver to the DNS server, the DNS server responds with either the IP address or an error. The DNS server hides the work that has to take place to get name resolution. The query that the resolver sends to the DNS server is called a **recursive query**. A recursive query means: Give me the answer or give me an error, but don't give me anything in between.

The DNS server then asks other name servers to help with resolution. The query that a DNS server sends to another name server is called an **iterative query**. An iterative query asks for the best you've got: If you don't have the answer to the whole question, please give me any resolution that you can help with. The iterative queries may be repeated several times while the DNS server just keeps asking other name servers, "Help me as much as you can." That is why other name servers will respond with the best that they do know. The iterative queries are hidden from the resolver; the resolver wants resolution but does not care how many name servers are helping with resolution.

The screen capture below shows the packet that is returned to Harry with resolution to www.sybex.com accomplished. Based on this response, Harry the resolver does not know how resolution occurred; he just gets the resolution he asked for—the IP address shown at the bottom of the screen capture. The packet shows both the question that was asked and the answer.

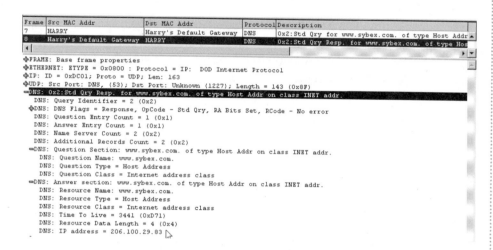

The DNS server might not be able to resolve the request. For example, imagine that Harry asks for resolution to fs1.sybex.com. The DNS server can resolve sybex and .com but cannot resolve fs1, so only an error is returned to Harry. The screen capture below shows the error being returned to Harry from the DNS server. The response says that the name fs1.sybex.com does not exist.

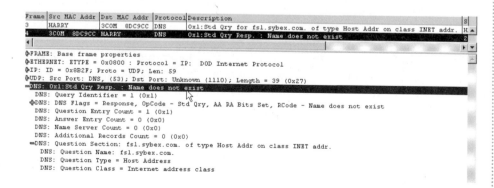

Maintaining a Database

One major task of the DNS server is to provide resolution for the resolvers that are configured to use that DNS server. Another major task is to maintain a database of host names and IP addresses. Then, when a query is made of the DNS server, it first looks in its database to see whether it can help with resolution. The administrator of a DNS server has to type in the host names and IP addresses in the database that the DNS server uses in resolving requests.

For example, an administrator for the sybex.com DNS server made an entry into a database at that server that www.sybex.com has the IP address of 206.100.29.83. After my DNS server got resolution to sybex.com, it queried the sybex.com DNS server for the IP address of www.sybex.com. The sybex.com DNS server responded with the correct address.

The .com server has an entry in its database that points any query for *any-thing*.sybex.com to the sybex.com DNS server. The sybex.com DNS server has the information needed to give resolution to *(anything the administrator wanted)*.sybex.com. The DNS administrator at Sybex typed these entries in the sybex.com DNS server's database, which is stored as a zone file. The administrator is in charge of the zone, and more specifically the zone file, for sybex.com. A zone file contains the names and IP addresses for this particular part of the domain name space. The administrator puts the records for sybex.com into a zone file called sybex.com.dns.

DNS is a service that can be run on different platforms and operating systems. The database that each DNS server uses is made of several files. Most DNS versions and implementations follow a standard called the Berkeley Internet Name Domain (BIND) implementation. The BIND implementation describes what files are necessary and what information the records in the DNS database must include.

Every DNS administrator maintains a DNS database. These databases are linked through the Internet to create a network of DNS databases. The DNS servers then work together to provide name-to-IP-address resolution and IP-address-to-name resolution. Because every administrator is maintaining their own database, and all the databases work together, successful DNS resolution is a collaborative effort.

Maintaining a DNS Server

A DNS administrator sets up and maintains the DNS database. DNS server software can be run on several operating systems. Depending on the operating system that is chosen, the administration methods differ slightly, but the basic concepts are the same. A server that the DNS service is run on is called a **name server**. There are three types of name servers, which are described in the following sections.

Primary Name Server

The **primary name server** holds the **master DNS database**. The administrator makes all updates to the master DNS database. The primary name server holds a **read/write** copy of the database. To add, delete, or modify any of the records in the DNS database, the administrator accesses the primary name server and modifies the master DNS database.

A primary name server is like an information operator with the master phone listing for her area. All modifications are made to this master phone listing. With just one copy of the DNS database on the primary name server, name resolution will take place just fine. However, an administrator has the option to assist the primary name server by setting up a **secondary name server**.

Secondary Name Server

A secondary name server holds a copy of the DNS database. This server provides resolution in the same way that the primary name server does.

Secondary name servers assist the primary name servers. Administrators set up secondary name servers for the following reasons:

Fault tolerance   If one server goes down or is unavailable, the other name server will be able to handle name resolution queries.

Load balancing   If a server becomes overloaded with name resolution requests, another name server will lighten the load.

Remote resolution   If you need to resolve an IP address from a remote site, a secondary name server can be placed at the remote location so that resolution can take place at that location without having to continually send traffic across WAN links.

name server
A server running the DNS service that can provide name resolution.

primary name server
The name server that holds the master DNS database.

master DNS database
The authoritative DNS database containing DNS records, where the administrator can modify records.

read/write
A file that can be read from and written to.

secondary name server
A name server that has a copy of the master DNS database.

fault tolerance
Taking into account any failures.

load balancing
Spreading the workload across servers.

DNS Zone Transfer

The secondary name server receives a copy of the master DNS database from the primary name server. The administrator does not make changes to the database on the secondary server; all updates must be made at the primary name server only. The secondary name servers hold a **read-only** copy of the DNS database. When the primary name server is updated, a copy of that database (zone file) is transferred to the secondary name servers.

Continuing the analogy of the information operator, the secondary name server is like another information operator. The second information operator gets a copy of the master phone list and can use it but can't update it. The second information operator helps with resolution just like the primary operator does.

The transfer of the database is called a **zone transfer**. A zone transfer moves the database from the primary name server to the secondary. Whenever a secondary name server comes online, it automatically initiates a zone transfer. The administrator also can set up a zone transfer to occur from a secondary to another secondary. The first transfer has to be from the primary name server to a secondary; then that secondary may transfer the database to another secondary.

The illustration below is an example of a DNS database being transferred. The primary name server performs a zone transfer to two secondary name servers, and one of the secondary name servers performs a zone transfer to a third secondary.

read-only
A file that can be read but cannot be modified.

zone transfer
The sending of a DNS database from one name server to another.

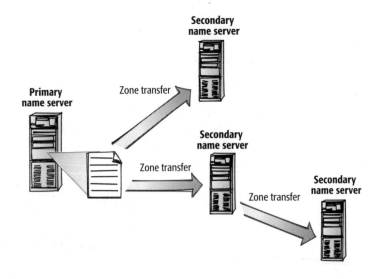

230

Caching-Only Server

A **caching-only server** contains no database. When the caching-only server comes online, it knows nothing. When the first query comes to it for resolution, the caching-only server must start at the root and work out all the levels of resolution. After it has resolved a URL, it has some information cached for the next query. The caching-only server quickly learns and caches the most commonly resolved queries. The caching-only server requires little setup and virtually no maintenance. When any DNS server is initially installed, it is essentially a caching-only server until you add the zone database.

A caching-only server is like an information operator not having a phone book. When the operator starts working, she must ask other operators for assistance on every query. As she resolves numbers, she jots notes to herself and gradually builds her own Rolodex. Soon she has the most frequently asked for names already resolved and handy.

Caching-only servers are excellent choices for remote offices connected by WAN links. Because there is no zone transfer when the caching-only server comes online, there is no initial bandwidth consumption.

Record Types in DNS

The DNS database is a collection of **records**. Several types of records can be included in the DNS database. The records are like cards in a Rolodex file. The first card describes the data in the Rolodex; it might contain the information about whose Rolodex it is and when it was created. Most cards in the Rolodex have a name, address, and phone number. The Rolodex might also include some other cards with various functions.

Some of the most common record types are:

- ◆ Start Of Authority (SOA) record
- ◆ A record
- ◆ CNAME record
- ◆ NS record
- ◆ PTR record
- ◆ MX record

Each is described in the following sections.

caching-only server
A name server that does not have a copy of a DNS database.

records
The information in the DNS database.

231

Start Of Authority (SOA) Record

A DNS database starts with a record called an **SOA record**. SOA stands for Start Of Authority, and there is only one SOA record in each zone database file. This record describes the zone in the domain name space that a particular database is authoritative over. In the Rolodex example, this would be the card that describes the card file, who it belongs to, when was it last updated, and other information about the data. In the Sybex DNS database, the SOA record describes the sybex.com zone, which is the zone that the Sybex database is authoritative over.

A Record

An **A record** is also called a Host record. This is the most common record type in a DNS database. The A record contains host names and IP addresses. This is like the cards in a Rolodex that have the actual names, addresses, and phone numbers.

CNAME Record

The term **CNAME** stands for Canonical name. Even though it has a fancy name, the record is simply a *code* name for an A record. Canonical names are aliases that have been entered into the DNS database. These records provide different ways to reference host records that are already in the database.

For example, say an administrator wants people to be able to get resolution to both fs1.sybex.com and www.sybex.com. Both have the same IP address. The DNS database already has an A record for www.sybex.com. So the administrator simply puts a CNAME record into the database for fs1 that points to the www A record.

In the Rolodex example, a card might be added for someone, and the card simply has a name and a note to go look at another card for the address or phone number. If my friend's nickname is "Pony," I can have a card that says "Pony" that points to the original card with his real name and number.

NS Record

An **NS record** indicates this and other name servers that are being used by this name server. An NS record exists for every name server that services the domain. Using the information operator analogy, an NS record has the phone number of all the operators that are using a copy of a particular phone book. This information will help them to contact each other.

PTR Record

A **PTR record** is used so that a query for the host name, not the IP address, can be resolved. If a query comes to the DNS server that says, "Here is the IP address; what is the host name?" the PTR record provides resolution. Every time an A record is added to the DNS database, a PTR record should also be added.

This would be similar to looking at a phone book and asking, "I have this phone number; whose number is it?" Or a modern example is the caller-ID feature that is available for your telephone. This service displays the name of the person who is calling as well as their phone number. If all it displayed were a telephone number, it would be an almost useless feature. It's when a reverse lookup is done and the name is displayed that the benefits of this call screening feature are realized.

Few applications are written that request a host name (the application knows the IP address, but would like to know the host name). The query that these applications send to the DNS server is called a reverse, or inverse, query. The DNS server examines the PTR records and responds with the host name that corresponds to the IP address. These PTR records are in a special zone called the **IN-ADDR.ARPA** zone. When a query comes to the DNS server requesting an inverse lookup, the DNS server can look in the IN-ADDR.ARPA zone for quick resolution.

MX Record

An **MX record** is a Mail eXchanger record. This record has the IP address of the server where e-mail should be delivered. For example, when e-mail is sent to andy@sybex.com, the DNS server at Sybex is queried for the address of the mail server at sybex.com. The DNS server looks for any MX records for sybex.com and returns the IP address of the mail server to where the mail should be transferred.

Other Record Types

An administrator could use other record types for their DNS database. Examples of such records include a WKS record which points to a WellKnown Service, or an RP record which indicates the Responsible Person for the database. The most common records, however, are those that were presented in this chapter.

Pointer (PTR) record
A record that aids with IP address-to-host-name resolution.

IN-ADDR.ARPA
Inverse Address from the ARPAnet; a zone used to keep PTR records.

Mail eXchanger (MX) record
A record that contains the address of the mail server.

Review Questions

Terms to Know

❏ DNS
❏ HOSTS.TXT
❏ SRI-NIC
❏ domain
❏ domain name space
❏ resolver
❏ root name servers
❏ cache
❏ recursive query
❏ iterative query
❏ name server
❏ primary name server
❏ master DNS database
❏ read/write

1. What is the name of the original file used to store host names and IP addresses?

2. What RFCs describe DNS?

3. What character represents the root of the domain name space?

4. What is the client called when asking for resolution?

5. How does the client know the IP address of the DNS server?

6. What type of query does the client send to the DNS server?

7. What type of query does the DNS server send to other name servers?

8. List three types of name servers.

9. What is the term used when a DNS database is copied from one name server to another?

_____

10. Can a secondary name server copy the DNS database to another secondary name server?

_____

11. Can a secondary name server copy the DNS database to a caching-only name server?

_____

12. What is the most common record type in a DNS database?

_____

13. What is the process of resolving an IP address to a host name called?

_____

Terms to Know
- ❑ secondary name server
- ❑ fault tolerance
- ❑ load balancing
- ❑ read-only
- ❑ zone transfer
- ❑ caching-only server
- ❑ records
- ❑ SOA record
- ❑ A record
- ❑ CNAME record
- ❑ NS record
- ❑ PTR record
- ❑ IN-ADDR.ARPA
- ❑ MX record

Chapter

13

Dynamic DNS

O ver the last couple of years, Dynamic DNS has become a standard method of updating resource records in a DNS database. Just as it makes sense to use DHCP for automatic IP address allocation, it makes sense to use Dynamic DNS. Recall that in Chapter 7, you learned how DHCP works. In this chapter, you will explore a technique that enhances DNS using DHCP.

In this chapter you will learn:

 What Dynamic DNS means

 How to configure a DNS and DHCP server to use Dynamic DNS

 How to configure a client to use Dynamic DNS

 How Dynamic DNS is used on the Internet

 The benefits of Dynamic DNS

What Is Dynamic DNS?

A DHCP server is set up to assign IP addresses automatically. This means that the administrator does not have to go to every desk and type in the IP address, subnet mask, default gateway, and other options. Instead, every time a DHCP client powers on or comes on to a network, this client broadcasts a request to find the DHCP server and get its IP address. This relieves the administrator of doing the tedious and error-prone work of typing in all the IP addresses.

Dynamic DNS
The process that allows the DHCP server to update the DNS database with new record information.

In contrast, you learned that DNS is statically updated. This means that the administrator has to actually access the DNS server to update DNS. To update DNS, the administrator must add the host name and IP address for a host name to get resolved in the DNS server's zone. The administrator updates the DNS database by adding an A record, which is the host record, and a PTR record, which is the reverse-mapping record. Now the DNS server can provide both name-to-IP-address resolution and IP-address-to-name resolution.

Dynamic DNS is very similar to the idea of an old-fashioned switchboard operator. No matter where you moved around in the company, as people called in and wanted to talk to you, the switchboard operator could switch that call to your current telephone line. The person on the other end didn't need to know which telephone line because it was the operator who switched the call to the correct line.

Likewise, Dynamic DNS allows the DHCP server and the DHCP clients to send updates to the DNS server. Updates to the DNS database are made without administrator intervention, and users don't need to know if an IP address changes or moves. As users get host-name-to-IP-address resolution, DNS will provide current and accurate information.

When DNS was originally designed (RFC 1034 and 1035), changes to the DNS database were expected, but not very often. The entries in the DNS database referred to hosts whose IP addresses were static. The designers of DNS could not have foreseen the incredible growth that the Internet has experienced or the increase in corporate and home networks. Many administrative tasks became automated, but DNS remained static. DHCP evolved to become the standard way of assigning IP addresses, and DNS needed to be enhanced to benefit from automated IP address assignment. Without Dynamic DNS, a DHCP server gave a dynamic IP address to a host, but other hosts couldn't get name-to-IP-address resolution to that host until the administrator updated DNS. In the past, there was no easy way around this for the administrator. Now, using Dynamic DNS, when a DHCP server gives out an IP address, it also updates DNS with this new information.

Dynamic DNS

NOTE

Dynamic DNS is described in RFC 2136, and the security for Dynamic DNS is described in RFC 2137.

Dynamic DNS uses the automation of DHCP to automate updates to the DNS database. The DHCP server is the key player in Dynamic DNS. The two pieces of information about a host that DHCP needs in order to update DNS are the IP address of the host and the fully qualified domain name (FQDN). Since the DHCP server has just assigned the IP address, the DHCP server knows the IP address of the host. To find the FQDN, the DHCP server looks inside the DHCP request packet. Remember that when a DHCP client is coming on to a network, the host uses broadcasts to find and lease an IP address from a DHCP server. The DHCP server knows the host name from looking in these packets, but the domain name is one of the options that the DHCP server assigns. Since the DHCP server assigns the domain, the DHCP server already knows the domain of the client. The DHCP server puts this information together and computes the fully qualified domain name.

For example, if the client's machine name is Harry, and a DHCP server in the SYBEX.COM domain is serving Harry the Host an IP address, the DHCP server computes the FQDN to be HARRY.SYBEX.COM. Now the DHCP server can register this information with the DNS server.

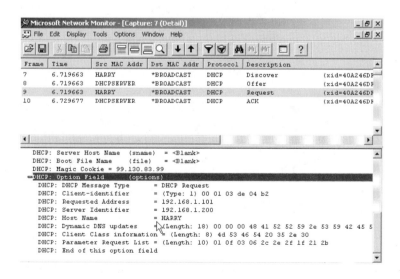

Notice the host name "Harry" in the DHCP option portion of the packet. This will be the first part of the FQDN. Also notice the Dynamic DNS update information.

After the DHCP server has finished leasing the address to the client, a DNS update record is sent to the DNS server. How much updating the DHCP server does and how much the client helps will vary. Dynamic DNS can be set up a couple of different ways. Remember, there are two records that will be updated, the A record and the PTR record. The options for Dynamic DNS include the following:

◇ DHCP server sends the PTR record, and the client sends the A record.

◇ DHCP server sends both PTR record and A record.

At the end of the IP address lease duration, the DHCP server will send another update request to the DNS server to remove both the PTR and the A records.

Harry the Host volunteers to send the A record, so Donna the DHCP Server only needs to send the PTR record. In the graphic below, the DNS server has been upgraded to a Dynamic DNS server—Debbie the Dynamic DNS Server in our example. The DHCP server must be configured to work with this new Dynamic DNS server.

Configure Windows 2000 Server for Dynamic Update

With Windows 2000 Server, the default setting is to have the DHCP server send the update request for the PTR record, and the Windows 2000/XP client to send the update request for the A record. If the administrator does not want the client to do the extra work of updating the DNS database, or would just prefer that the DHCP server do more of the processing, the default settings can be modified.

To modify the default settings in Windows 2000 Server, right-click the DHCP server entry in DHCP Manager and click Properties.

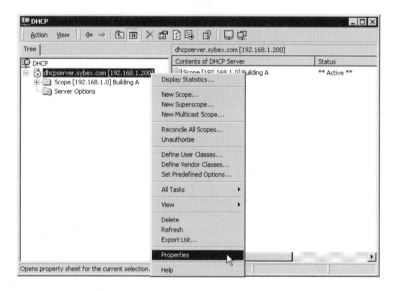

Click the DNS tab; this will show you the settings for using Dynamic DNS. The first choice, Automatically Update DHCP Client Information in DNS, must be selected to enable Dynamic DNS and for any of the other options to be available. The available options are:

- ◆ Automatically Update DHCP Client Information in DNS
    - ◆ Update DNS Only If DHCP Client Requests
    - ◆ Always Update DNS

◇ Discard Forward (Name-to-Address) Lookups When Lease Expires

◇ Enable Updates for DNS Clients That Do Not Support Dynamic Update

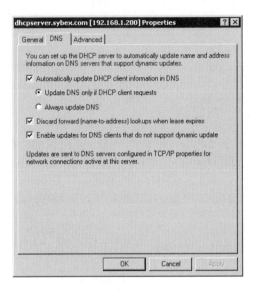

Each of these options will be discussed in the following sections.

Update DNS Only If DHCP Client Requests

This option is the default. During the lease negotiation, the client will request that it update its own A record and that the DHCP server update the PTR record. Therefore, the DHCP server has been "requested" to update the DNS database.

By choosing the Update DNS Only If DHCP Client Requests option,

◇ The DHCP server sends the PTR record update request.

◇ The client sends the A record update request.

Always Update DNS

If this option is selected, the DHCP server sends the update requests for both the A and the PTR records. An administrator may choose this option when the DHCP client is on a remote network and the local DHCP server can more conveniently send the update.

By choosing the Always Update DNS option,

- ◇ The DHCP server sends PTR and A record update requests.
- ◇ The client does nothing.

Discard Forward (Name-to-Address) Lookups When Lease Expires

This option is enabled by default, and it's a good idea for administrators to leave it checked. It sets the DHCP server to be in charge of removing the DNS entries when the lease expires. With this set, even if the client is not online when the lease expires, the DHCP server will request that both the A and PTR records are removed from DNS.

Enable Updates for DNS Clients That Do Not Support Dynamic Update

Before Dynamic DNS, DHCP clients did not negotiate to update DNS. Since there are still some legacy DHCP clients that were not written to use Dynamic DNS, having this option selected will force the DHCP server to update DNS for any clients that do not offer to. This option should be selected.

Statically-Assigned IP Addresses and Dynamic Update

Every time a Windows 2000 or XP client that has a statically-configured IP address comes onto a network, the client will register both its A and its PTR record. If an administrator changes the IP address, the client will send the update requests for the A and PTR records.

Configuring a Novell Netware Server for Dynamic DNS

A Novell NetWare DHCP server can be configured to update a Dynamic DNS server. The NetWare DHCP server sends the request for both the A and the PTR record to the DCHP server. Once configured, the NetWare DHCP server leases an IP address to a client and then sends the update requests to the DNS server.

To enable a NetWare DHCP server to send Dynamic DNS updates, the administrator has to configure the subnet address range. Using the DNS/DHCP Manager, there are three parameters that must be set. The first parameter to set is the range type. The range type must be set to either Dynamic BOOTP and DHCP or Dynamic DHCP.

The second parameter that must be configured is the DNS update option, which must be set to Always Update.

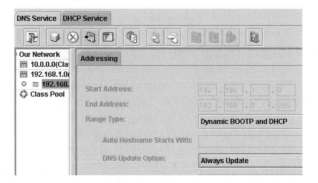

The last parameters involve choosing the subnet object that will activate Dynamic DNS and specifying the DNS zone for dynamic update. The NetWare DHCP server will also send the requests to remove the A and the PTR records when the lease has expired.

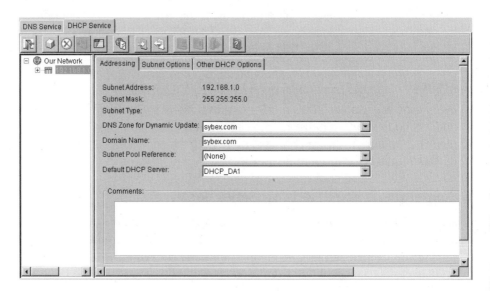

Configuring the Client for Dynamic DNS

Windows 2000 and Windows XP clients are set to update DNS by default. To modify this setting, the administrator must launch the Network and Dial-Up

Connections applet by right-clicking My Network Places and then choosing Properties. Then right-click the network connection that should be modified, and choose Properties.

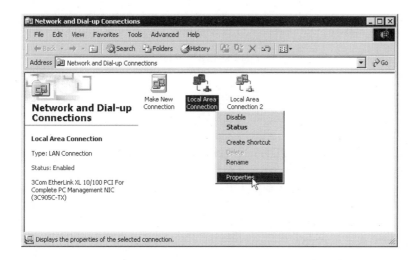

Then select TCP/IP on the Local Area Connection page, and choose Properties. From the TCP/IP Properties page, click the Advanced option. In the Advanced TCP/IP Settings page, choose DNS.

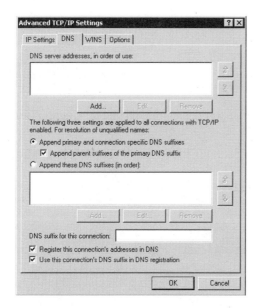

From this screen, choose whether to register the connection's address in DNS or use this connection's DNS suffix in DNS registration. If the Register This Connection's Addresses in DNS option is selected, then Dynamic DNS is enabled on the client, and the client will send the DNS update request for the A record using the FQDN and the IP address. If this option is not selected, the client will not send an update request.

If the Use This Connection's DNS Suffix in DNS Registration option is selected, the client will send the DNS update request using the first label of the computer name (like "Harry") and the DNS suffix (like "Sybex.com") for this connection. This option is useful if the DNS suffix differs from the domain name.

Another option that is available with Windows 2000 Server is secured dynamic updates, which lets the DNS server only accept registration requests from a computer that has an account in Active Directory. Once the A and the PTR records are in the DNS database, only the computer that sent the original registration request can send an update. The secure update feature will reject any updates sent from a DHCP server or client that are not encrypted. This option protects the zone and resource records against modification by unauthorized computers, and provides the ability to specify users and groups that are authorized to modify zones and resource records. To configure this option, open the Properties dialog box for the DNS server. On the General tab, set the Allow Dynamic Updates field to Only Secure Updates.

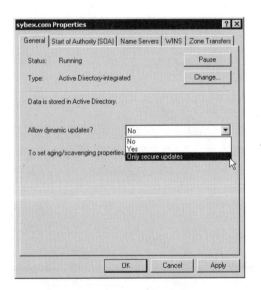

This option is only available when DNS is set to the Active Directory–integrated type. More information about secure Dynamic DNS is in RFC 2137.

Most DNS server's today support Dynamic DNS; some applications rely on Dynamic DNS. For example, Active Directory can use only a DNS server that supports Dynamic DNS. Active Directory dynamically registers services (SRV records), and then Active Directory clients query DNS for the SRV records to find the IP address of a service that it needs. A domain controller is an example of a service that the client will need the IP address for. During installation of Active Directory, the installation programs search out and confirm that the DNS server to be used supports Dynamic DNS. If the DNS server that was to be used does not support Dynamic DNS, the installer is given the option to install and begin using Microsoft's DNS.

Dynamic DNS on the Internet

Many ISPs use DHCP to deliver IP addresses to their customers. This makes it difficult for the home user to set up a Web site or FTP site on their home computer and to make it easily accessible to friends and family. It is difficult because every time the user connects to the ISP, their IP address may change. This makes it difficult for anyone to connect to a host when the IP address can change on any given day.

Rather than notify all of the family and friends of the new IP address, a home user can now subscribe to a Dynamic DNS server on the Internet. There are several of these DNS servers available that will allow Dynamic DNS updates from a home user when the host gets an IP address from their ISP's DHCP server. The home Web master can give the name of their site to friends and family, and each time the Web site comes online, a dynamic update is sent to a DNS server.

Benefits of Dynamic DNS

The benefits of using Dynamic DNS are realized by both administrators and users. The administrator no longer has to make constant and error-prone updates to the DNS database. Users will get resolution to information that is more current and accurate than what was possible with the old manual DNS database. Once configured, the Dynamic DNS transactions take place transparently. The users don't know about them, the users don't need to know about them, and the users don't need to do anything about them. As often as a host's IP address changes, the name of the host will be available in DNS. The users on the network will then be able to get name resolution to that host, even if that machine got a dynamic IP address just minutes ago that is different from the IP address it received several hours ago.

Review Questions

1. What are the two services that are necessary for Dynamic DNS?

2. What makes Dynamic DNS dynamic?

3. What is FQDN?

4. What resource records are added to the DNS database automatically?

5. In the default Dynamic DNS arrangement, which host sends which resource record update request?

6. When a lease expires on an IP address, which requests the resource records removed, the DHCP server or the client?

7. What happens if a client is using an older operating system that wasn't written to use Dynamic DNS?

8. When a Windows 2000 client comes onto the network and has a statically-assigned IP address, how does dynamic update occur?

_____

_____

Chapter

14

Windows Internet Naming Service (WINS)

I n the previous chapters, you learned that most applications are written to use host names and host name resolution. You also learned that some applications are written to use NetBIOS names and NetBIOS name resolution. In this chapter, you will learn more about a NetBIOS name resolution service provided by Microsoft called Windows Internet Naming Service, or WINS.

WINS is a local database of NetBIOS names and IP addresses. The WINS service provides resolution from the WINS database to its clients when a NetBIOS name-to-IP-address resolution is needed.

In this chapter you will learn about:

 NetBIOS applications

 NetBIOS name resolution without WINS

 NetBIOS name resolution with WINS

 WINS Manager

NetBIOS Applications

Many networks today are made up of a combination of workstations that use Windows 95/98, Windows NT, or Windows 2000 as their desktop operating system. A handful of applications have been written that use the NetBIOS names of these hosts instead of their host name. For example, a user on a network can open an application called Network Neighborhood and see the names of other workstations and servers. Network Neighborhood displays the NetBIOS names of other hosts.

When a Microsoft host is starting and building its TCP/IP stack, several NetBIOS services begin. These NetBIOS services will provide a service either to the local host or to other hosts in the network. Some of the NetBIOS services that a host may provide include the **workstation service** and the **server service**.

These services are like applications that are running on the host. The host automatically starts these services and offers them to other hosts. For example, the server service enables other hosts to connect to and share files from the host that is offering the service. The NetBIOS name and the service that are being offered must be unique on the network; no other host can be offering the same NetBIOS name and service.

NetBIOS Name Resolution Process without WINS

A computer's NetBIOS name needs to be resolved to an IP address for TCP/IP to communicate with that host. If the host cannot resolve the NetBIOS name to an IP address, communication will not occur. NetBIOS name resolution was developed many years ago for use without WINS. Microsoft TCP/IP clients can still use NetBIOS name resolution without WINS. However, WINS offers several improvements that you will learn about later in this chapter.

workstation service
A NetBIOS service that performs workstation activities such as using the local operating system.

server service
A NetBIOS service that performs server activities such as file sharing.

Name Registration

Before NetBIOS name resolution can take place, the NetBIOS hosts must go through a process of registering their NetBIOS names. The process of NetBIOS name resolution begins when a TCP/IP host that is running NetBIOS services starts; the host broadcasts a NetBIOS name registration packet that includes its NetBIOS name and the service that it offers. If any other host on the network receives the broadcast and has the same name, it sends back a **negative acknowledgment**. The registering host listens for any negative acknowledgments, and if none are received, the host assumes that it has a unique name. However, if a negative acknowledgment is returned, an error message is displayed telling the user that the NetBIOS name is already in use.

In the following screen capture, a name registration packet is being broadcast onto the network to register the NetBIOS name Harry. Notice that the name registration packet is *broadcast* from Harry.

```
182   HARRY        *BROADCAST   NBT      NS: Registration req. for HARRY          <03>             H
◄                                                                                            ►
⊕FRAME: Base frame properties
⊕ETHERNET: ETYPE = 0x0800 : Protocol = IP:  DOD Internet Protocol
⊕IP: ID = 0x3600; Proto = UDP; Len: 96
⊕UDP: Src Port: NETBIOS Name Service, (137); Dst Port: NETBIOS Name Service (137); Length = 76 (0x4C)
⊕NBT: NS: Registration req. for HARRY          <03>
```

As all the hosts come online and broadcast their NetBIOS names and services, there will be no duplicates. The host may be offering several NetBIOS services and will broadcast each. On a network, the second host that wants an existing NetBIOS name would not be able to start any NetBIOS services that already existed on the network. When a host powers down, or leaves the network, that NetBIOS name becomes available because another host can then come online and broadcast that name and the original name holder will not be online to generate a negative acknowledgment.

Suppose there is a conference and a requirement of the conference is that no two people have the same name. As new members walk into the conference room, they broadcast their names. Harry walks in, and in a very loud voice broadcasts, "I am Harry." All the other conference attendees examine their name tags to see whether their name is Harry. If someone else named Harry is already in the room, he'd yell back, "Sorry, Harry, I'm already here." Harry the newcomer would not be allowed to participate in the conference. As more people enter the conference room, they continue broadcasting their names, and the other attendees examine their name tags to make sure that there are no conflicts.

negative acknowledgment

An acknowledgment sent from a host or server that says, "I received your request and the answer is no."

253

The Conference—Name Registration without WINS

The illustration below shows Harry walking into a conference room and broadcasting that his name is Harry. The others check their name tags for any conflicts. Again, this is analogous to NetBIOS name registration.

NetBIOS name cache

Recently resolved NetBIOS names and IP addresses stored in RAM for rapid resolution.

NetBIOS name query

A packet asking for the IP address of a host with a particular NetBIOS name.

Name Resolution

Now you have learned how NetBIOS name registration takes place, the next issue is name resolution. When a host on a network wants to communicate with another host that is using a NetBIOS application, the initiating host uses the NetBIOS name resolution methods as described in Chapter 11.

The first place to look for NetBIOS resolution is in the **NetBIOS name cache**. Possibly the name was recently resolved or was configured with the LMHOSTS file to be permanently in NetBIOS name cache. If the NetBIOS name is not in NetBIOS name cache, and the host is not configured for WINS, a **NetBIOS name query** is broadcast.

The NetBIOS name query packet contains the NetBIOS name in question and the IP address of the originator. The name query is broadcast to the network asking for the owner of the name to respond with an IP address.

The screen capture below shows a host named Sally broadcasting a name query request (Query Req) for a node named Harry. Notice that the packet source is Sally and the destination is addressed to "Broadcast."

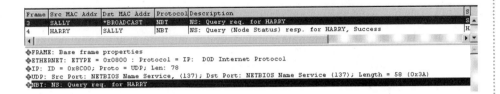

Each host examines itself as the name query broadcast is received. When the owner of the name recognizes itself as a match, a name query response is sent back to the originator of the query. The response includes the NetBIOS name and IP address of the destination. Now that the originator has the IP address of the destination, TCP/IP will begin the communication process with the destination.

The following screen capture shows the positive response that Harry sends back to Sally with his IP address in the last line of the screen capture. The source of the packet is Harry, and the destination is Sally.

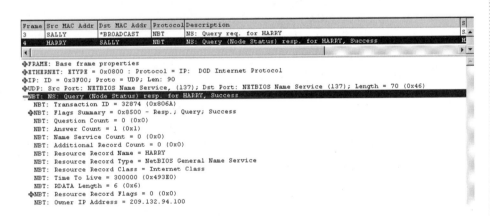

To continue with the example of the conference, suppose that everyone in the conference has a separate telephone. When one person wants to talk to another at the conference, the only way to get the other person's number is to broadcast for the person. If Sally wants to have a communication with Harry, she just shouts in the conference room, "Hey Harry, what's your number? My number is x531." As everybody in the room hears that name query broadcast, they examine their name tags. When Harry recognizes that Sally must be talking about him, Harry picks up his phone and calls x531. He says, "This is Harry. I understand that you want to talk with me; my number is x220." Now Sally, the originator of the name query, has Harry's telephone number and is able to begin communicating.

The Conference—Name Resolution without WINS

The following illustration shows Sally shouting for Harry in the same way that NetBIOS name queries are broadcast.

network bandwidth
The amount of data that can be put onto a network based on other communication traffic already using the wire.

This process of NetBIOS name resolution is efficient and works fine on a small network. As the network grows, however, this method becomes unacceptable. Imagine the conference in the preceding example with 10 people in the conference room. The number of broadcasts in the room would be acceptable and probably an efficient method of name-to-number resolution. If the coordinators of the conference decided to give free food and suddenly 1,000 people attended, the number of broadcasts would be out of control. Broadcast would then be an unacceptable and inefficient method of name resolution.

As networks got larger and it became obvious that broadcasting for NetBIOS name resolution was inefficient and consuming a great deal of **network bandwidth**, a solution was developed to rectify the problem. Imagine that conference room with 1,000 people and try to think of a more efficient way for people to get name resolution to one another's numbers.

NetBIOS Name Resolution Process with WINS

To decrease the inefficiency of using broadcasts to resolve NetBIOS names, the **NetBIOS name server** was created. A NetBIOS name server contains a dynamic database of NetBIOS names and IP addresses. WINS is a service that acts as a NetBIOS name server. The WINS service can be installed on a Windows NT server.

The IP address of the WINS server must be configured for any hosts that will use that WINS server. Since the administrator might not use a WINS server, the WINS IP address is an optional parameter of the TCP/IP configuration. An administrator can manually enter the IP address of the WINS server for every host, or if the network is set up to use DHCP, the WINS server address can be set up as an optional parameter that is supplied with the automatic IP address.

Name Registration

For a TCP/IP client that is configured to use WINS, the process of name registration changes a bit. Now, as the host is connecting to the network, rather than broadcast a name registration packet, the host sends a name registration packet directly to the WINS server. The name registration packet includes the NetBIOS name, IP address, and the NetBIOS services that the host is registering. The WINS server looks in the database to see whether another host has already registered that NetBIOS name. If there are no other entries with that NetBIOS name, the WINS server sends a positive acknowledgment back to the host.

Using WINS for name-to-IP-address resolution is similar to having a registrar at the conference described earlier in this chapter. The illustration below shows Rita the Registrar at the conference. Rita will handle registrations and resolutions.

NetBIOS name server
A server that registers and resolves NetBIOS names.

If you have any questions, ask Rita.

**Rita
Registrar of Conference**

Jim

Susan

Martha

Name Registration with WINS

The following screen capture shows a name registration request for the NetBIOS name Harry. The name registration is not broadcast; it is sent directly to the WINS server. The registration packet includes the name to be registered and Harry's IP address. Also in the screen capture, the second captured packet (frame 10) is the WINS server's positive response to Harry.

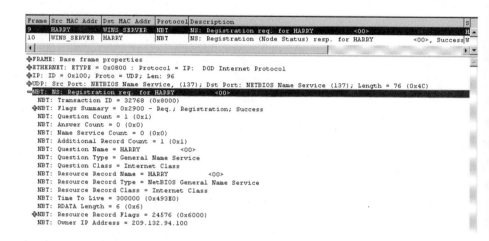

If the WINS server finds that a host has already registered that NetBIOS name, the WINS server sends a challenge. Three challenge packets are sent to the IP address of the host that registered that name. The challenge packets are simply asking, "Hey, are you still there?" If the host responds that it is still there and online, a negative acknowledgment is sent back to the other host that is requesting the registration. That host will then get an error message that a duplicate NetBIOS name exists. If the challenge goes unanswered, then the WINS server has to assume that the original host is no longer there. The server then updates the WINS database and sends a positive acknowledgment to the host requesting the registration.

If a host sends a name registration request to the WINS server and the WINS server does not respond, the host will resend the request up to three times before giving up. If the host gets no response from the WINS server after three tries, the host broadcasts the name registration request and listens for other hosts to send a negative acknowledgment. Therefore, when the new, better WINS service doesn't seem to be working, the client will go to the name registration method as if WINS didn't exist.

When we apply the WINS server to our conference example, name registration becomes a simple process. As people enter the conference room, they simply tell the registrar their names. As Harry comes into the conference, the registrar looks through the conference registration database and confirms that no one else in the conference is named Harry. If someone already has registered that name, the registrar calls their number and confirms that they are still at the conference. If no one answers at that number, the registrar will try two more times to be absolutely sure that they are no longer at the conference. If after three tries there is still no answer, the registrar updates the registration database with Harry's information and welcomes the new Harry to the conference with a positive name registration acknowledgment.

The illustration below shows Harry registering for the conference and the registrar looking at the database for any conflicts. Again, this is similar to NetBIOS name registration with WINS.

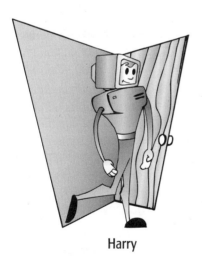

Harry

Rita
Registrar of Conference

Name Resolution

When using WINS, NetBIOS name resolution is a simple process that begins by sending the WINS sever a name query. Instead of broadcasting, a host that is trying to get NetBIOS name resolution simply sends a name query to the WINS server. The WINS server examines the WINS database and sends back either a positive or a negative response.

If the NetBIOS name being requested exists in the WINS database, the NetBIOS name and IP address are returned to the originator of the name query. This is a positive name query response. The host now has the IP address of the destination host and TCP/IP will begin communicating with that host.

The screen capture below shows two packets. The first packet (frame 1) is Sally's name resolution request being sent to the WINS server. The packet is not broadcast; it goes directly to the WINS server. The second packet (frame 2), which is expanded, shows the WINS server responding to Sally with the IP address for the NetBIOS name Harry.

If the NetBIOS name is not in the WINS database, the server sends a response to the originator of the request stating that the NetBIOS name is not registered. This is a negative name query response. When a negative name query response is returned to the originator of the name query, that host will continue with the next method of NetBIOS name resolution, which is to broadcast for name resolution.

In the conference room analogy, whenever someone wants to talk to someone else, they simply call the registrar. When Sally wants to talk to Harry, she calls the registrar. The registrar is able to look at the most current listing of attendees and give either a positive or negative response. In a positive response, the registrar returns the name and number to the originator of the name query. Sally can now contact Harry. If the registrar returns a negative response, which means that she does not have an entry for Harry, Sally will politely say thank you to the registrar, hang up the phone, and then broadcast for Harry. As long as the database is current, the registrar will be able to resolve most queries.

The following illustration shows Sally asking the registrar for Harry's number, in the same way that a host on the network will send a query to the WINS server to get NetBIOS name resolution to another host.

Now imagine that instead of just a couple of people at the conference, there are 1,000. This means there are 1,000 registrations and 1,000 people using the database for resolution. The chore of being the registrar could be overwhelming as the number of attendees grows. Doing both registrations and resolutions would be exhausting.

On a network, the WINS service consumes resources on the server on which it's installed. The number of WINS clients and the number of NetBIOS applications determines the overall draw on the server. It is estimated that one WINS server can service 10,000 clients. Although only one WINS server is necessary, it is recommended that a second WINS server be used for fault tolerance and redundancy. In any case, an administrator has to closely monitor the NetBIOS name resolution drain on the server resources. WINS servers can also be configured to share databases in a large internetwork.

Because WINS clients send registration and resolution requests directly to a WINS server, one WINS server can service many subnets. The name registrations and requests are not broadcast, so they will go through routers to the WINS server.

When a WINS client is properly shut down, the client sends a name release request to the WINS server. This lets the WINS server know that that NetBIOS name is no longer in use by that host. The WINS server marks that entry in the database as no longer in use. Now, when another host wants to register that NetBIOS name, the WINS server knows that it is available.

WINS Manager

To administer the WINS database, an administrator uses the WINS Manager utility. On a Windows NT server, the WINS service must be installed and the hosts configured to register with the WINS server. The WINS Manager is located by clicking Start ➢ Programs ➢ Administrative Tools ➢ WINS Manager.

Below is a screen capture of the WINS Manager utility. The entries in this WINS database include several NetBIOS names and IP addresses. This database will be used for resolution when any host that is configured to use it requests resolution. Some of the NetBIOS names that you may recognize include a few entries for Sally and the NT domain named Jumpstart.

static entry
A manual entry in the WINS database that is made by the administrator for a non-WINS client.

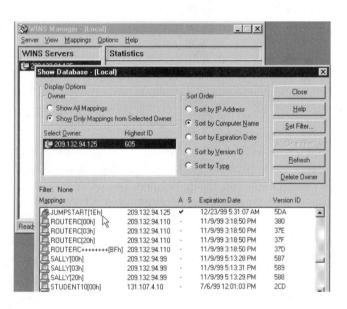

The entries include the NetBIOS name of the host, the IP address of the host, the expiration date, and the time of the entry. Another column shows the version of each entry. This hexadecimal version number starts at 1 and continues to increment as each entry is entered or updated. This is how the WINS service knows the most recent changes to the database. Every service that each NetBIOS host is registering must have a particular entry in the database; that is why there are multiple entries for each NetBIOS name.

On an internetwork that has non-WINS clients, an administrator may decide to manually enter the name of each non-WINS client into the WINS database. This is called a **static entry**. The benefit of configuring a static entry in the WINS database is that no host that registers with this WINS database can use the statically configured name. An additional benefit is that all the WINS clients can now get resolution to the non-WINS host.

To configure a static entry in WINS, enter the WINS Manager, click the Mappings menu, and choose Static Mappings, as shown below.

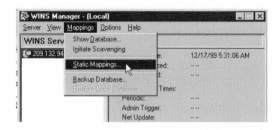

Click the Add Mappings button, then fill in the dialog box and click Add to complete adding an entry. In the Type field, you can specify the type of service that the non-WINS client is configured for and needs to have entered in the WINS database. In the screen capture below, a static mapping has been configured for the Administration server.

Now that the mapping has been configured, WINS will not let any WINS clients register with the name of ADMIN_SRV. If any WINS clients try to get resolution to ADMIN_SRV, the WINS database will be able to provide that resolution.

WINS provides an excellent service for automatically registering NetBIOS names and performing NetBIOS name resolution. Many networks today use WINS and a responsibility of many network administrators is to maintain WINS.

Review Questions

Terms to Know
- ❑ workstation service
- ❑ server service
- ❑ negative acknowledgment
- ❑ NetBIOS name cache
- ❑ NetBIOS name query
- ❑ network bandwidth
- ❑ NetBIOS name server
- ❑ static entry

1. What does WINS stand for?

2. Without WINS, how does name registration take place?

3. List two NetBIOS services.

4. If WINS receives a NetBIOS name registration, and that name has already been registered, describe what the WINS server does.

5. When a workstation not using WINS powers down, is a name release packet broadcast?

6. When a workstation using WINS powers down, is a name release packet sent to the WINS server?

7. If a WINS server replies to a host with a negative acknowledgment, what does the host do next?

8. Where is the first place that TCP/IP looks to resolve a NetBIOS name?

_____

9. Describe what a WINS server does when a registration comes in and there is already an entry for the NetBIOS name in the database.

_____

10. How does a TCP/IP host know where to find a WINS server?

_____

Chapter

15

IP Version 6

Throughout this book, you have looked at TCP/IP addresses used with Internet Protocol version 4. Because of the enormous growth of the Internet and other factors that you will learn about in this chapter, IP version 4 is going to be replaced by IP version 6.

Most of the principles you have learned in this book apply to IPv6; some have been updated and some replaced. It will be useful in working with IPv6 to have a good foundational knowledge of IPv4.

In this chapter you will learn about:

 The need for a new version of IP

 IPv6's form of addressing

 Plans for the proposed transition from IPv4 to IPv6

The Need for a New Version of TCP/IP

The Internet Protocol that is a standard today was created in the early 1970s. The current version is **Internet Protocol version 4 (IPv4)**. IPv4 has proven to be a stable and fully developed protocol; however, due to the enormous growth of the Internet, IPv4 is no longer viable. **Internet Protocol version 6 (IPv6)** will soon replace IPv4 as the Internet standard. IPv6 is also called **Internet Protocol, Next Generation (IPng)**.

IPng was proposed and recommended at an IETF meeting in July 1994 (in RFC 1752). The proposal to replace IPv4 as the Internet Protocol was accepted by the Internet Engineering Steering Group, and IPng became a proposed standard. In August 1998, the proposed standard was upgraded to draft standard. Many RFCs have been written about IPv6 and are available on the Internet for further examination.

The Name of the New Protocol

The reason that we are going from IPv4 to IPv6 and not IPv5 is that a protocol named IPv5 already exists and is referred to in RFC 1946 as ST2 and ST2+. IPv5 is not a replacement for IPv4 and has very limited use.

The Next Generation references *Star Trek, the Next Generation*. This protocol suite will replace IPv4 just as the Next Generation crew replaced the old crew of the USS *Enterprise*.

IPng is not just an IPv4 upgrade; it is an overhauled protocol. Many of the features are similar, and the foundational methods of IPv4 are still the same. However, the addressing is different, and the headers are more specialized and lighter. IPv6 provides more options, including more flow control and enhanced security.

Since early 1998, a testing and preproduction network for IPv6 on the Internet has been online. This network, called **6BONE**, has grown to more than 400 sites and interconnecting networks in 40 countries. With the 6BONE network stabilizing, a transition to IPv6 will begin soon. The transition to a total IPv6 network is expected to take up to 10 years. Once implemented, IPv6 should be the standard for decades. The transition is described later in this chapter.

Internet Protocol version 4 (IPv4)
The current version of IP that has been in use for over 20 years.

Internet Protocol version 6 (IPv6)
The formal name of the new version of IP that will be the new standard.

Internet Protocol, Next Generation (IPng)
The informal name of IPv6.

6BONE
The IPv6 backbone that is currently being used to build and test the IPv6 network infrastructure.

IPv6 Addressing

IPv4 is running out of network addresses, and routing tables are overflowing. In the early '90s, it was evident that something had to be done. Committees and teams were formed among many corporations and engineers. The result of the collaborative research and testing is IPv6. The design engineers have focused their improvements in the areas of addressing, efficiency, and enhanced security.

This section focuses on the addressing used in IPv6. The new protocol will provide many more IP addresses than the present version. And these new addresses will be written in hexadecimal form and will require a new type of notation.

IPv4 Addresses and IPv6 Addresses

In IPv4, there are 32 bits in every address. This means that there are approximately 4 billion unique IP addresses. This would have been enough addresses to support the original purpose of the ARPAnet. But as the ARPAnet grew into the Internet, and an enormous number of hosts connected to the network, IP addresses have been depleted.

IPv6 uses 128-bit addresses, which are exponentially larger than the address size of IPv4. Therefore, IPv6 supports a number of addresses that is 4 billion times the 4 billion addresses of the IPv4 address space. This works out to be:

IPv4 addresses (2^{32}):

4,294,967,296

IPv6 addresses (2^{128}):

340,282,366,920,938,463,463,374,607,431,768,211,456

This is an extremely large number of unique IP addresses. To put that number into an easier-to-comprehend concept, assume the Earth's surface is 511,263,971,197,990 square meters. Then, for every square meter of the surface of the Earth, there would be 665,570,793,348,866,943,898,599 unique IP addresses.

Harry—The Next Generation

The following illustration shows Harry the Host in the IPv4 world as one of a few hosts; but with IPv6, Harry will be one of a huge number.

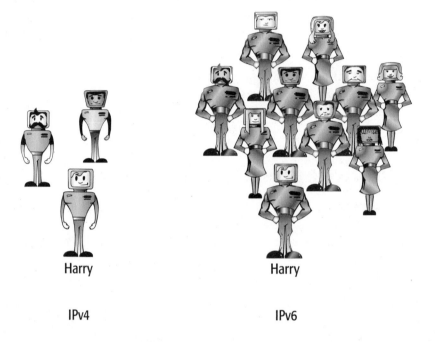

Harry

IPv4

Harry

IPv6

Why should we be able to use so many IP addresses? Did the designers go overboard? One plan proposed 64-bit addresses. But the designers of IPv6 determined that that might limit the growth of the network in the future.

Think of the future and the types of products that might need a unique IP address. It's possible to imagine that every item in your house will be connected to the Internet. You will be able to control air conditioning and heating through the Internet. Some other appliances that might be accessible to the Web include lighting, microwave ovens, refrigerators, automobile parts, cell phones, laptop computers, pagers, VCRs, and stereos. Because these appliances will be connected to the Internet, they will have a unique IP address.

Use your imagination to continue the list. Your Web-enabled refrigerator will be available to you and the manufacturer through the Web. Maybe you'll check the contents of the fridge through a Web browser before you leave work. Before you leave work, you'll access any item in your home over the Internet. You'll start dinner, adjust the temperature, and bring the car around to the front of the building. Is this possible? We'll see, but in any case, we'll have an addressing scheme that would provide enough addresses.

The New Hexadecimal IPv6 Addresses

In this book, you have looked at IPv4. These addresses are 32-bit addresses that look like this:

192.168.2.100

IPv6 addresses are 128-bit addresses and are written in hexadecimal form. You will recall from Chapter 3 that the hexadecimal numbering system uses the same 0 to 9 digits as decimal, then uses A, B, C, D, E, and F to represent 10, 11, 12, 13, 14, and 15. The decimal 16 is represented in hexadecimal as 10. The address below is an example of an IPv6 address taken from RFCs 1884 and 1924, which describe IPv6 addressing and encoding:

EFDC:BA62:7654:3201:EFDC:BA72:7654:3210

This is an example of the "full" IPv6 address wherein all 32 hex digits have a value that is significant. An IPv6 address with many 0s can be as short as eight hex digits. Because the IPv6 addresses are 128 bits in length, a new written standard has to be implemented. Using the IPv4 style of addresses, a 128-bit address would be represented by as many as 63 decimal numbers. Because that would be unreasonable, hexadecimal numbers are used to represent the binary addresses. Each section of hex characters represents 16 bits of the address. These 32 hex characters use 7 colons as separators. This address is referred to as a 39-character address (32 + 7). Some addresses will have several 0s within the address. For example:

1080:0000:0000:0000:0008:0800:200C:417A

To make notation of this address easier, the nonsignificant and leading 0s can be dropped. So the above address can be written as:

1080:0:0:0:8:800:200C:417A

Even this shortened address seems too long. Fortunately, we can shorten it one more time. Because the address has several consecutive 0s, we can drop those and just push the colons together. The above address can be written using the **double-colon notation** method as:

1080::8:800:200C:417A

---

double-colon notation

A shorthand method of writing IPv6 addresses without including non-significant 0s.

Double-Colon Notation

Whenever you see an address that uses double-colon notation, it won't be instantly obvious how many and which 0s are missing. Expanding an address that uses the double-colon notation is a two-step process for humans. First, write eight *x*s separated by colons, and replace the *x*s with values in the address that are to the left of the double-colon, moving from left to right. For example:

    1080:x:x:x:x:x:x:x

Then, starting from the furthest right side of the address, replace *x*s with values moving from right to left. For example:

    1080:x:x:x:x:x:x:417A

    1080:x:x:x:x:x:200C:417A

    1080:x:x:x:x:800:200C:417A

    1080:x:x:x:8:800:200C:417A

Now that the given values have been exhausted, replace each of the remaining *x*s with a 0.

    1080:0:0:0:8:800:200C:417A

TIP

An important rule in double-colon notation is that double colons can be used only once in an address.

An IPv4 address can be used within the IPv6 addressing scheme. The hexadecimal IPv4 address is placed in the last 32 bits of the IPv6 address. For example, the IPv4 address of

    192.168.2.100

within an IPv6 address is

    ::C0A8:0264

(which is using the double-colon notation for 0:0:0:0:0:0:C0A8:0264).

Converting decimal to hexadecimal is simply accomplished by using a calculator.

TEST IT OUT: CONVERTING IPV4 ADDRESSES TO IPV6 ADDRESSES

To convert an IPv4 to an IPv6 address, you first convert each section of the decimal address to hexadecimal. Then, because each hex value must be represented by two characters, you add a 0 to any values that have only one digit. Next, simply put the converted first and second octets together to form a four-character hex value. Finally, insert a colon and do the same for the converted third and fourth octet.

As an example, try converting 10.153.92.151 to an IPv6 address. The solution is:

1. Using a decimal to hex calculator, convert decimal 10 to hex:

   10 = A

2. Convert decimal 153 to hex:

   153 = 99

3. Convert decimal 92 to hex:

   92 = 5C

4. Convert decimal 151 to hex:

   151 = 97

5. Each of these hex values must be represented by two characters. Add a 0 to any values that have only one digit (A becomes 0A).

6. Put the hex digits together: 0A99:5C97

Now try this example: Convert 192.168.15.73 to an IPv6 address. The solution is as follows:

1. 192 = C0
2. 168 = A8
3. 15 = F
4. 73 = 49
5. F becomes 0F
6. Putting all the hex digits together, you have C0A8:0F49.

IPv6 Special Addresses

Many regulations apply to IPv6 addressing and many RFCs have been written about them. As the roll-out of IPv6 continues, many of these regulations will become common practice for administrators. Below are a couple of the more interesting regulations regarding special addressing concerns of IPv6.

The Unspecified Address

The address 0:0:0:0:0:0:0:0 is called the unspecified address. It must never be assigned to any host. It indicates the absence of an address. An unspecified address is used, for example, when an IPv6 host sends a packet seeking an address. The source address portion of the packet will contain the unspecified address. This is similar to a host sending a DHCP packet trying to discover an address.

The Loopback Address

The loopback address in IPv6 is 0:0:0:0:0:0:0:1. A host uses this address to send an IPv6 packet to itself. It can never be assigned to any host. This is similar to the IPv4 address of 127.0.0.1. Administrators use this address to aid in troubleshooting TCP/IP issues. As discussed earlier, an administrator can ping the loopback address to confirm that TCP/IP is bound correctly to the network card.

IPv6 Documentation

Many corporations and individuals are diligently working on the transition to IPv6. More than 180 RFCs have been published that reference this new standard. These RFCs cover everything from the inception of IPv6 to the transition plans. They include issues about addressing, header information, routing, and the organizations that will monitor IPv6.

These RFCs can be located by accessing the companion Web site for this book, which is referenced in Appendix D. In the next decade, network administrators will be called upon to aid in the transition to IPv6. The administrators who begin working in IPv6 soon will be in the greatest demand mid-transition. Therefore, it is important that network administrators get a handle on IPv6 as soon as possible. Training and hands-on experience will be invaluable. Several Web sites have been set up to involve volunteers in the IPv4 to IPv6 transition.

Improvements of IPv6

You learned in an earlier section about the dramatic increase of potential addresses that IPv6 will offer. Some of the other key improvements in IPv6 include:

◇ Enhanced security (described in RFC 1827).

◇ New types of packet addressing with multicast and anycast addressing.

◇ New IPv6 RFCs for protocols that have been discussed in this book, including DHCP, DNS, ICMP, IP, TCP and UDP. With the new IPv6 headers being streamlined, these other TCP/IP protocols have been improved.

Some redundant IPv4 header fields have been eliminated or made optional. The amount of resources used by every host and router to process a packet is reduced, which increases the amount of available bandwidth. Even though the IPv6 address is four times larger than an IPv4 address, the IPv6 headers are only twice as large. This means that packets are "slicker" and tighter without much extra, useless padding to slow them down.

Packets in IPv6 can have labels indicating that they belong to a certain flow, or group, of packets. Therefore, as the flow of packets moves through a router, the routers can keep certain similar packet types moving together, while other packets with a lower priority wait. This gives the sender the possibility of a **real-time** service. Such services include video conferencing and other communications that need to move through the Internet with the highest priority for almost immediate or real-time reception.

IPv6 describes rules for three types of addressing:

Unicast   One host to one other host. This is similar to much of the addressing that you have looked at in this book.

Anycast   One host to the nearest of multiple hosts. This type of address is used to send a packet to a group of hosts, but only the nearest host processes the packet. The idea is that the host that receives the packet can relay the information to the other hosts in the group. This type of addressing did not exist with IPv4.

Multicast   One host to multiple hosts. This type of address is similar to the multicast that you learned about in this book.

An IPv6 packet contains options that are specified as part of the header that is examined only at the destination, thus speeding up overall network performance.

real-time
A type of data that is available instantaneously. The term usually refers to video or audio conferencing.

unicast
A packet that is sent from one host to one other host.

anycast
A packet that is sent from one host to the nearest host within a group of hosts.

multicast
A packet that is sent from one host to many other hosts at the same time.

The Transition Plan to IPv6

RFC 1933 describes a plan to transition the existing IPv4 Internet to the new IPv6 Internet. A major consideration is how to convert the Internet into IPv6 without disrupting the operation of the existing IPv4 network. This proposal has a nickname of **SIT (Simple IPv6 Transition)**.

Simple IPv6 Transition (SIT)

The proposed plan to transition to IPv6.

The transition plan includes two phases. The first phase includes upgrading several components to the IPv6 level so that at the end of phase 1, there will be a combination of both IPv4 and IPv6 hosts and routers on the Internet. In the second phase of the transition, the remaining IPv4 addresses and components will be replaced, so that by the end of phase 2, there will be only IPv6 hosts and routers.

Some of the key objectives that SIT must comply with are detailed in the Simple IPv6 Transition proposal. These include:

- ◇ IPv6 and IPv4 hosts can coexist on the Internet during the transition. There will be no "cut-over" date, so IPv4 hosts can continue to operate on the IPv6 network.

- ◇ IPv6 routers and hosts can be deployed across the Internet in an independent fashion. Existing IPv4 hosts and routers may be upgraded to IPv6 at any time without being dependent on any other hosts or routers being upgraded.

- ◇ The transition will be as easy as possible for end users, system administrators, and network operators to understand and carry out. As existing IPv4 hosts or routers are upgraded to IPv6, they will continue to use their existing addresses in the IPv6 form.

- ◇ IPv6 will have minimal upgrade dependencies. DNS servers will be the first component to be upgraded to handle IPv6 addresses. There are no prerequisites to upgrading routers.

- ◇ IPv6 will have low startup costs. Budget considerations are always an issue. There must be little or no preparation work to upgrade existing IPv4 systems to IPv6, or to deploy new IPv6 systems.

The following illustration shows the upgraded protocol. Harry is working in a leaner, meaner, and more efficient network. Data transfer is faster, and security is enhanced.

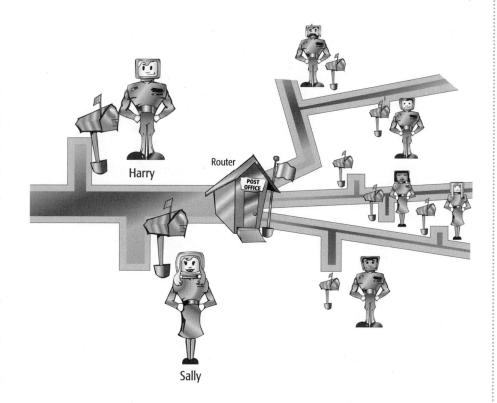

Review Questions

1. IPv4 uses _____ bit addresses.

2. IPv6 uses _____ bit addresses.

3. Write the following IPv6 address with the least amount of characters:
   109A:3210:0:0:0:0:0213:412B

   _____

4. Convert the following IPv4 address to an IPv6 address: 10.25.135.123

   _____

5. Convert the following IPv4 address to an IPv6 address: 192.168.31.4

   _____

6. Expand the following IPv6 address to display all 39 characters (colons count as a character) that are compressed with the double-colon notation:
   A013:1234:34::8:411A

   _____

7. List two reasons why a new protocol is needed.

   _____

8. What is the name of the proposed plan to transition IPv6?

   _____

9. Describe the phases of the IPv6 transition plan.

   _____

10. How long is the proposed transition expected to take?

_____

11. Convert the following IPv4 address to an IPv6 address: `172.20.25.16`

_____

12. Convert the following IPv4 address to an IPv6 address: `127.0.0.1`

_____

Appendix A

Answers to Review Questions

Chapter 1

1. ARPAnet

2. Any three of the following: No one point can be more critical than any other; it needs on-the-fly rerouting of data; it needs redundant routes to any destination; it can connect different types of computers over different types of networks; it cannot be controlled by a single corporation.

3. Host

4. A packet-switched network sends packets of data across the network independent of one another; each of the packets takes its own route. A circuit-switched network uses the same path, or circuit, for all data.

5. Request for Comments, a paper thoroughly describing a new protocol or technology

6. NCP

7. False; TCP/IP is a suite of protocols.

8. Internet Engineering Task Force, a governing body of the Internet

9. Any four of the following: It is a widely published, open standard; it is compatible with different computer systems; it works on different hardware and network configurations; it is a routable protocol; it has reliable, efficient data delivery; it has a single addressing scheme.

10. 1983

Chapter 2

1. A protocol is a set of rules for communicating that the sending and receiving hosts use when they send data back and forth.

2. A packet is a unit of data that is sent from an originating host to a destination host on a network.

3. The OSI model was created to break down the many tasks involved in moving data from one host to another.

4. Application, Presentation, Session, Transport, Network, Data-Link, and Physical

5. Application, Transport, Internet, and Network Interface

6. IPX/SPX, TCP/IP, AppleTalk

7. Packets

8. Headers

9. Data-Link; LLC (Logical Link Control) and MAC (Media Access Control)

10. Answers will vary.

11. Answers will vary.

Chapter 3

1. Any three of the following: MAC, Ethernet, physical, or NIC

2. FF:FF:FF:FF:FF:FF

3. IP, ARP, ICMP, IGMP

4. Logical addressing and routing

5. ARP

6. 2 minutes, and up to 10 minutes if used again

7. Broadcast, FF:FF:FF:FF:FF:FF

8. The hardware address of the host that sent the ARP request

9. Ping

10. Source IP address, source hardware address, destination IP address, and destination hardware address (set to FF:FF:FF:FF:FF:FF)

11. Source IP address, source hardware address, destination IP address, and destination hardware address

12. Ethernet, Token Ring, FDDI

13. The manufacturer "burns in" the address to a chip on the card when the card is manufactured.

14. 12 hexadecimal characters

Chapter 4

1. TCP (Transmission Control Protocol) and UDP (User Datagram Protocol)

2. TCP: Connection-oriented and guaranteed; UDP: Connectionless and not guaranteed

3. Three-way handshake

4. An acknowledgment

5. UDP does not wait for acknowledgments.

6. The application

7. UDP can transfer data faster.

8. TCP guarantees delivery of data.

9. 761

10. 768

11. TCP

12. It verifies that the packet was received correctly.

Chapter 5

1. At ports

2. 65,536

3. 1–1024

4. An FTP client logs into the FTP server and requests files by using TCP/IP. The FTP server sends the requested files back to the client by using TCP/IP.

5. An HTTP client sends a request to an HTTP server by using TCP/IP. The HTTP server sends the requested files back to the client by using TCP/IP, and the files are displayed with a Web browser application.

6. SNMP, Telnet, SMTP, and TFTP

7. A host can send packets only to the gateway, and the gateway then has the responsibility of sending on the packets to their destination.

8. Yes, a server can be running several services and listening at different ports for requests.

9. The standard for HTTP requests is port 80. To "hide" a Web site, an administrator can set the Web server to listen to any other port where standard requests are not made (the administrator can set it to listen only to port 8080 or port 8090, for example). In this way, only someone who knows that the Web server is listening at the hidden port can access the Web server.

10. Internet Assigned Number Authority (IANA)

11. 80

12. IP address, Transport layer protocol (TCP or UDP), and port number

13. A nice looking, easy-to-use application used to access an FTP server.

Chapter 6

1a. 195

1b. 165

1c. 155

1d. 231

2a. 0000 1010

2b. 0011 1001

2c. 0111 1111

2d. 1111 1111

3a. 1–127

3b. 128–191

3c. 192–223

4. A Class D address is used for multicasting. A Class D address is illegal as a host IP address, but is used for sending data to several hosts at the same time.

5. 254

6. 16,384

7. 16,777,214

8. An IP broadcast address

9. The network address

10. A host cannot have an address of all 0s or all 1s; such an address is always invalid.

11. $2N - 2$

Chapter 7

1. Manually and automatically

2. Discover, offer, request, and acknowledgment

3. All four

4. Hardware address of the client

5. Server address, offered IP address, client hardware address

6. To reserve an IP address for a particular hardware address. That host will always get the same IP address.

7. Most of the time. Only in a few situations—for example, when only a few hosts are on a network—should the administrator use manually configured addresses.

8. After 50 percent of the lease has expired

9. The DHCP client's hardware address is included in the offer.

10. Servers, printers, routers

Chapter 8

1. Network portion and host portion

2. Whether the destination is local or remote

3. Network portion

4. False; it is required.

5. 255.0.0.0

6. Not enough information was given to answer this question; you must know the subnet mask.

7. 255.255.0.0

8. Yes

   Source address—Network: 176.16, Host: 2.3

   Destination address—Network:176.16, Host: 4.5

9. No

   Source address—Network: 176.16.2, Host: 3

   Destination address—Network: 176.16.4, Host: 5

10. 255.255.255.0

11. No

Source address—Network: 192.168.1, Host: 3

Destination address—Network: 192.168.2, Host: 3

12. The host portion is 37.

13. The host portion is 1.37.

14. No

Source address—Network: 10.1.2, Host: 3

Destination address—Network: 10.1.3, Host: 4

Chapter 9

1a. 255.255.255.192

1b. 150.150.0.64, 150.150.0.128, 150.150.0.192

1c. 150.150.0.65–150.150.0.126

150.150.0.129–150.150.0.190

150.150.0.193–150.150.0.254

1d. Network: 150.150.255.128

Range of IP addresses: 150.150.255.129–150.150.255.190

1e. 1,022

1f. 62

2a. 255.255.255.128

2b. 151.151.0.128, 151.151.1.0, 151.151.1.128

2c. 151.15.10.129–151.151.0.254

151.151.1.1–151.151.1.126

151.151.1.129–151.151.1.254

2d. Network: 151.151.255.0

Range of IP addresses: 151.151.255.1–151.151.255.126

2e. 510

2f. 126

3a. 255.255.255.0

3b. 152.152.1.0, 152.152.2.0, 152.152.3.0

3c. 152.152.1.1–152.152.1.254

152.152.2.1–152.152.2.254

152.152.3.1–152.152.3.254

3d. Network: 152.152.254.0

Range of IP addresses: 152.152.254.1–152.152.254.254

3e. 254

3f. 254

4a. 255.255.255.240

4b. 200.200.200.16, 200.200.200.32, 200.200.200.48

4c. 200.200.200.17–200.200.200.30

200.200.200.33–200.200.200.47

200.200.200.49–200.200.200.62

4d. Network: 200.200.200.224

Range of IP addresses: 200.200.200.225–200.200.200.238

4e. 14

4f. 14

5a. 255.255.255.224

5b. 201.201.201.32, 201.201.201.64, 201.201.201.96

5c. 201.201.201.33–201.201.201.62

201.201.201.65–201.201.201.94

201.201.201.97–201.201.201.126

5d. Network: 201.201.201.192

IP address range: 201.201.201.193–201.201.201.222

5e. 6

5f. 30

6. Trick question; the address is invalid.

7. 255.255.255.192

8. 255.255.252.0

9. 255.255.254.0

10. 255.255.128.0

11a. 254

11b. 65,534

Chapter 10

1. Class B address exhaustion and overloaded routing tables.

2. It began assigning contiguous Class Cs.

3. 255.255.252.0

4. 255.255.240.0

5. 21

6. 1

7. 192.168.1.0/27

8. 192.168.1.0/28

9. 10.0.0.0/17

10. 176.16.0.0/17

Chapter 11

1. Host name resolution and NetBIOS name resolution

2. Local host, HOSTS file, DNS, NetBIOS name cache, WINS, broadcast, LMHOSTS file

3. NetBIOS name cache, WINS, broadcast, LMHOSTS file, HOSTS file, DNS

4. The IP address needs to be on the left.

5. Put an entry in the HOSTS file for www.sybex.com.

6. Add #PRE to the ACCT_SRV entry in the LMHOSTS file to have the name and IP address of ACCT_SRV always in NetBIOS name cache.

7. \SYSTEMROOT\SYSTEM32\DRIVERS\ETC

8. No, only NetBIOS names can be in the file.

9. The #PRE switch and the LMHOSTS file are used.

10. nbtstat –R

11. Host name resolution

12. Host name resolution

13. NetBIOS name resolution

14. HOSTNAME

Chapter 12

1. HOSTS.TXT

2. RFCs 1034 and 1035

3. A period

4. A resolver

5. IP address configuration has the address of the DNS server.

6. A recursive query

7. An iterative query

8. Primary, secondary, and caching-only

9. Zone transfer

10. Yes

11. No, caching-only servers do not have a copy of the database.

12. An A record

13. Inverse or reverse lookup

Chapter 13

1. DHCP and DNS

2. Resource records are updated in the DNS database automatically as the IP addresses are being allocated by DHCP.

3. FQDN stands for fully qualified domain name; it is the host's name combined with the domain name that the host is a member of (for example, HARRY.SYBEX.COM).

4. The A and the PTR records

5. The host sends the A record, and the DHCP server sends the PTR record.

6. The DHCP server

7. The DHCP server will request the update of both A and PTR records.

8. The Windows 2000 client sends the update requests to the DNS server.

Chapter 14

1. Windows Internet Naming Service

2. Broadcast

3. Workstation service and server service

4. The WINS server sends three challenges to the IP address of the NetBIOS name currently registered. If there is a response, the WINS server sends a negative acknowledgment to the newcomer; if there is no response to the challenge, the database is updated and a positive response is sent to the newcomer.

5. No

6. Yes

7. Broadcast

8. NetBIOS name cache

9. WINS sends a series of three challenges to the currently registered IP address. If there is a response, the new host cannot have that name. If there is no response, the new host can have the name.

10. The IP address of the WINS server is an optional parameter of the TCP/IP configuration.

Chapter 15

1. 32

2. 128

3. 109A:3210::213:412B

4. ::0A15:877B

5. ::C0A8:1F04

6. A013:1234:0034:0000:0000:0000:0008:411A

7. More addresses, enhanced security, greater efficiency

8. SIT, Simple IPv6 Transition

9. There are two phases. The first phase will have IPv4 and IPv6 coexisting on the same network, and the second phase will eliminate all of IPv4.

10. 10 years

11. AC14:1910

12. 7F00:0001

Appendix

B

Glossary

Numbers

$2^N - 2$ Equation used to figure out the number of subnets and hosts per subnet that can be created with a subnet mask. N is the number of bits that you are using for the subnet portion or the host portion of the address.

6BONE   The IPv6 backbone that is currently being used to build and test the IPv6 network infrastructure.

A

A record   Also called a Host record, it contains the names and IP addresses of hosts.

Acknowledgment   A packet sent by a host to confirm receipt of a packet. The sending host waits for an acknowledgment packet before sending additional data. The destination host sends acknowledgments as packets are received.

Address Resolution Protocol (ARP)   A protocol used to translate an IP address to a hardware address.

Alias   A simpler or alternative name for a host.

Anonymous   Account set up so that anyone can access files on an FTP server without a secret password.

Anycast   A packet that is sent from one host to the nearest host within a group of hosts.

Application layer   The top layer of the DoD and OSI models where applications listen for and respond to requests.

Application Programming Interface (API)   A common interface that enables programmers to write programs to a standard specification.

ARP cache   An area in RAM that holds recently performed IP-to-hardware-address resolutions.

ARP reply   A packet that is returned to the sender of the ARP request and that includes the IP address and hardware address that was requested.

ARP request   A broadcast packet that seeks to resolve an IP address to a hardware address.

ARPAnet   The Advanced Research Projects Agency's supernetwork—the predecessor of the Internet.

ASCII text file   A file that is stored as text only—no fancy characters. It can be edited with any text editor such as Notepad or Edit.

B

Bandwidth   The amount of data that can move through the cabling.

Binary   The base-2 number system that computers use to represent data. It consists of only two digits: 0 and 1.

Binary format   A compressed file format.

Broadcast   When broadcasting to get name resolution, the host "hollers" the name to be resolved onto the network.

Broadcast packet   A packet that is addressed to all hosts; the broadcast address is a universal address enabling all hosts to receive the packet. Routers will generally stop broadcast packets from moving on to another network.

C

Cache   Temporary storage of information that is accessed quickly.

Caching-only server   A name server that does not have a copy of a DNS database.

Canonical Name (CNAME) record An alias or code name for a host that already has an A record.

Circuit-switched network A network on which all data in a communication takes the same path.

Classful addressing system System of assigning IP network addresses in which addresses are allotted in well-defined blocks. The blocks of addresses in the classful system are Class A, B, C, D, and E.

Classless Inter-Domain Routing (CIDR) An IP addressing scheme that uses a slash followed by a number to highlight the network portion of an address instead of using a subnet mask.

Connectionless Communication that occurs without a connection being set up first.

Connection-oriented A type of protocol in which a connection is established and maintained until the application programs at each end have exchanged their message or messages.

Contiguous bits One bit following another.

Custom subnet mask A nonstandard subnet mask that a network administrator uses to make more efficient use of a network address by creating more subnets.

CuteFTP An easy-to-use FTP command interpreter application that turns your mouse clicks into FTP commands.

D

Decimal The base-10 number system that people use to represent data. It consists of 10 digits: 0, 1, 2, 3, 4, 5, 6, 7, 8, 9.

Default gateway A parameter included with the router's IP address that packets are sent to en route to a remote network.

Department of Defense (DoD) The branch of the United States military maintaining national defense.

DHCP acknowledgment (ack) The final step in using DHCP to lease a new IP address or to renew an IP address lease. A DHCP ack is broadcast for new IP address leases and sent directly to the DHCP client for renewals. The packet says, "It's a done deal! You can have this IP address, and here are some extra parameters that you can have."

DHCP discover The first step in using DHCP to lease an IP address. A DHCP discover packet is broadcast saying, "Hey, who is a DHCP server?"

DHCP offer The second step in using DHCP to lease an IP address. A DHCP offer packet is broadcast saying, "I'm a DHCP server; how would you like this fine address?"

DHCP request The third step in using DHCP to lease a new IP address and the first step in renewing an IP address lease. A DHCP request packet is broadcast for new IP address leases and sent directly to the DHCP server for renewals. The packet says, "Yes, I would like to have this IP address."

DHCP server A host running a service to lease IP addresses to other hosts. The DHCP server is configured by an administrator with the pool, or scope, of addresses to be leased.

Domain A unique portion of the name space in which an administrator creates an authoritative database of records to give resolution of names within the zone to an IP address.

Domain name space The entire inverted tree of Internet names.

Domain Name System (DNS) Distributed system used on the Internet to resolve host names to IP addresses.

Dotted decimal notation   The decimal representation of an IP address or subnet mask. Four decimal numbers separated by periods (or dots) is the preferred way to represent an address or mask.

Double-colon notation   A shorthand method of writing IPv6 addresses without including non-significant 0s.

Dynamic DNS   The process that allows the DHCP server to update the DNS database with new record information.

E

Encapsulation   The wrapping of a packet into the appropriate package or format.

Exclusion   An IP address that falls into a range of addresses to be leased, but that has been set by an administrator not to be leased.

F

Fault tolerance   Taking into account any failures.

File Transfer Protocol (FTP)   An application used to transfer files from one host to another and to store the files on the requesting host.

Firewall   An application that prevents certain types of data from passing from a public network to an internal, private network.

FTP command interpreter   A nice looking, easy-to-use application used to access an FTP server.

FTP command line utility   A non-mouse and non-fancy interface used to access an FTP server.

FTP server   Server on which an FTP server application is running to transfer files to clients.

FTP/TCP/IP   A packet that has an FTP header on top of a TCP header on top of an IP header.

G

Global option   A parameter that is set at the DHCP server and that applies to all scopes of IP addresses that this DHCP server serves.

H

Headers   Bits of information attached to each packet that usually include addressing and routing details; the information acts like a little sticky note on the packet.

Hexadecimal   A base-16 numbering system containing 16 sequential numbers (including 0) as base units before adding a new position for the next number; the hexadecimal system uses the numbers 0–9 and then the letters A–F.

Host   Any device (such as a workstation, server, mainframe, or printer) on a network or internetwork that has a TCP/IP address.

Host name resolution   The process of resolving a host name to an IP address.

HOSTNAME utility   A simple utility that determines the host name of the computer in which you are working.

HOSTS file   A file of host names and IP addresses.

hosts.txt   The original file that contained name-to-IP-address relationships.

HTTP/TCP/IP   A packet with an HTTP header on top of a TCP header on top of an IP header.

Hyperlink   Underlined word on a Web site that links to another document on that Web server or possibly on another Web server.

Hypertext Markup Language (HTML)   The file format of Web pages housed on a Web server that can be displayed in a useful format by a Web browser.

Hypertext Transfer Protocol (HTTP)   An application used to transfer files from one host to another and to display the files at the requesting host.

I

IN-ADDR.ARPA   Inverse address from the ARPAnet; a zone used to keep PTR records.

International Organization for Standardization (ISO)   The organization that ratified the OSI model.

Internet Assigned Numbers Authority (IANA)   An organization responsible for overseeing several aspects of the Internet.

Internet Engineering Task Force (IETF)   A governing body of the Internet.

Internet layer   Layer between the Network Interface and Transport layers of the DoD model; protocols at the Internet layer focus on addressing.

Internet Protocol version 4 (IPv4)   The current version of IP that has been in use for over 20 years.

Internet Protocol version 6 (IPv6)   The formal name of the new version of IP that will become the standard.

Internet Protocol, Next Generation (IPng)   The informal name of IPv6.

Internet routing tables   Tables that are maintained by Internet authorities and Internet Service Providers (ISPs) that provide the information for routing packets on the Internet.

Internetwork   Several smaller networks connected together.

IP address   An address that IP uses to identify a unique network and host.

Iterative query   A question asked with the expectation that the best information available will be returned so that more queries can be sent based on that information.

L

LAN Manager   A networking product that was the predecessor of Microsoft's Windows NT.

Layer   A portion of the OSI model that is used to categorize specific concerns.

LMHOSTS file   A file containing NetBIOS names and IP addresses that is used for name resolution.

Load balancing   Spreading the workload across servers.

Local host   A step in name resolution wherein a host examines its TCP/IP configuration to see whether the name being resolved is its own.

Local network   Hosts that are on the same side of a router are considered on the same local network. Two hosts on the same local network have the exact same bit values in the network portion of their IP addresses.

Logical address   This address can be modified; it refers only to the host.

Loopback   An address that is used for diagnostic purposes, to test the TCP/IP stack of a TCP/IP host.

M

Mail eXchanger (MX) record   A record that contains the address of the mail server.

Master DNS database   The authoritative DNS database containing DNS records. The administrator can modify records in this database.

Microsoft TCP/IP client Any TCP/IP host that has installed and configured Microsoft's TCP/IP client software. This accounts for most TCP/IP hosts.

Multicast A packet that is sent from one host to many other hosts at the same time.

Multicast address A reserved IP address that Internet Group Management Protocol (IGMP) uses for streaming data. No one host can have this address, but several can receive data by listening to it.

N

Name resolution The process of finding the IP address for the name of a computer.

Name server A server running the DNS service that can provide name resolution.

Name Server (NS) record A record that lists the IP address of a name server.

`nbtstat` A utility used to monitor the names that are in NetBIOS name cache.

Negative acknowledgment An acknowledgment sent from a host or server that says, "I received your request and the answer is no."

NetBIOS Network Basic Input Output System; a program that enables applications on different computers to communicate within a Local Area Network.

NetBIOS name cache Temporary cache storage for NetBIOS names and IP addresses that have been resolved. The names and addresses are stored in RAM for rapid resolution.

NetBIOS name query A packet asking for the IP address of a host with a particular NetBIOS name.

NetBIOS name resolution The process of resolving a NetBIOS name to an IP address.

NetBIOS name server A server that registers and resolves NetBIOS names.

NetBIOS names The names given to a computer that is running a Microsoft operating system.

Network Address Translation (NAT) An application that translates the IP address of the sending host to another IP address while relaying the TCP/IP data to another network.

Network administrator A person who installs, monitors, and troubleshoots a network.

Network bandwidth The amount of data that can be put onto a network based on other communication traffic already using the wire.

Network Control Protocol (NCP) The protocol used before TCP/IP.

Network interface card (NIC) A piece of hardware that is used to connect a host to a network; every host must have one in order to connect to a network.

Network Interface layer Lowest layer of the DoD model, it acts as a host's connection, or interface, to the network.

Network topology Describes how a network is connected and how each host knows when and how to transmit and receive data.

O

Octet Eight bits of data.

Open Standards Interconnection (OSI) model A seven-layer model used to break down the many tasks involved in moving data from one host to another.

P

Packet A unit of data that is prepared for transmission onto a network.

Packet-switched network   A network on which the data in a communication takes several paths.

Parsing   Reading through a file looking for specific data.

PC DOS   PC operating system used with early PCs that could only address up to 640K of RAM. This limitation lead to severe issues, as more RAM was needed.

Peer-layer communication   A type of communication in which each layer of the sending host communicates with the same layer of the receiving host.

Ping   Packet InterNet Groper; a software utility that tests connectivity between two TCP/IP hosts.

Pointer (PTR) record   A record that aids with IP-address-to-host-name resolution.

Ports   Numbered addresses where requests are sent and where applications listen for requests. Ports are numbered 1–65,536.

Primary name server   The name server that holds the master DNS database.

Protocol stack   Protocols that send and receive data.

Protocol suite   A combination of protocols.

Protocols   Rules or standards that govern communications between hosts.

Proxy server   An application that relays TCP/IP traffic from one network to another while changing the IP address of the sending host.

R

Read/write   A file that can be read from and written to.

Read-only   A file that can be read but cannot be modified.

Real-time   A type of data that is available instantaneously. The term usually refers to video or audio conferencing.

Records   The information in the DNS database.

Recursive query   A question asked with the expectation that the response will be either the complete answer or an error, nothing less.

Remote network   A network other than the one that the host is on; a remote network is on the other side of a router. Two hosts on remote networks have different bit values in the network portion of their IP addresses.

Request for Comments (RFC)   A paper thoroughly describing a new protocol or technology.

Reserved IP address   An IP address that cannot be used as a valid host address.

Resolve   To translate a logical to a physical address.

Resolver   A client that is trying to resolve a host name to an IP address.

Root name servers   Powerful name servers that contain addresses of the top-level name servers.

Router   A host that interfaces with other networks and can move packets from one network to another.

Routing   The process of determining which is the next path to send a packet so that it gets to its destination.

Routing table   A table that contains the addresses indicating the best routes to other networks.

S

Scope   A pool of IP addresses that a DHCP server leases to DHCP clients.

Scope option   A parameter that is set at the DHCP server that applies to only one scope of IP addresses.

Secondary name server   A name server that has a copy of the master DNS database.

Sequence numbers   Numbers in a header that indicate the order of packets. If packets get out of order en route to the destination host, this numbering system enables packets to be rearranged in order at the destination host.

Server service   A NetBIOS service that performs server activities such as file sharing.

Shares   A feature of several operating systems that is used to designate local resources that will be accessible across the network.

Simple IPv6 Transition (SIT)   The proposed plan to transition to IPv6.

Socket   IP address : TCP or UDP : port number.

Source-quench   An ICMP packet that is sent to slow down the transmission at the source.

Standard subnet mask   Also called a default subnet mask. For Class A = 255.0.0.0, for Class B = 255.255.0.0, and for Class C = 255.255.255.0.

Stanford Research Institute Network Information Center (SRI-NIC)   The site of early Internet growth and host-name maintenance.

Start Of Authority (SOA) record   The first record in a DNS database; it describes the database.

Static entry   A manual entry in the WINS database that is made by the administrator for a non-WINS client.

Stream   A series of packets sent without waiting for acknowledgments.

Subnet   A smaller network created by dividing a larger network.

Subnet bits   Bits used in the subnet mask to extend the number of bits available for the network portion of the IP address.

Subnet calculator   A software calculator that figures out subnet masks, valid networks, number of hosts, and host ranges. Several are available for download on the Internet.

Subnet goggles   A fictional set of goggles that IP wears when looking at an IP address to determine whether an address is local or remote.

Subnet mask   A parameter included with every IP address that highlights the network portion of the IP address.

Supernetted subnet mask   A subnet mask that uses a supernet notation.

Switch   A character or set of characters used to further enhance a command.

T

Three-way handshake   A three-step conversation initiated by TCP to set up a connection between hosts.

time to live (TTL)   The amount of time that the lease on an IP address is valid.

Transmission Control Protocol (TCP)   Protocol at the Transport layer that is connection oriented and guarantees delivery of packets. TCP is responsible for ensuring that a message is divided into the packets that IP manages and for reassembling the packets into the complete message at the other end.

Transmission Control Protocol/Internet Protocol (TCP/IP)   The suite of protocols that when combined create the "language of the Internet."

U

Unicast   A packet that is sent from one host to one other host.

Uniform Resource Locator (URL)   The address of a Web site that a user can surf to.

User Datagram Protocol (UDP)   A protocol offering a limited amount of service when messages are exchanged between hosts. No connection is set up and no acknowledgments are expected.

W

WAN connection   A connection between two LANs (Local Area Networks) is a WAN (Wide Area Network) connection.

Web browser application   A client application used for surfing the Web. Examples are Netscape Navigator and Microsoft Internet Explorer.

Web server   Server on which an HTTP server application is running; users can surf to this server and request that files be transferred and displayed.

Well-known ports   Port numbers 1–1,024, which are reserved for certain applications.

Windows Internet Naming Service (WINS)   Microsoft's NetBIOS name server that keeps NetBIOS names and IP addresses in a database and later gives name resolution.

Workstation service   A NetBIOS service that performs workstation activities such as using the local operating system.

Z

Zone transfer   The sending of a DNS database from one name server to another.

Appendix
C

Acronym
Expansion Guide

Acronym	What It Stands For
ack	acknowledgment
API	Application Programming Interface
ARP	Address Resolution Protocol
ARPA	Advanced Research Projects Agency
ARPAnet	Advanced Research Projects Agency Network
ASCII	American Standard Code for Information Interchange
BIND	Berkeley Internet Name Domain
bit	binary digit
CNAME	canonical name
DHCP	Dynamic Host Configuration Protocol
DNS	Domain Name System
DoD	Department of Defense
FDDI	Fiber Distributed Data Interface
FTP	File Transfer Protocol
HTML	Hypertext Markup Language
HTTP	Hypertext Transfer Protocol
IANA	Internet Assigned Numbers Authority
ICMP	Internet Control Message Protocol
IETF	Internet Engineering Task Force
IGMP	Internet Group Message Protocol
IP	Internet Protocol
IPng	Internet Protocol, Next Generation
IPv4	Internet Protocol version 4
IPv6	Internet Protocol version 6
IPX/SPX	Internetwork Packet Exchange/Sequenced Packet Exchange
ISO	International Organization for Standardization
ISP	Internet Service Provider
LAN	Local Area Network

Acronym Expansion Guide

Acronym	What It Stands For
LLC	Logical Link Control
LMHOSTS	LAN Manager Hosts
MAC	Media Access Control
MX	Mail eXchanger
nak	negative acknowledgment
NCP	Network Control Protocol
NetBIOS	Network Basic Input Output System
NIC	Network Interface Card
NS	name server
OSI	Open Standards Interconnection
Ping	Packet InterNet Groper
RAM	random access memory
RFC	Request for Comments
SIT	Simple IPv6 Transition
SMTP	Simple Mail Transfer Protocol
SNM	subnet mask
SNMP	Simple Network Management Protocol
SOA	Start Of Authority
SRI-NIC	Stanford Research Institute Network Information Center
TCP	Transmission Control Protocol
TCP/IP	Transmission Control Protocol/Internet Protocol
TFTP	Trivial File Transfer Protocol
TTL	time to live
UDP	User Datagram Protocol
URL	Uniform Resource Locator
WAN	Wide Area Network
WINS	Windows Internet Naming Service
WWW	World Wide Web

Appendix D

What's on the Web Site

So much has been written about TCP/IP that to include all the relevant documentation in one book would be impossible. A *TCP/IP JumpStart* Web site has been set up to give you quick and current references to documents that have been discussed in this book, as well as to other Web sites of interest.

How to Access the *TCP/IP JumpStart* Companion Web Site

To access the *TCP/IP JumpStart* companion Web site:

1. Open a Web browser window and go to the Sybex Web site (www.sybex.com).
2. Go to the Catalog Site Index area and click in the Search box.
3. Type **4101**, which is the ISBN number of this book, or type **TCP/IP JumpStart**, the title.
4. From the *TCP/IP JumpStart* book page on the Web site, click the Links button.

What You'll Find on the Web Site

The *TCP/IP JumpStart* Web site serves as a current reference to many materials that a TCP/IP administrator, programmer, or instructor would need to access. Your exploration of TCP/IP documentation, tools, and utilities on the Internet can start at the *TCP/IP JumpStart* Web site. The Web site is updated regularly and includes links to information described in the following sections.

Requests for Comments

Throughout the book, I make many references to Requests for Comments. Many times, as an administrator or programmer, you will want to refer to the original or latest RFC to get more detailed information about a protocol. If you have never read an RFC, you're in for a treat. The *TCP/IP JumpStart* Web site has links to all RFCs that have been published.

Subnet Calculators

Administrators need to be able to determine the proper subnet, valid network, and correct host addresses based on the number of hosts and the number of networks that they work with. In this book, you were taught how to manually determine this information. To double-check your work, or maybe just to make it easier, the Web site has links to several subnet calculators.

Further Reading on IP Version 6

In Chapter 15 of this book, you learned about the next version of TCP/IP. IP version 6 is currently being tested and deployed, and the links on the companion Web site provide valuable, current information about this protocol.

Many of the linked Web sites have interesting articles about the history and growth of the Internet. Some sites include cool tools, such as one for tracing your route around the Internet.

Special Note to Instructors

For instructors, the *TCP/IP JumpStart* Web site has a link to an Ancillaries page, which provides you with free support materials, including a bonus exam, syllabus, and PowerPoint slides for classroom lectures. Ask your Sybex Sales Rep for free access information.

Index

Symbols & Numbers

#PRE switch in LMHOSTS file, 209
2^N - 2, 169, 294
6BONE, 268, 294

A

A record, 232, 294
  dynamic update, 240, 242–243
acknowledgments, 58, 294
  and delivery guarantee, 60
  DHCP acknowledgment packet, *125*, 295
  negative, 253, 298
acronyms, 304–305
Active Directory, 247
Address Resolution Protocol (ARP), 42,
  43–46. *See* ARP (Address Resolution
  Protocol)
addressing scheme, 12, 18. *See also* IP
  addressing
Advanced Research Projects Agency
  (ARPA), 4
Advanced TCP/IP Settings dialog box,
  DNS tab, *245*, 245–246
alias, 201, 294
anonymous FTP user, 71, 294
Anycast, 275, 294
API (Application Programming Interface),
  194, 294

APIPA (Automatic Private IP Addressing), 12&
AppleTalk protocol suite, 19
Application layer (DoD), 29, **68–75**, 294
  FTP (File Transfer Protocol), **71–73**
  HTTP (Hypertext Transfer Protocol),
    74–75
  ports and sockets, **67–70**
    well-known ports, **70**
Application layer (OSI), 25, 28
Application Programming Interface (API),
  194, 294
ARP (Address Resolution Protocol), 42,
  43–46, 294
ARP cache, 43, *43*, 294
ARP packets, **46**
ARP reply, 45, *46*, 46, 294
  ping to examine, 48
ARP request broadcast, 43, 46, *46*, 294
  ping to examine, 48
  to resolve hardware address, **44–45**
ARPA (Advanced Research Projects
  Agency), 4
ARPAnet, **4–5**, 294
  cessation, 7
  requirements, 5
ASCII text file, 294
  HOSTS file as, 200
audio streaming with IGMP, 50–51
Automatic Private IP Addressing
  (APIPA), 128

B

andwidth, 256, 294, 298
  name resolution broadcast and, 207
erkley Internet Name Domain (BIND), 228
inary file format, 71, 294
inary numbering system, 36,
    80–82, 294
  converting decimal to, **84–89**
    with bit value method, 84–85
    with calculator, *88*, 88–89
    with division method, 86–87
  converting to decimal, **83**
  counting in, 138
IND (Berkley Internet Name
    Domain), 228
it, 83
it value method, for decimal to binary
    conversion, 84–85
roadcast, 294
  of NetBIOS name query, 254–255, 256
roadcast packets, 37, 294
  subnetting rules and, 151

C

ache, 224, 294
  NetBIOS name cache, **203–204**
aching-only server, 231, 294
alculator, for decimal to binary
    conversion, *88*, 88–89
erf, Vint, "A Protocol for Packet Network
    Interconnection," 7
hecksum, in UDP header, 61
IDR (Classless Inter-Domain Routing),
    96, **186–187**, 295
rcuit-switched network, *9*, **9**, 295
asses of IP addresses, **92–96**
  class A, **92–93**
    subnet masks, 171
    subnetting, 161–162
  class B, **94**
    problems from, **181–182**
    subnet masks, 172
    subnetting, 163–164
  class C, **95**
    subnet masks, 173
    valid hosts, 165–167
  class D, **96**
  class E, **96**
  custom subnet masks, 143
  limitations, 180
  standard subnet masks, **142–143**
classful addressing system, 180, 295
classless addressing system, 186
client. *See also* Microsoft TCP/IP client
  for FTP, 71
  Windows configuration for dynamic
    DNS, 244–247
CNAME (Canonical Name) record,
    232, 295
.com domain, 221
command prompt, to run HOSTNAME
    utility, 199
communication, host-to-host, 7
connection-oriented communication, 56,
    58, 295
connectionless communication, 57, 295
  UDP (User Datagram Protocol) for,
    61–63
contiguous bits, 295
  in subnet mask, 155
Control Panel (Windows XP), 103, *103*, *104*
Crocker, Steve, 6
custom subnet masks, **148–170**, 295
  creating additional networks, 150
  creation, **151–170**
    calculating number of networks and
      hosts, 169–170
    determining maximum number of
      hosts on networks, 153
    determining number of subnets
      needed, 152–153

range of valid host IP addresses,
158–160
subnet mask determination,
153–156
valid network addresses, 157–158
subnetting rules, 150–151
CuteFTP, 73, 295

D

Data-Link layer (OSI), 27, 28. *See also*
Network Interface layer (DoD)
data transfer, protocols and, 18
database for DNS, **228**
A record, 232, 294
dynamic update, 240, 242–243
CNAME (Canonical Name) record,
232, 295
MX (Mail eXchanger) record, 233, 297
NS record, 232, 298
PTR (pointer) record, 233, 299
dynamic update, 240, 242–243
Start of Authority (SOA) record, 232, 300
decimal numbering system, 36,
80–82, 295
converting binary to, **83**
converting to binary, **84–89**
with bit value method, 84–85
with calculator, *88*, 88–89
with division method, 86–87
default gateway, 40, 42, 295
in Windows NT, 113
DHCP (Dynamic Host Configuration
Protocol), **116–117**, 238
leases, 121, **126–128**
IP address renewal, **127–128**
setting duration, **130**
obtaining address from server,
118–125
DHCP acknowledgment packet,
124–125, *125*, 295

DHCP discover packet, 118–119,
119, 295
DHCP offer packet, 119–121, *121*, 295
DHCP request packet, 121–123,
123, 295
reserving DHCP IP addresses, **129**
setting scopes and options, **131**
setup in Windows NT, 111
DHCP server, 116, 295
in Dynamic DNS, 239
UDP to search for, 62–63
Windows 2000 configuration for
dynamic update, **241–247**, *242*
diagnostics. *See* troubleshooting
division method, for decimal to binary
conversion, 86–87
DNS (Domain Name System), **202**,
219–233, 295. *See also* Dynamic DNS
completing resolution, **226**
database
automatic updates, 239
maintenance, **228**
record types, **231–233**
on the Internet, **221**
querying name servers, **224–225**
what it is, **220**
DNS server
maintaining, **229–233**
caching-only server, 231
primary name server, 229
secondary name server, 229
querying, **223**
Windows XP settings to indicate, 106
DNS zone transfer, **230**, *230*
DoD (Department of Defense), 4, 295
reference model, **29**
domain, 221, 295
domain controller, 247
domain name space, 221, 295
dotted decimal notation, 90,
139–140, 296

double-colon notation, 271,
272–273, 296
Dynamic DNS, **237–247**, 296
benefits, 247
on Internet, 247
Windows 2000 server configuration,
241–247

E

edu domain, 221
electrical appliances, IP addresses
for, 270
encapsulation, 20, 296
Ethernet address, 36
exclusions, 296
from DHCP scope, 131

F

failure recovery, as TCP design goal, 8
fault tolerance, 296
secondary name server for, 229
firewall, 48, 296
flexibility, of TCP/IP, 3
FTP (File Transfer Protocol), **71–73**,
72, 296
port for, 70
FTP command interpreter, 71, 73, 296
FTP command line utility, 71, 296
FTP server, 296
FTP/TCP/IP packet, 72, 296
FTP Voyager, 73

G

gateway. *See* default gateway
global option, for DHCP scope, 131, 296

H

handshake, three-way, **58–59**, 300
hardware address, 35, **36–37**
ARP request broadcast to resolve,
44–45
determining, **42**
resolution of IP address to, 43
target, 37
hardware, independence as TCP design
goal, 8
headers for packets, 20, 296
IP (Internet Protocol), 39
from Network Interface Layer, 35
TCP (Transmission Control Protocol), 63
sequence numbers, 60
UDP (User Datagram Protocol), 61, 63
hexadecimal numbering system, 36,
81, 296
for IPv6 addresses, 271
host, 3, 296
interaction with Network Interface
layer, 34
host name resolution, **193**, **196–212**, 296
broadcast, **206–207**
cycle, 212, *212*
DNS (Domain Name System), **202**
HOSTS file, **200–201**
LMHOSTS file, **208–209**
local host process, **198–199**
NetBIOS name cache, **203–204**
NetBIOS name resolution vs., **195**
WINS (Windows Internet Naming
Service), **205**
host-to-host communication, 7
Host-to-Host layer. *See* Transport layer
HOSTNAME utility, **198–199**, 296
hosts, 18
number on network, 153
HOSTS file, **200–201**, 296

hosts.txt file, 220, 296
HTML (Hypertext Markup Language), 74, 297
HTTP (Hypertext Transfer Protocol), **74–75**, 297
   port 80 for requests, 69
HTTP/TCP/IP packet, 74, 296
hyperlinks, 74, 296

I

IANA (Internet Assigned Number Authority), 70, 181, 297
ICMP (Internet Control Message Protocol), **47–48**
   ping to examine packet, 48
IETF (Internet Engineering Task Force), 6, 297
IGMP (Internet Group Management Protocol), **49–51**
IN-ADDR.ARPA zone, 233, 297
installing IP addressing, **102–117**
   manual configuration, **102**
   on Windows 95/98, **114–116**
   on Windows 2000, **106–110**
   on Windows NT, **110–114**
   on Windows XP, **103–106**
Internet, 2
   growth, 180
   origins, **4–5**
Internet Assigned Number Authority (IANA), 70, 181, 297
Internet Control Message Protocol (ICMP), **47–48**
   ping to examine packet, 48
Internet Engineering Task Force (IETF), 6, 297
Internet Group Management Protocol (IGMP), **49–51**
Internet layer (DoD), 29, **38–51**, 297
   IP (Internet Protocol), **39–42**

Internet Protocol, Next Generation (IPng), 297. *See also* IP (Internet Protocol) version 6
Internet Protocol (TCP/IP) Properties dialog box, 105–106, *106*
   for manual IP address assignment, 109, *109*
Internet routing tables, 181–182, 297
   supernetting and, **183–185**
internetwork, 12, 13, 297
InterNIC, reserved IP addresses, 93
interoperability of TCP/IP, 3
IP (Internet Protocol), **39–42**, 297
   hardware address determination, **42**
   local or remote destination, **40–41**
IP (Internet Protocol) version 6, **267–277**, 297
   addressing scheme, **269–274**
     future possibilities, 270
   converting IPv4 addresses to, 273
   documentation, **274**
   improvements of, **275**
   special addresses, **274**
   transition plan, **276–277**
   Web documents about, 309
IP addressing, 38, **80–97**, 297. *See also* DHCP (Dynamic Host Configuration Protocol); name resolution
   allocation, **180–182**
   CIDR (Classless Inter-Domain Routing), 96
   classes, **92–96**
     custom subnet masks, 143
     standard subnet masks, **142–143**
     summary, **97**
   converting IPv4 to IPv6, 273
   dotted decimal notation, 90
   installation and assignment, **102–117**
     manual configuration, **102**
     on Windows 95/98, **114–116**
     on Windows 2000, **106–110**

on Windows NT, **110–114**
on Windows XP, **103–106**
numbering systems, **80–89**
reserved, 49
resolution to hardware address, 43
P broadcast address, 93
Png (Internet Protocol, Next Generation), 268, 297
Pv5, 268
PX/SPX protocol suite, 19
SO (International Organization for Standardization), 23, 297. *See also* OSI reference model
erative query, 226–227, 297

K

ahn, Bob, "A Protocol for Packet Network Interconnection", 7

AN Manager, 209, 297
ayers in OSI model, 23, **24**, 297
    mnemonics for remembering, 27
    responsibilities, **25–27**
ading zeros, in binary number conversion, 89
ases in DHCP, 121, **126–128**
    discarding forward lookups after expiration, 243
    setting duration, **130**
LC (Logical Link Control) sublayer, 27
MHOSTS file, **208–209**, 297
ad balancing, 297
    secondary name server for, 229
ocal Area Connection Properties page (Windows 2000), *107*
ocal Area Connection Properties page (Windows XP), *105*
ocal host, 297

local host process, in name resolution, **198–199**
local network, 297
    identifying, **139–141**
    as packet destination, 136
logical address, 39, 297
Logical Link Control (LLC) sublayer, 27
loopback address, 93, 274, 297

M

MAC (Media Access Control) address, 36
MAC (Media Access Control) sublayer, 27
Mail eXchanger (MX) record, 233, 297
master DNS database, 229, 297
memory, ARP cache in, *43*, 43
Microsoft TCP/IP client, 298
    host name, 196
    name resolution steps, 195
    NetBIOS name cache, **203–204**
Microsoft TCP/IP Properties dialog box (Windows NT), IP Address tab, *113*, 113
Microsoft TCP/IP Properties dialog box, WINS Address tab, *204*
multicast address, 49, 96, 275, 298
multicast packet, 298
multimedia streaming, 51
MX (Mail eXchanger) record, 233, 297

N

name release request, to WINS server, 261
name resolution, **191–215**, 298
    basics, **192–193**
    broadcast, **206–207**
    DNS (Domain Name System), **202**, **222–228**
    host name resolution, **193**
        cycle, 212, *212*
    HOSTS file, **200–201**

LMHOSTS file, **208–209**
local host process, **198–199**
NetBIOS name cache, **203–204**
NetBIOS name resolution, **194**, **213–215**
  vs. host name resolution, **195**
WINS (Windows Internet Naming
  Service), **205**
name servers, 229, 298
  querying, **224–225**
NAT (Network Address Translation),
  93, 298
nbtstat command, 209–211, *210*, 298
NCP (Network Control Protocol), 4, 298
  limitations, 7
negative acknowledgment, 253, 298
negative name query response, 260
net view command, 213, *215*
NetBIOS, 298
NetBIOS applications, **252–263**
  NetBIOS name resolution with WINS,
    257–261
    name registration, 257
  NetBIOS name resolution without
    WINS, **252–256**
    name registration, 253
  WINS Manager, **262–263**
NetBIOS name cache, **203–204**, 254, 298
  pre-loading entries, 209
  viewing contents, 209–211, *210*
NetBIOS name query, 254, 298
NetBIOS name resolution, **194**,
  213–215, 298
  cycle, 214–215, *215*
  vs. host name resolution, **195**
NetBIOS name server, 257, 298
NetBIOS names, 298
  in LMHOSTS file, 208
NetBIOS scope ID, 204
NetWare, HOSTS file, 201
network
  6BONE, 268, 294
  circuit-switched, **9**, *9*, 295

packet-switched, **10**, *10*, 299
  functioning of, 11
Network Address Translation (NAT),
  93, 298
network administrator, 2, 298
Network and Dial-Up Connections
  window (Windows 2000), 106
network bandwidth, 256, 294, 298
Network Control Protocol (NCP), 4, 298
  limitations, 7
Network dialog box (Windows 95/98),
  Configuration tab, *114*
Network dialog box (Windows NT)
  Identification tab, *110*, *112*
  Protocols tab, *112*
network interface cards (NIC), 36
Network Interface layer (DoD), 29,
  34–37, 298
Network layer (OSI), 26
Network Neighborhood, 252
network topology, 34, 298
NIC (network interface card), 36, 298
Novell, 19
Novell Netware server, configuration for
  dynamic DNS, 243–244, *244*
NS record, 232, 298
numbering systems, 36, **80–89**

O

octal numbering system, 81
octets, 90, 298
open standard, TCP/IP as, 12
operating systems, support for TCP/IP, 2
OSI (Open Standards Interconnection)
  reference model, **23–28**, 298
  vs. DoD model, 29
  layers, 23, **24**
    mnemonics for remembering, 27
    responsibilities, **25–27**
  use, **28**
overhead, minimization as TCP/IP goal, 8

acket InterNet Groper. *See* Ping (Packet InterNet Groper)
acket-switched network, **10**, *10*, 299
  functioning of, 11
ackets, 10, **20–21**, *21*, 298
  DHCP
    acknowledgment packet, 124–125, 295
    discover packet, 118–119
    offer packet, 119–121
    request packet, 121–123
  DHCP acknowledgment packet, *125*
  for DNS query, 226
  for IPv6, 275
  TCP portion, 57, *57*
  UDP portion, 57, *57*
arsing, 201, 299
 DOS, 180, 299
er-layer communication, 28, 299
hysical address, 36
hysical layer (OSI), 27, 28
ng (Packet InterNet Groper), 47, 196–197, 299
  packets, **48**
orts and sockets, **67–70**, 299
  for HTTP, 74
  for UDP, 61
  well-known ports, **70**, 301
PRE switch in LMHOSTS file, 209
esentation layer (OSI), 26, 28
imary name server, 229, 299
inters, reserved IP addresses for, 129
otocol stack, 1, 2, 19, 299
otocol suite, 1, 2, 299
  examples, 19
otocols, 1, 2, 299
  need for, **22**
  packet movement by, **20–21**, *21*
  questions answered by, 19
  what they are, **18–21**
proxy server, 93, 299
PTR (pointer) record, 233, 299
  dynamic update, 240, 242–243

Q

querying
  DNS server, **223**
  iterative or recursive, 226–227
  name servers, **224–225**

R

RAM, ARP cache in, *43*, 43
RAND Corporation, 4
read-only, 299
  DNS database as, 230
read/write, 299
  DNS database as, 229
real-time, 275, 299
records, 299
  DNS types, **231–233**
recursive query, 226–227, 299
redundancy, as ARPAnet requirement, 5
reliability, 56
remote network, 40, 299
  identifying, **139–141**
  as packet destination, 136
remote resolution, secondary name server for, 229
reserved IP addresses, 49, 93, 299
  class E as, 96
resolve, 299
resolver, 222, 299
RFCs (Requests for Comments), **6**, 299
  761 for TCP, 63
  768 for UDP, 63
  801 for NCP to TCP transition, 7
  849 for hosts.txt file, 220
  959 for FTP, 71

1034 for DNS, 220, 238
1035 for DNS, 220, 238
1060 for well-known ports, 70
1700 for well-known ports, 70
1752 for IPng, 268
1878 for subnet addressing, 151
1884 on IPv6 addressing, 271
1924 on IPv6 addressing, 271
1933 for transition to IPv6, 276
1946 on IPv5, 268
2136 for Dynamic DNS, 239
2137 for Dynamic DNS security,
    239, 246
for IPv6, 274
Web site links, 308
root name servers, 223, 299
routability
    on-the-fly, 5
    of TCP/IP, 3, 8, 12
routers, 40, 147, 299. *See also* default
    gateway
    name resolution broadcast and, 206
    and reserved IP addresses, 93, 129
routing, 299
    Internet layer for, 38
routing table, 41, 299

S

scope for DHCP, 117, 300
    setting, **131**
scope ID, NetBIOS, 204
scope option, 300
secondary name server, 229, 300
secured dynamic updates of DNS, 246
Select Network Component Type dialog
    box (Windows 2000), *107*
Select Network Protocol dialog box
    (Windows 95/98), *115*
Select Network Protocol dialog box
    (Windows 2000), *108*

Select Network Protocol dialog box
    (Windows NT), *111*
sequence numbers, 300
    in TCP header, 60
server service, 252, 300
servers
    for FTP, 71
    reserved IP addresses for, 129
Session layer (OSI), 26
shares, 213, 300
shutdown, and DHCP lease, 128
SIT (Simple IPv6 Transition), 276, 300
SMTP (Simple Mail Transfer Protocol), 75
SNMP (Simple Network Management
    Protocol), 75
    port for, 70
SOA (Start of Authority) record, 232, 300
sockets, 69, 300
software, independence as TCP design
    goal, 8
source-quench packet, 47, 300
SRI-NIC (Stanford Research Institute
    Network), 220, 300
standard subnet masks, 142–143, 300
standards, need for, **22**
Stanford Research Institute, 5
Start of Authority (SOA) record, 232, 300
static entry in WINS database,
    262–263, 300
statically-assigned IP addresses, and
    dynamic update, 243
stream of data, 300
    sending audio and video with IGMP,
        50–51
    sending to multiple hosts, 49
subnet, 148, 300
subnet bits, 150, 300
subnet calculator, 151, 300, 309
subnet goggles, 300
subnet mask, 300

ubnet masks, 39. *See also* custom
  subnet masks
  class A, 171
  class B, 172
  class C, 173
  local or remote network identification,
    139–141
  network and host, **138–139**
  standard for classes, **142–143**
  supernetted, 185
  what it is, **136–141**
  in Windows NT, 113
upernetted subnet mask, 300
upernetting, **183–185**
witches, 300
  in LMHOSTS file, 209

CP (Transmission Control Protocol), 56,
  58–60, 300
  data organization and delivery
    guarantee, 60
  ports, 69
CP/IP (Transmission Control
  Protocol/Internet Protocol), 1, 301
  advantages, **12–13**
  birth, **7**
  companion Web site, **308–309**
  design goals, **8**
  and DoD model, **29**
  features, 3
  installing on Windows 95/98, **114–116**
    manual assignment of IP address,
      115–116
  installing on Windows 2000, **106–108**
  installing on Windows NT, **110–114**
    manual assignment of IP address,
      112–114
  installing on Windows XP, **103–106**
    manual assignment of IP address,
      103–106

Microsoft client, 298
  host name, 196
  name resolution steps, 195
  NetBIOS name cache, **203–204**
  need for new version, **268**
  what it is, **2–3**
testing. *See also* troubleshooting
  127. IP address for, 93
text file format, 71
TFTP (Trivial File Transfer Protocol), 75
  port 69 for, 69, 70
three-way handshake, **58–59**, 300
Transport layer (DoD), 29, **56–57**
  TCP (Transmission Control Protocol),
    58–60
  UDP (User Datagram Protocol), **61–63**
Transport layer (OSI), 26
troubleshooting
  127. IP address for, 93
  HOSTNAME utility for, 199
  ICMP to perform, 47
  loopback address for, 93, 274
TTL (time to live), 300
  for DHCP lease, 126
  setting duration, 130

U

UDP (User Datagram Protocol), 56, 57,
  61–63, 301
  ports, 69
Unicast, 275, 301
United States Department of Defense
  (DoD), 4, 295
  reference model, **29**
University of California at Los Angeles, 5
University of California at Santa Barbara, 5
University of Utah, 5
Unix, HOSTS file, 201
unspecified address (IPv6), 274
URL (Uniform Resource Locator), 74, 301

V

vendors, support for TCP/IP, 3
video streaming with IGMP, 50–51

W

WAN connection, 301
    subnet address for, 153
Web browser, 301
    HTTP for, 74
Web browser application, 74
Web server, 74, 301
Web sites
    connection process, 74–75
    for *TCP/IP JumpStart*, **308–309**
well-known ports, **70**, 301
WellKnown Service (WKS) record, 233
WildPackets, IP Subnet Calculator, 149, *149*
Windows 95/98
    DHCP on, 108
    HOSTS file, 201
    IP addressing installation, **114–116**
        manual assignment of IP address,
        115–116
Windows 2000
    client configuration for dynamic DNS,
        244–247
    DHCP server configuration for
        dynamic update, **241–247**
    HOSTS file, 201
    IP addressing installation, **106–110**
        manual assignment, **109–110**

Windows (Microsoft), calculator, *88*,
    88–89
Windows NT
    HOSTS file, 201
    IP addressing installation, **110–114**
        manual assignment, **112–114**
Windows XP
    client configuration for dynamic DNS,
        244–247
    HOSTS file, 201
    IP addressing installation, **103–106**
WINS (Windows Internet Naming
    Service), 49, **205**, 301
    IP addressing installation, 49
    NetBIOS name resolution with,
        257–261
        name registration, 257–259
    NetBIOS name resolution without,
        252–256
        name registration, 253
    static entry in database, 262–263
WINS Manager, **262–263**
WINS server, limits on clients, 261
WKS (WellKnown Service) record, 233
workstation service, 252, 301

Z

zeros, leading, in binary number
    conversion, 89
zone file, for DNS server database, 228
zone transfer, 230, *230*, 301

TELL US WHAT YOU THINK!

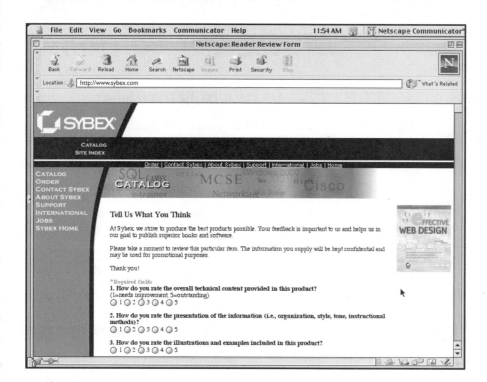

Your feedback is critical to our efforts to provide you with the best books and software on the market. Tell us what you think about the products you've purchased. It's simple:

1. Visit the Sybex website
2. Go to the product page
3. Click on **Submit a Review**
4. Fill out the questionnaire and comments
5. Click **Submit**

With your feedback, we can continue to publish the highest quality computer books and software products that today's busy IT professionals deserve.

www.sybex.com

SYBEX Inc. • 1151 Marina Village Parkway, Alameda, CA 94501 • 510-523-8233

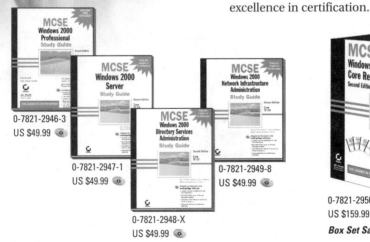